LIVING WITH(OUT) BORDERS

CATHOLIC THEOLOGICAL ETHICS IN THE WORLD CHURCH

James F. Keenan, Series Editor

Since theological ethics is so diffuse today, since practitioners and scholars are caught up in their own specific cultures, and since their interlocutors tend to be in other disciplines, there is the need for an international exchange of ideas in Catholic theological ethics.

Catholic Theological Ethics in the World Church (CTEWC) recognizes the need to appreciate the challenge of pluralism, to dialogue from and beyond local culture, and to interconnect within a world church not dominated solely by a northern paradigm. In this light, CTEWC is undertaking four areas of activity: fostering new scholars in theological ethics, sponsoring regional conferencing, supporting the exchange of ideas via our website (catholicethics.com), and publishing a book series.

The book series will pursue critical and emerging issues in theological ethics. It will proceed in a manner that reflects local cultures and engages in cross-cultural, interdisciplinary conversations motivated by mercy and care and shaped by shared visions of hope.

Living with(out) Borders

Catholic Theological Ethics on the

Migration of Peoples

Edited by

Agnes M. Brazal

and

María Teresa Dávila

ORBIS BOOKS
www.orbisbooks.com

TOGETHER IN GOD'S MISSION OF MERCY

Founded in 1970, Orbis Books endeavors to publish works that enlighten the mind, nourish the spirit, and challenge the conscience. The publishing arm of the Maryknoll Fathers and Brothers, Orbis seeks to explore the global dimensions of the Christian faith and mission, to invite dialogue with diverse cultures and religious traditions, and to serve the cause of reconciliation and peace. The books published reflect the views of their authors and do not represent the official position of the Maryknoll Society. To learn more about Maryknoll and Orbis Books, please visit our website at www.maryknollsociety.org.

Library of Congress Cataloging-in-Publication Data

Names: Brazal, Agnes M., editor.
Title: Living with(out) borders : Catholic theological ethics on the
   migration of peoples / edited by Agnes M. Brazal and María Teresa Dávila.
Other titles: Living without borders
Description: Maryknoll: Orbis Books, 2016. | Series: Catholic theological
   ethics in the world church ; #4 | Includes index.
Identifiers: LCCN 2015043788 | ISBN 9781626981669 (pbk.)
Subjects: LCSH: Emigration and immigration—Religious aspects—Catholic
   Church. | Globalization--Religious aspects—Catholic Church. | Christian
   sociology—Catholic Church. | Catholic Church--Doctrines.
Classification: LCC BX1795.E44 L58 2016 | DDC 241/.62—dc23 LC record available
   at http://lccn.loc.gov/2015043788

Im memory of the more than 40,000 women, men, and children,

who perished in arduous migrant crossings over land and seas since 2000.

CONTENTS

Part VII: A Future with(out) Borders

Acknowledgments

With gratitude to the twenty-four scholars from seventeen countries, whose works speaking to the challenges and hopes of migrants' lives is shared in these pages.

This book series has been conceived by the Planning Committee of the Catholic Theological Ethics in the World Church (CTEWC) after two successful cross-cultural conferences in Padua (2006) and Trent (2010). We are grateful to the committee for their suggestions and advice for this volume, which is the fourth in the book series. We mourn deeply, however, the loss of one of our Planning Committee members, Lucas Chan, SJ (1968–2015) who passed away in 2015, and whose publications on Scripture and ethics and leadership in organizing the first Pan-Asian Conference of moral theologians in Asia (2015) remain vital for Catholic theological ethics in Asia and the world.

Special mention is likewise due to James F. Keenan, SJ, whose leadership in global theological ethics is committed toward fostering a truly global conversation, especially by providing a space where the voices of those in the peripheries can be heard.

Finally we are thankful to our publisher, Orbis Books and our editor, James Keane, for his patience and commitment to the timely publication of this volume.

INTRODUCTION

Agnes M. Brazal and María Teresa Dávila

Borders establish boundaries of "one entity from another." In discourses on migration, borders may refer to regional or national boundaries, sociocultural or religious identities, political or economic distinctions, racial, gender/sexual orientation divides. In establishing identities, borders simultaneously include and exclude; but borders can also be porous or rigid. Postcolonial Asian theologian Kwok Pui-lan prefers the term *border-passage* to *border-crossing* to highlight the fact that the crossing is something that is not finished once and for all, and that the migrant can constantly move from one to the other.[1]

These *borders* the migrant is confronted with can be linked to the concept of citizenship and entitlement to rights. In her article, "Incompleteness and the Possibility of Making," Saskia Sassen argues that "citizenship is an incompletely theorized contract between the state and the citizen."[2] This allows for modifications in our notion of citizenship and, in particular, who is the rights-bearing citizen. The key protagonists in these shifts are the "outsider and the excluded" who challenge the normative definition with "new types of claims across time and space." Examples of such changes in the past are the granting of voting rights to non–property-owning citizens and women, and marriage rights to gays and lesbians.

Another element that is important to note when speaking about *borders* and *rights* of migrants/refugees (forced migrants) is that it is only in the modern period that political membership was articulated in the context of the nation-state. In Europe, citizenship discourse emerged from the context of Greek city-states and cities in the Late Middle Ages. Globalizing forces today are effecting changes in the authority of nation-states, and the redeployment of citizenship markers beyond the citizens of a nation-state through the United Nations, international, and regional conventions. For example, the partial rights granted to irregular or undocumented migrants (e.g., right to be justly paid for work done) by the International Convention on the Rights of All Migrant Workers and Their Families (1990)[3] have become effective for countries that have ratified the convention, thus constituting them as "informal citizens."

In this globalizing context, the essays in this volume analyze ethical challenges and claims to rights arising from various and intersecting border passage experiences of migrants, and examine them in the light of the Christian tradition. The movement of peoples has always been a key concern for Catholic social teaching.[4] Its consistent emphasis on the rights of people on the move and particular attention to

1

distinct migratory situations has been a helpful tool for those seeking to address concrete situations of suffering due to the migratory experience. And yet, ever more complex challenges have appeared in the last two decades, particularly in the intensification of conflict within and across borders since September 11, 2001. An intensification of conflict within and across borders, an increasing number of people on the move for employment, leisure, educational, and/or medical opportunities, environmental refugees, and people persecuted because of their gender, as well as the growth in the movement of particularly vulnerable people (children, young girls, and women), present an expansion in distinct and complex ethical demands.

The essays represent seventeen different national or regional contexts, considering the challenges posed by a broad array of situations—domestic or temporary/circular migration, refugees, tourists, trafficked people, formerly sending countries turning into receiving countries or vice-versa—and taking cognizance of the two poles in the circuit of migration—the situation in the receiving and the sending communities. They draw both from the experiences of concrete peoples whose hopes for lives with dignity know no bounds and from the breadth of the Catholic tradition. At times these two sources may seem to have little to say to each other or perhaps even contradict each other, as in the case of the empowerment of the *baklâ* (queer) whose subversion of boundaries of sexual identity confounds and challenges classic notions of essentialism in Catholic thought.

Part I focuses on "Global Migration: A Sociological Perspective" with an essay from **Saskia Sassen**, a reputable theorist of globalization and international human migration. In her provocative thesis, Sassen argues based on the experience of migration to and within Europe that loose border controls do not necessarily lead to the "invasion" of immigrants. Her essay investigates the factors that "make" the migrant: economic (e.g., systematic recruitment of employers, "development effect" of foreign investment and export-oriented growth in developing countries); politico–military (e.g., bridges built with former colonies, the existence of bases); wars that produce refugees and internally displaced peoples; the attraction of cultural–ideological zones; and the globalization of networks of human trafficking. She points out that people do not necessarily move from poorer to wealthier regions even with more porous borders.

Part II on "Human/Cultural Rights of Asylum Seekers/Refugees and Labor Migrants" begins with an essay of **Nader Michel** on the plight of Sudanese refugees who fled to Egypt because of the civil conflict between North and South Sudan. Even as a signatory to the ratification of the UN 1951 Geneva Convention on refugee status and right to asylum, Egypt restricted the refugees' access to schools, national medical insurance, and rationed food, which had the effect of rigidifying social, political, economic, racial, and religious divisions. With the return of freedom of mobility between the two countries in 2004, and with more stories of positive personal encounters between Sudanese and Egyptians, perceptions are gradually changing.

An emerging driver in the displacement of peoples is climate change and environmental degradation. Climate change was not caused and its effects not bounded by a single nation-state; rather, these cross borders. **Maryanne Loughry** examines the case of the Carteret Islanders in the Pacific, referred to by international media as the world's first climate refugees. While the Catholic Church considers them de facto refugees, there is no international convention or legally binding agreement that defends the rights of these peoples on the move.

The Jesuit Refugee Service (JRS) is the Society of Jesus's response to the plight of refugees. **Diego Alonso-Lasheras** discusses the work of Centro Astalli, the product of a joint effort with the Church of Rome "to defend and serve the human rights of refugees." Drawing from the Ignatian sense of "consolation," Alonso-Lasheras affirms the ministry of Centro Astalli and JRS in general as fostering "consolation in action" both for the refugees and the volunteers, who grow in faith, hope, and charity as they serve the refugees.

Peter Štica reports on migration in the Czech Republic, which—with the fall of the Iron Curtain—has shifted from being an emigrating country to an immigrating or receiving country. And with this dissolution of one border, a new *border* arose: that between immigrants from the European Union and those granted asylum, on the one hand, and temporary workers from third country (neither Czech nor European Union), on the other. Because of policies that privilege circular migration and the attachment of a residence permit to a specific occupation, temporary workers find themselves particularly vulnerable the moment their job assignments end. They become irregular migrants, and their status for access and participation is diminished and compromised. Štica calls for policy reforms grounded in human rights, which would include long-term integration of migrants as well as transparency regarding the real labor demands of the country.

Part II ends with a more philosophical–theological essay from **William O'Neill** who delves into the politics of exclusion as fostered in communitarian and liberal discourses. In communitarian ethics, community tends to be based on blood affinity or kinship, and rights is generally restricted to such "concrete other," while in liberal ethics, rights is ascribed to sovereign individuals, but the respect for the "generalized other" does not necessarily lead to a feeling of moral obligation toward forced migrants. Since rights are tied to one's citizenship, the loss of a home or nation is almost like the loss of one's humanity. O'Neill argues that hospitality, read through the lens of an option for the poor, is a "more inclusive" idiom for understanding the rights of forced migrants in a way that can better guide US policy.

Part III, "Gendered and Embodied Borders," begins with a sobering look at the violence against young women in the "single transnational space" formed by the proximity of El Paso (USA) and Ciudad Juarez (Mexico). **Nancy Pineda-Madrid** presents the combination of sex trafficking and feminicide—violence against women because of and through their gender—as a particularly gruesome expression of the violence that materializes exponentially along the border, where multiple jurisdictions; languages; state, national, and international laws; and deep inequality coexist. Attention to these acts of violence and the commitment to their just resolution by the different parties involved can be a measure of the ability of bordering towns, state, and church jurisdictions to attend to the particular vulnerabilities found in this most complex of borders. Pineda-Madrid suggests that the broken bodies of women represent the crucified body of Christ. Just as Christian discipleship depends on remembering this crucified body, Pineda-Madrid suggests that the re-membering of the murdered women by families, churches, and communities is a central step to healing from a crime many would rather keep silent and unknown.

Alexandre Andrade Martins delves into the health issues of Bolivian and Haitian migrants in Brazil. Though both nationals and migrants have access to the same quality health care in Brazil, migrants are more vulnerable because of the precarious conditions in which they live and work, and the lack of a specific classification that they are migrants; thus the absence of attention to their particular needs—the language barrier, the health profile coming from a different country—and the health personnel's lack of training to deal with foreigners. The Catholic social teaching on human dignity, preferential option for the poor, common good, and solidarity that leads to justice, impels Christians to be sensitive to the (health) needs of the migrants, especially the vulnerable ones. Martins presents the Brazilian Catholic Church response through the *Pastorais sociais,* social ministry of the Catholic communities, by giving examples of three groups and their work—the Pastoral of the Migrant, Pastoral of Human Mobility, and Pastoral of Health.

Christine Gudorf highlights temporary circular migrants who increasingly have assumed a female face with the feminization of migration. Employed mostly as domestic workers or as maids on cruise ships, with some tricked or seduced into sex work, they suffer from various forms of exploitation, such as sexual abuse, extended working hours, crowded rooms, and the lack of protection, from sending governments because of the fear of losing a big source of national income, their remittances. On the one hand, she proposes that the church in receiving countries help lobby for legal reforms and the ratification of international instruments that protect migrants' rights. On the other hand, the church in the sending country can lobby for necessary legal reforms in recruitment processes, and help potential migrants and their families discern the pros and cons of migration, cope with the separation, and manage well the finances.

The effects of migrations on families remain one of the biggest challenges to migration ethics. Part IV, "Cross-border Marriages and Migrant Families," begins with an essay by **Regina Wentzel Wolfe** who investigates the challenge of internal migrations in China. The *Hukou,* a long-standing registry system dividing urban from rural residents, holds people in untenable living and working situations against their will. As she observes, families' aspirations and hopes for a better life are curtailed by their inability to pass the fruits of their labor on to the next generation regardless of how hard they work or study.

The particular victimization of women migrants within the context of transnational families is at the heart of the analysis from **Kristin Heyer**. She lifts up *familismo*—which places high value on relations in the family and community as well as intergenerational kinship networks—as both a helpful and dangerous concept in understanding gender dynamics among Latin American migrants in the United States, where the family is viewed as offering protection to women threatened by harsh working conditions and abuse, while at the same time limiting women's agency in patriarchal networks of relation. She offers a creative engagement with the role of the family in Catholic social teaching that transcends some of the more traditional gendered assumptions.

Gemma Tulud Cruz completes this section by taking a very close look at a known, but often poorly examined, phenomenon affecting a growing number of families globally—cross-border marriages. While the increase in cross-border marriages can be attributed to the ease with which people can now cross regional, national, and international borders, Cruz puts the spotlight on the influence of the proliferation of commercially arranged marriage migration and a "marriage strike" against a patriarchal institution among more educated East Asian women, leaving rural men in search of a traditional wife elsewhere. Cruz observes gaps between the experience in cross-border marriages and church teachings, and posits a growing understanding of gender mutuality over complementarity as one possible corrective that will help the church speak more relevantly to this experience.

Virtues are an integral element in discussions of migration ethics. Part V, "Virtues in the Migration Context," offers innovative perspectives encouraged by emerging contexts that should challenge previous discussion on the topic. **Mauricio Alarcón Burbano** showcases the empowerment of Haitian associations in Ecuador since the Haitian earthquake of 2010. Noting deep difficulties at integration, most notably language barriers, but also racial and ethnic differences, Alarcón highlights how leaders of Haitian associations exhibit the virtue of fortitude, moving forward in their service to Haitian communities, even when they do not enjoy an ecclesial home or host for their associations.

In the context of Tanzania, **Deogratias Rwezaura** takes a page from former president Julius Nyerere, exploring the concept of *ujamaa* (extended familyhood) to expand on possible policies of solidarity and hospitality for refugees. Rwezaura argues that a welcome without rights or participation hinders integration, and negatively impacts both refugees and host communities. He then uses these insights to propose reforms to refugee policies in contemporary East Africa.

Speaking of the virtue of hospitality in the tourism industry, **Patrick McCormick** turns the tables on the typical discussions focused on hosts to a discussion emphasizing hospitality on the part of guests. McCormick contends with the ignorance of most international travelers and guests with regard to the poor conditions of workers in the tourism industry, the meager wages earned by most, sex trafficking, the unjust distribution of gains from fast-paced tourism development projects, and their negative environmental impact. Travelers are invited to participate in "fair-trade tourism" where hospitality calls for deeper awareness, solidarity with workers, and collectively challenging labor and other regulations in the tourism industry.

Peter Phan closes this part on virtues with the challenge of memory and remembering in the life of migrants. What is the role of memory for those who would rather forget the dangerous and unjust situations from which they came? Exploring the centrality of remembering in the Bible as well as memory and forgiveness in contemporary theories of reconciliation, Phan proposes that "right remembering" on the part of the migrant people and communities, done in relationship with sending and host countries, is an essential step in the work of building just communities for all that take seriously people's past experiences and hope for the future.

Part VI, "Theo-anthropological Reflections," articulates insights and challenges on what it means to be human in the context of migration and in the light of the Christian faith **Prem Xalxo** writes of tribal girls doing domestic work in the metropolitan cities of India. Uprooted from their communities, Xalxo cites as major challenges helping them maintain a sense of human dignity, equality, justice, and pride in their tribal identity and communitarian spirit. These often-trafficked tribal girls suffer multiple vulnerabilities as they are isolated in their positions, often subjected to physical and sexual abuse by the owners of the home where they serve, with no recourse to justice. Because their situation in India falls outside the purview of civil law, Xalxo suggests that the church's role in giving hope to the tribal girls by empowering tribal communities and the defense of human rights is significant, including working directly with international agencies fighting for the rights of domestic workers.

Michael Sepidoza Campos employs the *baklâ* (queer) experience as trope to illuminate the life of the undocumented migrant and of incarnational events. Both closeted, and living with the threat of displacement, queer and migrant bodies are situated in a "third space" of being neither here nor there. Both queers and migrants question the concept of nation and identity; and the state is regarded as the "closet" that both contains and expels with its multiple openings unwanted bodies. When used as trope for a theology of the diaspora, this double movement of belonging and expulsion resists the fetish for interpreting incarnational events in terms of stability or ontology in favor of "reorienting divinity toward irruption."

The Venezuelan experience described by **Rafael Luciani** evidences how rapidly a nation can transition from a host to a sending country, albeit, of asylum seekers, and the challenges this implies. Reflecting on Venezuela as having experienced being both a host and a sending country, Luciani proposes the *itinerant* identity of Jesus as a model for humanity and, in particular too, for hosts and guests alike. The itinerant journey relativizes attachment to a particular identity, culture, or ideology; allows one to encounter "others" and be challenged by them; encourages the building of filial relationships; and consequently reinserts one into a bigger family.

Part VI closes with the difficult challenge posed by **Nontando Hadebe**, who, writing from the context of South Africa, and drawing from disability studies, highlights the ugliness of racism and xenophobia in a country still healing from the wounds of the apartheid regime. She sees an alignment between the Trinity and their vernacular discourse on *Ubuntu*—human being and becoming as intimately related and dependent on the being and becoming of others. The Ubuntu Trinity is a model for inclusive and just communities; it signals a way to shape structures and communities of inclusion amid fear and dislike of difference.

Part VII, "A Future with(out) Borders," wraps the discussion on the overarching yet critical conversation of the meaning of state borders when the movement of peoples across them is at its highest rate in human history. **David Hollenbach** reviews political philosophical arguments in favor of open borders and the latter's scriptural basis. He then turns to arguments on the moral relevance of the nation-state, which not only allows people to govern themselves but also protects the human dignity of those living in it. Hollenbach asks how key ethical concepts, such as the distinction of an order of love, particularities of ethnicity, and other characteristics, play into the role of borders in the life of nations and in the care of vulnerable migrants. He concludes by suggesting some priorities: the refugee who has crossed one's border, the refugee who fled because of the military offensives initiated by one's country, migrants who do jobs nationals would not take, and migrants from countries with historical (colonial/neocolonial) relations with one's country.

Maryanne Heimbach-Steins pushes the boundaries of the conversation on "porous" borders by arguing that the current challenge forces the transcendence of political, ethnic, economic, racial, or religious boundaries. Heimbach-Steins argues that the border is a "basic structure of human existence"; the ethical challenge is how to transcend borders. Her proposed migration ethic of liminality provides—based on the recognition of the other—a moral compass in the transcendence of borders. The biblical impulses that she has identified to nourish this ethics of liminality include our creation in God's image, the gospel of God incarnate in Jesus, the Exodus as a liberation experience, and our relation to God as strangers.

We understand that the scenarios and contexts of migrations and borders that are represented in these essays include both perennial questions about human dignity as well as contemporary challenges that can shift in one, half, or even one-quarter of a generation. One thing they make decidedly clear is that addressing these challenges within the Christian tradition calls for a contextual, indeed, an incarnate response, one where migrants' lives and concerns intersect and interrupt the church, nongovernmental organizations, nation-states, and regions. These essays will challenge readers from a variety of contexts to appreciate and examine his or her role at each level of charity and responsibility.

Notes

1. D. N. Premnath, ed., *Border Crossings: Cross-Cultural Hermeneutics* (Maryknoll, NY: Orbis Books, 2007).

2. Saskia Sassen, "Incompleteness and the Possibility of Making: Towards Denationalized Citizenship?" *Political Power and Social Theory*, 20 (2009): 229.

3. Office of the United Nations for High Commissioner for Human Rights, http://www2.ohchr.org.

4. The rights of families to seek employment, sustenance, and safety has been affirmed beginning with Pope Leo XIII's *Rerum Novarum* (1891). Pius XII's Apostolic Constitution *Exsul Familia Nazarethana* (1952) focused entirely on care for the migrant family, tracing key migratory patterns of the past one hundred years, and advocating for the rights and pastoral care of newly created migrants. With John XXIII's *Pacem in Terris* (1963) and Paul VI's *Octogesima Adveniens* (1971), the church aligns itself with the right of people to migrate, enshrining the rights of migrants over against the sovereignty of borders. Since then, the work of the Pontifical Council for the Pastoral Care of Migrants and Itinerant People (est. 1970) along with the efforts of local bishops conferences periodically have made statements highlighting the ever evolving plight of people on the move.

Part I

Global Migration:

A Sociological Perspective

THE MAKING OF MIGRATIONS

Saskia Sassen

There was a time, notably in the 1950s and into the 1970s, when migration had clear features, which made it a somewhat easily identifiable process.[1] The generic subject of this period for much, though not all, of the world was *the immigrant*. Particular countries stood out in scholarly discussions, notably the United States and Canada; much of Northern Europe; Australia; Israel; and, for South American immigrants, Argentina and Brazil.

Today, trafficked people and refugees dominate the flows and the debate. I would argue that the generic subject in much of Europe today is the asylum seeker, even if a good number of arrivals are immigrants. On the other hand, in the United States it is still immigrants, even if a rapidly growing number should be recognized as refugees and asylum seekers. Finally, partly left out of the mainstream discussion about people on the move are the massive numbers of the long-term and short-term displaced, many inside their own country, with an overall estimate of over fifty-two million by 2013.[2] As I have argued elsewhere, many if not most of the internally and internationally displaced will never go back home, because home is now a war zone, a plantation, or a new private gated community. It becomes increasingly inadequate to capture the status of this vast population by the designation *displaced* as they are now all, mostly, refugees. Nor does the language of migration capture what is happening in the Mediterranean, in the Andaman Sea, and in Central America. It is a different event, possibly profoundly different. It may well be a first signal of an emerging future, when even more people will be on the move, not because they are in search of a *better* life but because they are in search of *bare* life. These are the expelled.[3]

From a broader perspective, immigration and refugee flows take place within larger geographies of empires or powerful countries, which have indirect control over a space beyond their borders. Here I focus on immigration partly because my concern is to show the considerable degree of structuring in these flows, something we cannot say about the flows of refugees and asylum seekers. Still, much of the data often include the latter in the numbers for migrants, as I indicated earlier. On the other hand, the estimated fifty million environmentally displaced people are counted as migrants, rather than as refugees, which is a more accurate term. Nor do the estimated twenty-one million victims of forced labor globally (an underestimated figure) easily appear in the numbers for migrations and refugees, even though over ten million of these forced-labor workers are part of those flows.

In the first section, I examine the cross-border geographies within which diverse historical and current migrations take place, geographies shaped by larger cross-border dynamics. In the second section, I use the migrations to Europe and within Europe to examine how this tendency toward patterning holds even in a small continent with multiple countries next to each other. Given these features, Europe serves as a natural experiment: we might expect a weaker effect from older imperial arrangements such as the well-known cases of Algerians migrating to France, Indians to the United Kingdom, or Indonesians to the Netherlands.

More Shaping That Meets the Eye

Organized recruitment by employers or governments (often on behalf of employers) lies at the origin of many immigration flows, both in the 1800s and today.[4] The dynamics of who recruits whom in terms of countries tends to be shaped by prior political–economic bonds (e.g., colonialism, military invasions, or current foreign investment, and other cross-border operations by firms in the context of economic globalization). Thus, most migrants from India went to the United Kingdom in the postwar decades, while most Algerians went to France: that is to say, each group traveled the bridge built by their former colonial power. In brief, receiving countries have typically been participants in the processes leading to the formation of international migration.

Increasingly significant are today's multiplying global imaginaries, which are partly a function of Western economic and media dominance and have their own way of constructing bridges. Eventually, over time, most migration flows gain a certain autonomy from the organized recruitment mechanisms that may lie at their origin, paving the way for so-called chain-migration, that is to say, that the bridges to specific countries have been built and migrating becomes a simpler, more routinized choice.

Thus, in the case of the large mass migrations of the 1800s, these emerged as part of the formation of a trans-Atlantic economic system binding several nation-states through economic transactions and wars, particularly war-induced flows of people. This trans-Atlantic economy was at the core of US development. There were massive flows of capital, goods, and workers, and there were specific structures that produced this trans-Atlantic system. Before this period, labor movements across the Atlantic had been largely forced, notably slavery, and mostly from colonized African and Asian territories.

The Netherlands and Belgium both received significant numbers of people from their former colonial empires. They also received foreign workers from labor-exporting countries such as Italy, Morocco, and Turkey. Switzerland similarly received workers from traditional labor-exporting countries: Italy, Spain, Portugal, Yugoslavia, and Turkey. All three countries originally organized the recruitment of these workers, until eventually a somewhat autonomous set of flows was in place. Sweden has long received most Finnish emigrants. Also in Sweden as in the other countries, there was a large expansion of the recruitment area to include workers from the traditional labor-exporting countries on the Mediterranean.

The renewal of mass immigration into the United States in the 1960s, after five decades of little or no immigration, took place in a context of expanded US economic and military activity in Asia and the Caribbean Basin. The United States is at the heart of an international system of investment and production that binds these various regions. In the 1960s and 1970s, the United States played a crucial role in the development of a world economic system. It passed legislation and promoted international agreements aimed at opening its own and other countries' economies to the flow of capital, goods, services, and information.[5]

This central military, political, and economic role contributed both to the creation of conditions that mobilized people into migrations, whether local or international, *and* to the formation of links with the United States that subsequently were to serve as unintended bridges for international migration. This bridging effect was likely strengthened by the Cold War context and the active promotion of the advantages of open democratic societies. One, albeit controversial, interpretation is that these patterns show us that measures commonly thought to deter emigration—foreign investment and the promotion of export-oriented growth in developing countries—seem to have had precisely the opposite effect, at least in the short and middle run.[6] Among the leading senders of immigrants to the United States in the 1970s and 1980s were several of the newly industrialized countries of South and Southeast Asia whose extremely high growth rates are generally recognized to be a result, initially, of foreign direct investment in export manufacturing. A parallel analysis may be drawn with respect to the *development* effect of the North American Free Trade Agreement on Mexican emigration to the United States: ongoing and new emigration, and, eventually, stabilization in thirty years.

Additionally, specific forms of internationalization/globalization of capital observed with the implementation of restructuring policies by the International Monetary Fund and World Bank contribute to build direct and indirect bridges between countries of origin and the United States via investment. Long before the current phase of globalization, the implantation in the 1960s and onward of Western development strategies eventually became major factors generating emigration. Significant to mobilizing people into emigration was the setting up of export-processing zones and large-scale acquisitions by foreign governments and corporations of rural land, mostly to develop plantations. Both the industrial and agricultural set-ups were extremely labor intensive, thereby mobilizing vast numbers to the pertinent zones. The consequences of such development strategies led to the replacement of small-holder agriculture with export-oriented commercial agriculture, to the westernization of educational systems, to the destruction of national industrial sectors, and a massive corresponding rise in imports of consumer goods. All of these contributed to mobilize people into migration streams—regional, national, transnational.

In short, the making of bridges for the flow of capital, information, and high-level personnel from the center to the periphery created the direct and indirect conditions for growing emigrations that used those *bridges*. These emigrations included those of local professionals who had learned the ropes of the trade through employment in the West's imposition of restructuring programs, and they included the emigrations of small farmers and shopkeepers, and factory owners who had lost everything due to the entry of large corporations into their traditional local markets.[7] The administrative, commercial, and development networks of the former European empires, and the newer forms these networks assumed under the Pax Americana and subsequently, along with the explicit/formal making of global systems (international direct foreign investment, export processing zones, wars for democracy), create bridges for the flow of capital, information, and high-level personnel from the center to the periphery, and, more importantly, the flow of migrants. The postwar influx of people from the Commonwealth into Britain was partly shaped by the fact that England and Englishness were much present in the Commonwealth. This way of narrating emigration captures the ongoing weight of colonialism and postcolonial forms of empire on major processes of today's globalization, including specifically those binding emigration and immigration countries. The major immigration countries are not innocent bystanders; the specific genesis and contents of their responsibility will vary from case to case and period to period.

Invisible Borderings of Migration Flows and Spaces

Notwithstanding the fuzzy edges of the diverse categories in play, immigration flows have historically tended to have geographic, temporal, and institutional boundaries that indicate a definition of the *where, when,* and *who* of immigration. These cross-country regularities contribute to a far more qualified understanding of immigration and hence of policy options. Clearly, this also depends on the type of legislation states engage in. One critical issue is that governments and policy makers should recognize that there is patterning to migration flows and considerable understanding concerning what engenders a new migration flow as well as the likelihood that migrants might prefer circular migration much more than current policy recognizes.

In what follows, I focus on Europe in some detail as a test of the larger arguments of the prior section, to wit, that international migrations happen within larger geographies shaped by past imperial projects. Europe can function as a sort of natural experiment to examine some of the historical trends that have shaped migration flows. Compared to other major continental recipients of migrants, such as North America, Australia, and South America, Europe contains an enormous diversity of countries in a relatively compact continent, with many borders easy to cross, particularly in today's post-EU era. One could argue easily that migrants of a given nationality might explore many countries within Europe and thereby exit those inherited imperial geographies.

.

I discuss here a few trends that engage diverse facets of the larger empirical situation that gets at the issue of international migrations as happening inside larger imperial geographies and a few related questions. It is impossible in this short essay to reference the vast scholarship on intra-European migrations and migrations to Europe from outside the continent. Among useful and continuously updated sources are Eurostat and the International Organization for Migration.

1. *Emigration mostly encompasses a small share of a country's population.* Except for those who are driven to migrate due to war or environmental destruction, we now know that most people are quite reluctant to leave their home villages or towns. Again, here we need to distinguish between refugees and emigrants, even if in some cases the distinction is vague. Most Mexicans have not left their country and moved to the United States, nor have most Poles left Poland and gone to Germany or the United Kingdom, nor will most Algerians try to come to France. In fact, the evidence shows that when there is a massive flow, it often is due to direct persecution or war in the home country.

The considerable patterning of migrations, described in the first section of this essay, underlines these features. Thus, most emigrants from Russia and other former Soviet-sphere countries who went to Germany in the early 1990s after the wall came down were ethnic Germans, mostly from Russia, and Roma people from Romania. These were two populations with very specific though also very different reasons for migrating. They fit into the category of individuals and groups who are determined to leave the country they are in (pent-up demand) and will come no matter what, but do so within a space shaped by earlier histories. There is a grey area of potential emigrants who may or may not leave, depending on pull factors. But the vast majority of people in a poor country are not likely to consider emigration.

These types of patterns were already evident in the nineteenth century, which is worth noting since at that time borders were basically not controlled because the state lacked the technical capacities to do so. Another sort of natural experiment is today's European Union, where nationals can easily move to another country and there is still considerable variation in earnings levels across member states, thus an added incentive to move to high-wage countries. But EU figures for both the pre- and post-enlargement period show little cross-country migration among EU residents, with numbers hovering at about 6 percent of the EU population until quite recently. The overall inference is that most people do not want to leave their countries, even if they are poorer than other countries.[8]

2. *Immigrants are typically a minority of a country's population.* Continuing with the above but focusing on receiving countries in some detail, shortly after the 2004 expansion of the European Union that incorporated several countries that had long been emigration countries, the much-feared invasion by citizens of poor European countries did not quite materialize. This is an interesting period regarding migration because the terrible wars in Iraq and Syria had not quite started, and there were far fewer asylum seekers and refugees than in the last few years. One can

thus isolate the fact that suddenly citizens from several poor European countries were free to move to several rich countries.

Yet by 2006 the much-feared pent-up demand did not materialize. According to Eurostat, in half of the EU25 countries nonnationals were under 5 percent of the population in 2006, two years after the opening of borders, and many of these were from the original European Union. Generally, nonnationals were only over 10 percent of the population in Luxembourg, and, mostly due to long-term former Soviet residents, in Latvia and Estonia. Further, a good share of nonnationals came from other EU countries.

In the preenlargement period, immigrants were 5 percent (18.8 million) of the EU population. Then and today, most immigrants are from other European countries. Third-country immigrants count for a minority of the total European population. Not even today's significant numbers of refugees and asylum seekers change this fact, even though the numbers have increased over the last three years due to the wars in the Middle East and diverse parts of Africa.

It is not unusual for immigration countries to develop cultures of fear around immigrants, even when they are the same phenotype and language group, as the case of Irish immigrants made clear in the United States and the United Kingdom.[9] This can escalate sharply when there is a difference of religion and of cultural practices. For instance, the eight major preenlargement EU countries had a total immigrant population of 2.5 million from the Maghreb. This was 13.3 percent of the total immigrant population in the European Union, and less than 1 percent of the total European population. But it has not kept it from engendering considerable debate around questions of cultural and religious obstacles to incorporation, even long before the invasion of Iraq in 2003 radicalized some long-term resident Muslims.

3. *There is considerable return migration,* except when the military–political situation in countries of origin makes this unfeasible or when immigrants are undocumented and would have trouble returning—thus they become unwilling full-time captives of the immigration country. For example, we now know that about 60 percent of Italians who left for the United States around the turn of the century, returned to Italy, a fact rarely mentioned in the typical immigration account in the United States, where the assumption is that they did not want to leave. The incidence of cross-border residence by EU nationals has declined since 1970, partly as a function of the return of Italian, Spanish, and Portuguese immigrant workers to their home countries once they were free to come and go. The current crisis, especially in Spain and Greece, has once again promoted outmigration from these countries, but it often takes the form of circular migration. Before the current wars in parts of North Africa, there was generally considerable circular migration in the Mediterranean; this was also the case in North America, until the US government militarized the border with Mexico. The effect has been to transform part-time resident immigrants into forced full-time residents.

This suggests that when it is easier for migrants to circulate between country of origin and country of immigration, they spend more of their time in their country of origin than is the case today with tight border controls, assuming that the country of origin is not a war zone. Return migration may become a different phenomenon—not a definitive return, but a circular movement. It calls for considering the sending and receiving areas as part of a single economic, social, and political system. It is within this system that immigrants make their own individual decisions and take action.

4. *One important tendency is toward the formation of permanent settlements for a variable share of immigrants, but never all.* This tendency is likely even when there are high return rates and even when a country's policies seek to prevent permanent settlement. We see this happening in all countries receiving immigrants, including extremely closed countries such as Japan (with often irregular immigration from the Philippines, Thailand, and other Asian countries, as well as legal immigrations from several Latin American countries) and Saudi Arabia as well as in the more liberal Western nations.

Irregular immigrants are likely to be part of any immigration, no matter what political culture and particular migration policies a country adopts. *Unauthorized immigration has emerged as a generalized fact in all Western economies in the post–World War II era*, including Japan. This has raised a whole set of questions about the need to rethink regulatory enforcement and the sites for such enforcement. Although the fact of such unauthorized immigration suggests that it is possible to enter these countries no matter what policies are in place, the available evidence makes it clear that the majority of unauthorized immigrants are from the same nationality groups as the legal population and are typically fewer in number than the legal population. Again, this signals a measure of boundedness in the process of unauthorized immigration and the possibility that it is shaped by similar systemic conditions as the legal population, thereby similarly limited in its scope and scale.

5. *Immigration is a highly differentiated process.* It includes people seeking permanent settlement and those seeking temporary employment who circulate back and forth. The two major patterns that are emerging today are circular migration and permanent settlement. Circular migration was a key pattern in the nineteenth century before border controls were instituted in any systematic way. We also know that there was a significant increase in the permanent resident immigrant population after borders were closed in EU countries in 1973–74, suggesting that some of this growth might not have occurred if the option of circular migration had existed. Much migration has to do with supplementing household income in countries of origin rather than with permanent settlement. Given enormous earnings differentials, a limited stay in a high-wage country may be sufficient.

One important question is whether recognizing these differences might facilitate the formulation of policy today. There is a growing presence of immigrants who are not searching for a new home in a new country; they think of themselves as moving in a cross-border and even global labor market. We know that when illegal immigrants are regularized, they often establish permanent residence in their country of origin and work a few months in the immigration country, an option that becomes available when they can circulate more freely. We know that some of the Polish women who now work as cleaners in Berlin out of financial necessity only want to do this work for three or four months a year and then return to their hometowns. This is also the case with some of the African migrants in Italy. The share and numbers of those who seek to become permanent residents seems to be considerably smaller than the numbers of the total resident foreign population suggest.

Conclusion:
Who, Then, Is the Migrant?

This diversity of connections, both old and current, that underlie the patterning evident in international migrations, unsettles the image of *the immigrant* as a stranger who appears at our border uninvited. And that is also why the current events in the Mediterranean and the Andaman Sea are different from the migrations of the post–World War II period and also older migrations in the Americas.

Elsewhere I have sought to understand if there were massive movements from poor to rich areas when the states had not yet gained full control over their borders, when they lacked the technical and bureaucratic capacities to control borders.[10] I used the intra-European migrations of the nineteenth century as a type of natural experiment to answer this question because there were many rich and many poor places, the distances were not so long, and states did not control their borders well. But also under these conditions, there were no massive movements from poverty to prosperity. Why, when there were so many poor in some regions, when there was inequality in wages and work opportunities between regions, and when there were no border controls, why did not all poor, or the vast majority of them, migrate to the sites of prosperity?

In Europe as in many other regions, labor migrations took place within systemic settings even when tight border control was not at issue. Further, there are multiple mechanisms contributing to their size, geography, and duration. From a macrosocietal perspective, these can be seen as akin to equilibrating mechanisms. Labor migrations never became mass invasions, and the historical patterns displayed suggest they are part of a system conditioned by these mechanisms. Enormous excess inflows by immigrants are not part of the history of labor migrations in Europe. Neither can today's numbers be construed as an invasion.

The importance of recruitment and networks, often spatially circumscribed networks, the frequency of circular migrations that connected specific places of origins with specific destinations over long periods of time, all of these signal the extent to which migrations are embedded in, and shaped by, specific systems. Important to the current debate and panic is the fact that these features were there long before states were able to control their borders: thus, the shaping effect is not simply a consequence of immigration policy as such. There typically is something in addition to the will of individual migrants that contributes to form and sustains migratory flows. Very often it is the existence of one or another kind of geopolitically specified system.

Such systems can be characterized in a multiplicity of ways: economic (e.g., the Atlantic economy of the 1800s, the European Union, the North American Free Trade Agreement); politico–military (the colonial systems of several European countries, US involvement in Central America); transnational war zones (e.g., formation of massive refugee flows as a result of major European wars); cultural–ideological zones (e.g., impact in socialist countries of the image of Western democracies as offering the *good life* to each and all). Today we can add the globalizing of, often, old networks for the trafficking of people.

There is a second pattern that those earlier nineteenth-century intra-European migrations allow us to see. Even though *immigrants* had the same phenotype and broadly speaking European culture, they were discriminated against. Immigrants were marked as *the other*. These were times when population growth was slow, mortality high, labor shortages acute, and population growth was generally seen as enormously desirable. But immigrants were seen as undesirable by many sectors of the larger society. If we add to this the fact of systemic shaping in the geography, duration, and size of labor migrations, it does become evident that, beyond issues of fairness and social justice, people are able to misunderstand or ideologically override their actual needs. Today the argument against immigration may be focused on questions of race, religion, and culture; and this may seem very rational.

But, in fact, in my sifting of the historical and current evidence, they are new contents for an old passion: the racializing of the outsider, of the *other*. Today the *other* is represented, stereotyped as from a different race, religion, and culture. Yet equivalent arguments were made in the past when migrants were of the same broad religious, racial, and cultural group: they were seen as not fitting in the receiving society, as having bad habits and the wrong morals.[11] Migration is typically a move between two worlds, even if it is in a single region or country—such as East Germans moving to West Germany who were seen as a different ethnic group, one with undesirable traits.

While immigrants and refugees at various times reached significant numbers and were seen as *others* even if Europeans, the experience of *invasion* and flows that are out of control does not seem to have been dominant images till the aftermath of World War I. The formation and strengthening of the interstate system brought to the fore questions of border control. Both the definition and the actual condition of refugee that comes out of the aftermath of World War I are functions of the existence of an increasingly formalized interstate system; they are only weakly centered in broader notions of human rights and the right to asylum as a universal human right.

For much of the nineteenth century *immigrant* was a category that was constituted differently from today because the question of border control was less central to state sovereignty than it became with World War I. Similarly, the category *refugee* was constituted differently even when we see the beginnings of mass refugee movements in the 1880s. The centrality of border control emerges partly as a function of the development of state capacities for full border control and general control over its territory. The will to regulate all spheres of activity marks this new era in the history of the state. The other side of this coin was the strengthening of the interstate system. Today, with the emergence of EU-wide institutions, the weakening of the interstate system and the end of the Cold War, immigrants and refugees coming from poorer countries are once again conflated as one broad category of people basically driven by economic need. The current experience and perception is probably closer to that of the nineteenth century than it is to the period spanning the two wars and much of the Cold War.

A third major issue is an elaboration of the proposition that labor migrations are embedded in larger systems. That is to say, it is not simply a matter of the poor deciding to come to rich countries; if this were the case, we should plan on well over three billion people engaging in such movements when in fact today there are only about seventy million who have migrated to the rich countries, which is under 3 percent of all the poor. So, poverty itself is not enough to explain emigration. It is of little help for politicians to think that all the poor will come. It is incorrect, and it leads to the wrong policies. Establishing whether labor migration is an integral part of how an economic and social system operates and evolves is, in my view, critical. The logic of this argument is as follows: If immigration is thought of as the result of the aggregation of individuals in search of a better life, immigration is, from the perspective of the receiving country, an exogenous process, one formed and shaped by conditions outside the receiving country. The receiving country is then saddled with the task of accommodating this population. If poverty and overpopulation grow, there may be a parallel growth in immigration, at least potentially. The receiving country's experience is that of a passive bystander to processes outside its domain and control, and hence with few options but tight closing of frontiers if it is to avoid an *invasion*.

When immigration is conditioned on the operation of the economic system in receiving countries, it gets inserted into the spaces and periods of growth, or, in certain cases, into particular phases of decline and reorganization. This was the case in the United States when sweatshops replaced unionized jobs during deindustrialization in the 1970s and 1980s. In Europe's many immigration phases and diverse patterns across countries, the new migrations of the post–WWII period of rebuilding destroyed countries met a strong need for workers in basic sectors: agriculture and construction. In today's Europe, especially after the war in Iraq, the context is radically different: it is marked by refugees from diverse wars and by a strong sense of injury and injustice among the second and third generation of immigrants, many now citizens.

Immigration happens in a context of socioeconomic inequality between sending and receiving countries, but this inequality by itself is not enough to explain emigration. This inequality needs to be activated as a migration push factor— through organized recruitment, neocolonial bonds, etc. Most poor countries in the world have long been poor and often not seen emigration. Poverty by itself is not enough to explain emigration. In post–World War II Europe, migrant workers were actively recruited. And it was the economic, political, and social conditions in the receiving country that set the parameters for immigration flows and where the immigrants wound up working. It was the emergence of a second generation and changes in labor needs that contributed to the closure of immigration in most Western European countries in the early 1970s. This in turn generated a flow of undocumented migrants.

And then came today's wars in the Middle East and many parts of Africa. This was the beginning of a whole new phase, one where refugees and undocumented desperate men, women, and children sought refuge. This happened in a context where a good number, though not all, of the descendants of that first post–World War II generation were unemployed, racialized, angry. Religion in this context can be a major activator of politics. Yet all along most first-, second-, and third-generation immigrants were fully integrated into the tissue of civil society. This is where we are now: a majority well-incorporated and growing numbers of the second- and third-generation youth, angry because more and more doors are closing in a context of growing inequality and ongoing economic crisis.

Immigration flows may take a while to adjust to changes in levels of labor demand or to saturation of opportunities, but eventually they always have tended to adjust to the conditions in receiving countries, even if these adjustments are imperfect. Thus, there was a decline in the rate of growth of Polish immigration into Germany once it was clear that the opportunities were not as plentiful, and a circular migration replaced permanent migration in many East to West flows, including from the former East Germany to West Germany. The size and duration of flows is shaped by these conditions. It is not an exogenous process that is only shaped by poverty and population growth elsewhere and hence is autonomous from the accommodation capacities of receiving countries.

If size and duration are partly shaped by conditions in receiving countries, then the possibility of reasonably effective immigration policies also exists. Managing a patterned and conditioned flow of immigrants is a rather different matter from controlling an *invasion*. Implementation of an effective policy does not necessarily mean perfect synchronization between conditions in the receiving country and immigrant inflow and settlement. This will never be the case. Immigration is a process constituted by human beings with will and agency, and with multiple identities and life trajectories beyond the fact of being seen, defined, and categorized as immigrants for the purposes of the receiving polity, economy, and society. There is no definitive proof in this matter. But there are patterns, and there are past patterns, that have lived their full life. And they can tell us something about the extent to which immigration has consisted of a series of bounded events, with beginnings and endings, and specific geographies—all conditioned by the operation and organization of receiving economies, polities, and societies.

Notes

1. For further sources on the main issues discussed in this essay, see the following (all by Saskia Sassen): *Guests and Aliens* (New York: New Press, 1999); *The Mobility of Labor and Capital* (Cambridge: Cambridge University Press, 1988); *Expulsions: Brutality and Complexity in the Global Economy* (Cambridge, MA: Harvard University Press/Belknap Book, 2014).

2. *UNHCR, Global Trends 2012* (Geneva: UN High Commissioner for Refugees, 2013).

3. Saskia Sassen, *Expulsions: Brutality and Complexity in the Global Economy* (Cambridge, MA: Harvard University Press 2014). The term *displaced* comes from the UN agency in charge of refugees generally, used to describe internal refugees in a country, who are assumed to be able to return to their homes once the particular conflict is over.

4. For a discussion on this specific aspect for several European countries in the 1700s and 1800s, see Sassen, *Guests and Aliens,* chaps. 1–3.

5. This argument is developed at length in Sassen, *The Mobility of Labor and Capital.*

6. I develop these two issues at length in ibid., chaps. 1, 2, 4, and 5.

7. This is also at the heart of the debate in India today, about opening the Indian economy to the large corporate food chains, which is expected to have massive effects on a country where very small and modest enterprises and shops take care of basic consumer needs.

8. I have examined this in great detail for the 1800s and onward in my book *Guest and Aliens,* chaps. 1–3.

9. See Sassen, *Guests and Aliens,* chapter 3, for an examination of a range of places and periods that saw brutal attacks on immigrant workers even though most immigrants were the same religious and phenotype group as those of the receiving country. Thus, when Baron von Haussman was rebuilding parts of Paris, he needed more workers and brought in Catholic German and Belgian workers. The French saw these as the *wrong* type of Catholics and attacked them. I found hundreds such incidents involving the same religion but different nationalities within Europe. This signals that it is more than self-evident differences at work in these racializations.

10. Sassen, *Guests and Aliens.*

11. For a discussion on racialization and othering as it pertains to current issues in migrations, see María Teresa Dávila, "Racialization and Racism in Theological Ethics: 'Facing History' as a Pillar for a Catholic Ethic Grounded on the Preferential Option for the Poor and an Incarnational Anthropology," in *Catholic Theological Ethics: Past, Present, and Future,* ed. James Keenan (Maryknoll, NY: Orbis Books: 2011), 307–21; Rita Dhamoun and Yasmeen Abu-Laban, "Dangerous (Internal) Foreigners and Nation Building: The Case of Canada," *International Political Science Review* 30, no. 2 (2009): 163–83; and Helga Leitner, "Spaces of Encounter: Immigration, Race, Class, and the Politics of Belonging in Small-Town America," *Annals of the Association of American Geographers,* 102, no. 4 (2012): 828–46.

Part II

Human/Cultural Rights of

Asylum Seekers/Refugees

and Labor Migrants

The Sudanese Refugees in Egypt

A Tale of Encounters and Failures

Nader Michel, SJ

War has raged between the army of the government of North Sudan and the Sudan People's Liberation Army of the South since the 1980s, especially during the 1990s, and until 2011. This is the longest lasting civil conflict in Africa and has forced hundreds of thousands of southern people to leave their homes and seek refuge in neighboring countries, mainly in Egypt. It began in 1983 after the government of Khartoum broke the peace agreement of 1972 and imposed *Sharia* (Islamic Law) on the South as well as on the North of Sudan. The outbreak of the war in Darfur in 2003 brought more waves of refugees. Sudanese refugees may have reached two to three million—five million according to some estimates. Those who arrived from the South were mainly Christians. A small number of them, not more than 35,000 people, fulfilled the criteria of the UN High Commissioner for Refugees (UNHCR) to be formally considered as refugees, and so they were able to benefit from the medical services available in centers affiliated to the UNHCR, such as Caritas Egypt,[1] to move freely in Egypt, and especially to petition to be relocated to other countries, such as the United States, Australia, or Canada.

At the end of 2005, about 3,500 Sudanese people—whole families including infants, from different tribes, both Christian and Muslim—gathered in Mustafa Mahmoud Place in Cairo, in front of the headquarters of the UNHCR, to apply pressure in the hopes of being admitted as refugees. As one of the refugees, Rebecca, said, "they did not want to stay in Egypt, neither to go back to Sudan, because for many there was no home to go back to."[2] After three months of establishing themselves there, the police came to dislodge them, but the refugees' leaders refused the many warnings of the police. It ended in a horrible and terrifying scene; many lost their lives, and many more were injured, while others were taken to prison and badly treated. This tragic incident still marks the spirit and the memory of the Sudanese in Egypt.

Until 1995, the Sudanese people could travel to Egypt without a residence visa and benefit from health and schooling facilities, but in that year, Egypt accused the Sudanese government of being involved in an assassination attempt against then President Mubarak in Addis-Ababa, and Sudanese people were forced afterward to apply for an entry visa before arriving in Egypt. The Egyptian government provided no education, health, or nutritional services to the Sudanese refugees, and the great majority were helped by private organizations and Christian churches.

Challenges and Difficulties

The Sudanese refugees had suffered religious discrimination and persecution in their own country. They came from rural areas, and few of them had finished their secondary education. Almost all of them had sought refuge in Khartoum before they were compelled to leave because of the growing difficulties in finding jobs and the many vexations they were suffering from the government and the police. Arriving in Cairo, they found a noisy overcrowded city (sixteen to eighteen million), so they were forced to live among a huge number of people different in color, culture, and religion, in a country suffering from a difficult economic situation with an unemployment rate reaching 20 percent.

The first challenge that the refugees faced was finding appropriate housing, and rapidly they formed clusters living together in some districts of Cairo where churches, considered as main landmarks for refugees, were not far, or in neighborhoods where rent might be more affordable for them. The main Cairo districts (Abbaseya, Ain Shams, Zeitoun, and Maadi) where many Sudanese, mainly Christians, were settled are located on Metro Line 1, a fact that helped their mutual support and access to work. Other refugees found housing in the informal district Arbaa wa Nus, a few kilometers outside Cairo. In this district, dozens of people may live in the same apartment and share one toilet. The Sudanese settled in Cairo districts according to their tribal origin; for example, the Nuers and the Dinkas were concentrated at Abbaseya, and the Fur at Medinet Nasr.

In the popular districts where the Sudanese lived, many Egyptians accused them of being the cause of increasing rent. But in fact, the Sudanese complained of being treated unequally by Egyptian homeowners, and they rented houses at prices higher than Egyptians did. In order to afford the rent, many families lived together in the same apartment, each occupying a room. Relations with their Egyptian neighbors varied; they might be distant and discrete, or close and friendly. Here, too, religion played a positive role in bringing people together despite their racial and cultural differences. Being Christian in Egypt or Sudan is a factor of social discrimination that creates bonds of proximity and solidarity between those suffering the same destiny. Many Egyptian Christians showed spontaneous sympathy toward their coreligionists who fled persecution in their own country.

The Sudanese had to compete with Egyptians for scarce job opportunities and worked mainly in the informal sector or sold traditional goods in the streets. After some time, many Sudanese people relied on subsidies they received from relatives who had immigrated to Western countries, and afterward they became reluctant to accept work. Wherever the Sudanese lived, the presence of the refugees raised fears among Egyptians who had the feeling of being in front of a phenomenon of invasion.[3] In fact, they brought money to the country by working in the informal sector and by receiving monetary remittances from abroad,[4] but the Egyptian economy was not able to cope with the great migratory influx.

In almost all cases, because the Sudanese were not able to provide previous school reports and birth certificates for their children, and the parents themselves oftentimes lacked the valid residence permits, the children were not admitted into public schools, which were already overcrowded and offering only a mediocre level of instruction. Thousands of Sudanese children did not receive any education. Because of scarce resources, many Sudanese children who were admitted dropped out of school to do odd jobs and bring money to their households. Christian refugees, though to a lesser degree than in Sudan, still experienced discrimination because of their religion. They had greater difficulties in integration, being both black and Christian in a Muslim and Arab city.

In addition to housing, schooling, and economic difficulties, refugees had to face many negative racial prejudices from the Egyptians. In the streets, people called them dark, chocolate, or used other insults. Some women complained of sexual harassment, verbal or physical.[5] The racial discrimination against the Sudanese has historic roots; since 1898, when a joint British and Egyptian army defeated the Mahdiyya movement, many Sudanese people came to Egypt, but they were engaged in low-status social jobs, as doorkeepers or waiters. They were seen as "inferiors both racially and culturally."[6] However, these racial feelings were not present everywhere.

Many refugees felt they were trapped in a vicious cycle, one that started with poverty and was perpetuated by their inability to provide higher education to their children. This was even more complicated by the position of the UNHCR that prevented them from leaving for the United States, Canada, or Australia. Sudanese refugees were condemned to remain in Egypt without hope or a possible dream of a better future. One refugee, Melissa, described the situation in these words:

> You would think I would be used to rejection, so the sound of still another door closing behind me, as if my life was a long corridor of closed doors. More doors will open, and already I can hear the click as these doors shut too, and yet I keep my eyes open. I keep waiting for new doors to open.[7]

Some Sudanese people turned to alcohol and other drugs. Some tried their luck in Israel, but they frequently ended up as victims of smuggling gangs between the borders of Egypt and Israel. The refugees either lost their money or their lives, and only a few arrived at their destination. Those who remained alive were put in prison. From time to time, the media reported on scandals of organ theft from Sudanese and other African refugees. Many refugees were afraid of going alone to any hospital. In other cases, some refugees were approached to sell their organs by organized networks of organ traffickers.

Ethnic and Tribal Models in the Midst of Cairo

Almost all the refugees retained a keen interest in the history and culture of their home country and followed the news coming from home closely. It was a means of preserving their identity and transmitting it to their offspring. For others, the memories of the painful events that pushed them to leave their country did not leave any room for nostalgia about returning to Sudan. They chose to live in clusters as a way to cope with the identity crisis caused by the loss of "kin, home, community, and other spaces of relatedness."[8]

Two phenomena, complementary in their meaning and opposite in their appearance, marked the identity discourse of the Sudanese in Egypt. On one hand, the Sudanese, whatever their tribal, racial, or religious differences, affirmed their roots: "we are Africans, we are not Arabs." On the other hand, they also often strongly asserted their ethnic and tribal origins, as well as their distinct cultural traditions. In doing so, they sought to preserve their identity in the face of the challenges they were experiencing in their new society. Sudanese women continued to wear their traditional colorful robes, wrapped around their bodies in a way completely different from the customs of the majority of Egyptian women (who typically wear veils). Religious celebrations, as well as social events, were accompanied by joyful music and dance, both of which are not usual in Egyptian worship services.

The growing number of Sudanese people in Cairo reinforced their resolve to prove their differences and to proclaim their identity against all kinds of pressures from society. Recalling the tribal structure and its community bonds was one of the tactics of defense and self-affirmation. Nevertheless, the tribal system has undergone some change in this urban setting; as the refugees came and went frequently, the chief was elected for a limited period, and not chosen for life on the basis of his moral authority, as is done in Sudan. In other words, the tribal system functioned as an association in the city, offering different types of services to the members of the group and defending their rights. Yet rivalry and the partitions between tribes remained. Liturgical services were held in different tribal languages, and people traveled from different parts of the city to attend liturgical services in their own language. Few Sudanese attended Mass in the Coptic rite, the rite of many Christians in Egypt.

The Churches: Sudanese Home in a Foreign Land

In the context of a different culture, an indifferent government, and a restricted UNHCR, the churches rapidly became the main centers where Sudanese people found real refuge, and reconstructed their social communities according to their way of living and thinking. The war had taught Sudanese people, as Rebecca said,

> to use religious values as a means for survival, to understand how to cope with what was going around them, and to cope with the challenges they faced . . . In fact, religious fervor in Sudan was to a great extent measured by the pain that people suffered as result of the war.[9]

One of the refugees, George, spoke about his long and painful suffering in these words:

> Many innocent people lost their lives, children became orphans, families were broken up, and people like me were torn away from their homes and from the people they loved. And yet there are some happy endings to this war story. I know, because I am alive to tell it . . . I want the Sudanese to realize that the solution to our problems is not guns, but God. It is only through God that we can find peace in this world.[10]

The challenges that the Sudanese met in their new society turned them more and more toward churches and religion, and many priests and pastors witnessed an increase in the expression of religious belief as a way to retain faith and hope, and to face fear, despair, as well as material challenges. Mahzouz, a Sudanese refugee said,

> we prayed to God to help us, and to stop the war, but it never comes to an end. God seems to have abandoned Sudan and Africa. Africans saw each other as the enemy, and turned on their own brothers. The truth is that only peace is going to save us, and that this peace is going to come from within, from Africa itself, from each individual African.[11]

Sunday Masses became an important moment in their lives to defend their racial and cultural identity, and to access information on the situation in their original homes. The liturgical celebrations became not only the main space of expression of faith in the Lord who saves but also the occasion to rebuild communitarian bonds. The churches provided space and opportunities for faith formation and renewal and social encounters, as well as for work training programs, and even for political awareness and mobilization. The churches became beehives: at one corner classes for catechism and at the other corner a hiring center that processed requests for available work. Many had an office for medical care or for distributing food, clothing, and other goods. The priests and pastors also helped create space for the refugees in Egyptian society by offering opportunities for housing and jobs.

Many laypeople were engaged in church activities and services, and continued their religious formation in available centers such as the High Institute for Religious Sciences,[12] called Sakakini, next to the Sacred Heart Parish in Cairo, run by the Comboni Fathers. To some degree, there was competition between different churches to attract Sudanese people to their congregations by offering services and money. Catholic parishes (although Anglican parishes played an active part also) had an important role in the assistance offered to Sudanese refugees.[13] Many churches developed schools that followed the Sudanese curriculum to help children and young adolescents continue their education and be prepared for the future. St. Luanga School at Sacred Heart Parish, for example, enrolled one thousand students.

In some churches, like St. Andrew in Maadi, workshops for handicrafts, like masks, bags, or paintings, offered work opportunities for the refugees. These products were sold to Westerners who could afford the expensive prices.

As time passed, the Sudanese began to create spaces of social interaction other than the churches. Not far from the churches and near the large Sudanese populations, they opened small shops to provide Sudanese food, clothes, and cultural products such as music and other local goods. Restaurants became places of encounter and discussion. Associations emerged to deliver educational and medical services to the refugees. They served as a place to guide newly arrived people, and they provided English courses to prepare the Sudanese for their dreamed new life in a third country. By these means, the Sudanese tried to reach out to the society in which they lived and to establish their symbolic landmarks in it. They created their own territory, though modest, in Cairo.[14]

After the tragic incident of Mustafa Mahmoud Place, many Sudanese refugees realized that their hopes to be resettled in the United States, Canada, or Australia had vanished, and they were not able—despite the peace treaty between the South and the North of Sudan signed on June 1, 2004—to go back to their homeland. A new and dangerous phenomenon emerged: Sudanese youth gangs committing violent acts and stealing from other refugees. The churches in Cairo therefore began programs for these teenagers, providing formal education but also activities, such as art, music and sports, and tried to reach out to this youth population. Rumors emerged that the government of Sudan was backing these gangs and providing financial means to fuel the fighting between them in order to undermine the future of the youth and of the South of Sudan as a whole.

Despite the fact that these attempts to help the youth involved in the violence did not always bring the expected results, Mishca, one of the refugees who worked for the youth enrolled in the gangs, said,

> I learned to transcend the automatic reaction of self-pity and anger, and began to find solutions despite the seemingly endless problems of refugee life. I learned to have hope and now, as I grow older, I am sure of one thing: God arranges whatever happens or is going to happen to me and everything is under His control, so I am not afraid of the future. I pray to God that we can make positive changes to keep our teenagers from joining the gangs, that we can end the violence that we came to Egypt to escape.[15]

Partitions, Bridges, and Contacts

Initially when they arrived in Egypt, the Sudanese refugees considered it as a transitional step, a sort of waiting area, before reaching the land of their dreams. The lack of structures of assistance deepened their alienation. They did not know much about Egyptian traditions and ways of living, and they were not always eager to learn. The divide between Egyptian and Sudanese communities was almost total, leading to exclusion, confinement, and isolation. The Sudanese chose to regroup and organize themselves in homogenous communities, coming from the same region, speaking the same language, and practicing the same religion.[16]

In this context, acquiring the formal status of refugees offered the Sudanese a legitimation for their presence on the Egyptian soil. They were able to build up an identity that allowed them to make contact with Egyptians and showed that they were not exploiting the country's resources but only asking for their rights, with a clear and declared intention not to settle in Egypt. The decision of UNHCR in June 2004, to put an end to the designation of formal refugee status after the conclusion of the cease-fire between the North and the South of Sudan, definitely shattered the hope of traveling to a new and rich country. During the sit-in of Mustafa Mahmoud Place in December 2005, the Sudanese chiefs refused gestures of solidarity from Egyptians because it countered the image of being refused in Egypt and their great need to be settled in a third country.

Whatever the great difficulties encountered by both Sudanese and Egyptians, the everyday reality was not always dire. There were many cases of adaptation and mutual acceptance. While it was not a real integration, it was not a case of complete marginalization.[17] Mainly through the services provided by the churches, Sudanese women were able to find work in Egyptian houses as cleaners and babysitters; and after some time, Egyptian people specifically requested Sudanese women because they appreciated their reserve and their diligence to duty. Many men worked in shops, offices, and construction. Relations of trust, confidence, and mutual appreciation began between individuals of both Egyptian and Sudanese communities. Through these contacts, a new perception of the culture and habits of the other was made possible, and although limited in its extent, they influenced somewhat the general opinion of both populations. In some cases, Egyptian managers sought the Sudanese to work in their establishments. Some of the Christian Egyptians either joined groups of volunteers that helped church services or hired the Sudanese to work in the available informal sector.

A Missed Opportunity:
A Tale of Encounters and Failures

The Sudanese in Egypt are an uprooted people who struggle for their survival and the preservation of their cultural and religious identity. They came from a painful past and were facing an uncertain future. Many went back to their country after the declaration of the new state of South Sudan on January 9, 2011. Yet the dilemma persists, as one refugee, Melissa said:

> Our current dilemma is whether we should stay in Egypt or return to Sudan. Although the peace treaty was signed, peace is not yet a reality in my home country, though I wish it were. There is still war in Darfur and between various tribes. The tension and fierce competition between politicians

for important positions in the system is fierce, and extreme poverty and desperation lead to corruption. . . . Officially, there is peace but in reality there are landmines waiting in the fields, there is tension between tribes, between government officials and people, there is corruption and no infrastructure, medicine, or good schools.[18]

The Egyptian government ratified in 1980 the 1951 Geneva Convention on refugee status and right to asylum, its protocol of 1967, as well as the Constitution of the Organization of African Unity that relates to right of asylum. Nevertheless, the government restricted access of refugee children to schools; national medical insurance; and the delivery of ration procurement for sugar, oil, rice, and tea. In January 2004, Egypt and Sudan signed an agreement that guarantees the freedom of circulation, residence, work, and property to citizens of both countries. In February 2005, under pressure from the Egyptian National Council for Motherhood and Childhood, the Ministry of Health decreed that all foreigners resident in Egypt may have access to primary health care. The ratification of international conventions has never been implemented by laws that organize the refugees' life and their access to different services, and despite all the official decrees and agreements, the everyday fate of the refugees has not been ameliorated or alleviated.

Not only is the Egyptian government indifferent to the fate of the Sudanese refugees, but also the Egyptian church, in its major branch, the Coptic Orthodox (six to eight million), and the Coptic Catholic, a small but active minority (150,000), has not taken an active part in helping the Sudanese refugees. The priests, pastors, and religious sisters who are involved in helping the refugees and organizing services for them are mostly non-Egyptians. The Sudanese are a foreign people served by foreigners. The Egyptian church as an institution has not realized that the care of Sudanese people constitutes her own mission. She continues to operate as if there is not a social and ecclesial challenge, consisting in the presence of this great number of displaced people due to persecution, torture, violence, and poverty. Stories of the sufferings of the Sudanese refugees remained confined in their own enclosed circle and have not reached the conscience of the Egyptian church, or at least have not reshaped the understanding of her mission to bring comfort and support to suffering people.

In other words, the encounters failed to a large extent on the institutional level but were made possible through individual relations and experiences. Although they were not all a success story, many of them allowed Sudanese and Egyptian people to meet, come to know each other, and appreciate the human treasure that each one of them was carrying. These numerous individual encounters bridged, in some way, gaps between the two people, and offered the opportunity to both of them to bring the culture and richness of the other to their own people. Experiences were conveyed to that person's group through stories the person was telling about his or her life, and the self-disclosures that person was making about the changes that happened in his or her perception and comprehension of the other. These positive tales brought light and color to the large canvas that described the fate of the Sudanese refugees in rather dark lines. The general negative discourse about the situation of the Sudanese in Egypt was mitigated by more discrete, private, and individual stories about successful human encounters.

Those Sudanese who overcame their initial difficulties and found their way in Egyptian society are now more integrated. A new way of being Sudanese in Egypt is emerging after years of struggles, sufferings, and mutual misunderstandings and ignorance of the other, a way that is brighter and more balanced. Egyptian and Sudanese mentalities are slowly changing. Egyptians have become more accustomed to the presence of the Sudanese, and more welcoming, despite the persistent differences between the African and the Mediterranean cultures. The Sudanese have certainly acquired a greater knowledge of the Egyptian mentality and society, and developed a better creativity in adapting themselves to Egyptian society. They have passed this on to their children, to ensure for them a better perspective and life through integration. Might the future bring more successful encounters and fewer failures?

Notes

1. Since I work as a doctor at the Caritas clinic in Cairo's popular district of Matareya, I have many opportunities to encounter Sudanese refugees. I was also asked by the Comboni Sisters of Sacred Heart Parish to assist those injured after the December 1995 Mustafa Mahmoud Place clashes.

2. Nora Eltahawy, Brooke Comer, and Amani Elshimi, eds., *Voices in Refuge, Stories from Sudanese Refugees in Cairo* (New York: American University in Cairo Press, 2009), 44–45.

3. Fabienne Le Houérou, "Living with Your Neighbor: Forced Migrants and Their Hosts in an Informal Area of Cairo," in *Arba wa Nus, Diaspora in Cairo: Transient Presence and Transient Territory Conference* (Cairo: CEDEJ, AUC FMRS Department, 2004).

4. http://www.panapress.com.

5. Jane Kani Edward, *Sudanese Women Refugee: Transformations and Future Imaginings* (New York: Palgrave Macmillan, 2007), 183.

6. Ibid., 182.

7. Eltahawy, Comer, and Elshimi, *Voices in Refuge*, 64.

8. Stephanie I. Riad Akuei, "Cultural Mindfulness amongst the Dinka Displaced by War: Cairo as Potent Place to Points Beyond," http://www.aucegypt.edu/fmrs/Research/Akuei.pdf, cited in Eltahawy, Comer, and Elshimi, *Voices in Refuge*, 126.

9. Eltahawy, Comer, and Elshimi, *Voices in Refuge*, 40.

10. Ibid., 76.

11. Ibid., 93.

12. I taught many Sudanese students in this institute, especially courses on the social teaching of the Catholic Church.

13. Marilou Terrien, *Les réfugiés soudanais au Caire* (Lyon: Université Lyon 2, Institut d'Etudes politiques, 2005–2006), 8.

14. Ibid., 47.

15. Eltahawy, Comer, Elshimi, *Voices in Refuge*, 122.
16. Terrien, *Les réfugiés soudanais au Caire*, 36.
17. Ibid., 37.
18. Eltahawy, Comer, Elshimi, *Voices in Refuge*, 62–63.

Sailing the Waves on Our Own

Maryanne Loughry

Catholic social teaching has always taken a strong stance on refugees, asylum seekers, and migration, and in keeping with the principle of subsidiarity, the Catholic Church has taken the lead in identifying these people in regular encounters through the ministry of pastoral care. This has led to the Catholic Church embracing new categories of forcibly displaced people as they have emerged and become of concern in local settings. One such category that has been identified in recent times is people who are forced to leave their homes and communities because of environmental degradation and climate change.

As often happens with newly identified categories of people in need, many are slow to recognize not only the needs of these affected people but also their rights and entitlements. For people affected by environmental degradation and extreme climate events, this has been made all the more complex by ongoing debates about the science of climate change and arguments about who is responsible. Climate change has serious human rights ramifications and states have been slow to recognize their obligations to mitigate the harmful effects of human activity on the environment by reducing the greenhouse gases (GHG) released into the atmosphere. States need to be called on to ensure that their responses to climate change are consistent with their human rights obligations under domestic and international law. This year's much anticipated encyclical by Pope Francis on the environment promises to be one more way that Catholic social teaching champions the human and cultural rights of humans.

In the Pacific, regional governments and churches have always been aware that populations living on small islands struggle to have meaningful livelihoods and, in recent times, to feed their families and meet other fundamental human rights because of factors such as population overcrowding, fresh water shortages, poverty, and slow-onset environmental degradation. Today, however, because of more frequent extreme weather events, Pacific island communities are struggling to find sustainable solutions for these ongoing challenges. Frequent extreme weather events now commonly result in family and community members moving to other islands or the mainland for security, education, and employment, often leaving behind a few family members to attend to the ancestral family land. However, unlike ancient times, when relocation was easier and more readily accommodated, today's islander people are increasingly finding themselves in unfamiliar urban settings with uncertain futures.

As early as 1992, on the occasion of the fortieth anniversary of the establishment of the office of UN High Commissioner for Refugees (UNHCR), the Pontifical Council for the Pastoral Care of Migrants and Itinerant People, and the Pontifical Council "Cor Unum" jointly produced a statement of the Catholic Church's teaching on refugees: *Refugees: A Challenge to Solidarity*.[1] This document recognized that the refugees the Catholic Church referred to in its social teachings were a more inclusive group than those defined in the 1951 UN Refugee Convention[2] as a person who

> owing to a well-founded fear of being persecuted for reasons of race, religion, nationality, membership of a particular social group or political opinion, is outside the country of his nationality and is unable or, owing to such fear, is unwilling to avail himself of the protection of that country; or who, not having a nationality and being outside the country of his former habitual residence as a result of such events, is unable or, owing to such fear, is unwilling to return to it.

While embracing the UN definition of a refugee, *Refugee: A Challenge to Solidarity* went further and highlighted *de facto refugees*, victims of armed conflict, erroneous economic policies, and natural disasters, as people of concern to the Catholic Church.

Today these victims of natural disasters include populations displaced by climate change and environmental degradation. A comprehensive understanding of the characteristics of victims of natural disasters can be found at the Centre for Research on the Epidemiology of Disasters (CRED), located at the Université Catholique de Louvain (UCL), Belgium. Annually CRED registers all forms of global disasters, and in 2012 it registered 357 naturally triggered disasters resulting in 124.5 million victims worldwide.[3] Today, most of these naturally triggered disasters are viewed through the lens of climate change and its resulting displacement.

The number of people estimated to be affected by climate change is vast. Estimates of the numbers of climate-change displaced people have fluctuated wildly, with some suggesting up to two hundred million displaced should global warning "take hold."[4] What these exact numbers will be in the future remains uncertain. Calculating the number of people displaced and on the move has always been notoriously difficult to predict. Whether people are moving, directly or indirectly, because of climate change and environmental degradation is also very difficult to calculate due to the multiple possible causal factors in play. Additionally, many will only be displaced short term, whereas others will need permanent relocation because of the loss of their homes and land.

Possibly even more significant for Christians is the fact that most of these displaced people are poor. The effects of climate change are now seen as factors that are superimposed on existing population's vulnerabilities. People affected by climate change and environmental degradation have reduced access to drinking water, their health is negatively affected, and they experience significant threats to food security. For many there is a reduction of land mass for cultivation;[5] all of these are known drivers for deeper poverty and migration.

Pope Francis in his 2013 Apostolic Exhortation *Evangelii gaudium* has put the poor front and center for all Christians. At the very beginning of his first exhortation, Pope Francis laments the fact that when the Christian's interior life becomes caught up in self-interests and concerns, there is no place for the poor.[6] He especially elaborates the necessity for inclusion of the poor in society in paragraphs 186 through to 216 of *Evangelii gaudium*, extolling how important it is to be attentive to the cry of the poor and to come to the aid of the poor. Indeed, this emphasis is seen as a marker of Pope Francis's papacy. Further, in the same exhortation, Pope Francis has singled out new forms of poverty and vulnerability in which Christians are called to recognize the suffering Christ: the homeless, the addicted, refugees, indigenous people. In the same paragraph, he writes of migrants presenting a particular challenge, calling himself the pastor of a church without frontiers.[7] Climate-change displaced people are the very exemplars of the poor and vulnerable that Pope Francis is highlighting.

Very early in his papacy, on his first official visit outside of Rome, Pope Francis visited the Italian island of Lampedusa off Sicily. This small island is the landing place for refugees and migrants traveling by boat to Europe and "seeking a better life."[8] These migrants and refugees come from countries such as Eritrea, Nigeria, Syria, Mali, Gambia, Guinea Bissau, and Senegal. They come in hope of entering what some call Fortress Europe. They have taken the dangerous journey because for the vast majority there is no other pathway. They are blocked from obtaining visas through the regular migration pathways.

Pope Francis went to Lampedusa to pray with those who had come by boat. Aware that thousands of people were arriving by this dangerous means and that many other thousands had perished en route, he went to pray, celebrate Eucharist, and to thank the local community and other civil society groups who provide hospitality to these migrants and refugees. In his homily that day, Pope Francis spoke of a culture of well-being that now pervaded society, resulting in most people being indifferent to the plight of these poor, indifferent to refugees and migrants. He emphasized the globalization of indifference[9] where people have come to be indifferent to the suffering of others. In his homily on Lampedusa, Pope Francis lamented the lack of attentiveness to our world, our failure to protect what God has created, and our lack of concern for others.

It is now recognized with more authority than ever that our world is experiencing significant climate change with immense impacts on populations; while this was formerly a contested area of science, governments and climate scientists are now more than ever acknowledging this reality. The authoritative 2014 Intergovernmental Panel on Climate Change (IPCC) report is unequivocal in concluding, "Human interference with the climate system is occurring and climate change poses risks for humans and natural systems."[10] The IPCC is a scientific intergovernmental body established in 1988 by two UN organizations: the World Meteorological Organization and the United Nations Environmental Program (UNEP) to assess the scientific, technical. and socioeconomic information relevant for the understanding of the risk of human induced climate change.[11] The 2014 IPCC report is a review of all of the published scientific reports on climate change, and contends that since the last report in 2007, there has been a large increase in the published material being reviewed resulting in a substantially larger knowledge base and strengthening the IPCC's capacity to make assertions on climate change with ever increasing levels of confidence.

In spite of the work of the IPCC and other research bodies, climate-change skeptics still abound. And like all global issues of our time, the issue is complex. In relation to climate change and displacement, this complexity is characterized by the difficulty in ascertaining the degree of influence of environmental factors and climate change on peoples' decision to move given the multiple causal factors that impact people's decision to relocate.

Accepting that climate change and its associated environmental degradation are predicted to displace millions of people in the coming years,[12] and contribute to world poverty, what are some of the ethical questions behind climate-change displacement? Christians need to ask how our approach to ecology informs our understanding and response to climate change, and furthers our response to climate-change induced displacement.

In many nation-states, the poor are low carbon emitters, yet they are bearing the brunt of human interference on our climate and environment. They are the ones who are asked to adapt their lifestyle to adjust for climate change while corporations and governments resist mitigation. There is also no covenant or legal agreement that defends the rights of these migrants whose movement is induced by climate change.

One way into this ethically complex topic and the questions posed above is to look at a case study of a situation of displacement that is happening now, one that is of concern to many internationally and to the Catholic Church in particular.

A Case Study of Fifty Years

Sailing the Waves on Our Own is the anglicized name of Tulele Peisa, a Pacific nongovernmental organization located in Bougainville, Papua New Guinea. With the assistance of the Catholic Church of Bougainville, Tulele Peisa is working with Pacific Islanders who immediately need to be relocated from their small island communities due to the impact of rising sea levels on their land. Why are the Catholic Church and this nongovernmental organization engaged in this role? For more than fifty years, the plight of the Carteret Islanders has been known, researched, and documented. Indeed the people of the Carteret Islands have even been identified and characterized in the international media as the world's first climate refugees,[13] yet for decades they have struggled to have their needs adequately resourced so as to be able to plan for their future with dignity. Relocation to a more stable environment is still a dream for most of them.

The people of the Carteret Islands are one of the many small island populations recognized in the earlier 2007 IPCC report[14] as being extremely vulnerable to the effects of climate change. The government of Papua New Guinea and the Autonomous Bougainville Government have agreed that residents of the Carteret Islands (approximately six thousand inhabitants) need to be resettled to the Papua New Guinea mainland because of environmental degradation, salt water inundation, and food insecurity, all of which are exacerbated by accelerating climate change.

The Islanders' vulnerability is particularly exacerbated by what appears to be limited adaptive capacity and adaptation options by the affected people and their government. This is exacerbated by the high adaptation costs relative to Papua New Guinea's gross domestic product.

A Little History: Fifty Years Ago

The reality is that the effects of climate change and resulting displacement are not new to this population and many others. For the Carteret Islanders, their difficulties surviving on their small atolls was acknowledged as early as 1963, when Catholic missionaries wrote to the then district commissioner reporting an acute food shortage following a coconut failure.[15] In this correspondence, the Catholic mission offered suitable land for possible relocation of the Carteret Islanders to the Bougainville mainland. In the following year, the office of the Bougainville district reported that the Carteret Island had a population in 1964 of 716 people, and that there was little doubt that there were periods of time when the Carteret Islanders had insufficient food for their needs.[16]

Thirty Years Ago

In the early 1980s, the North Solomon Provincial Government planned to overcome the problem of population overcrowding and food insecurity on the atolls through a resettlement scheme. An atolls resettlement committee was established in 1982, and a site was identified in the Kuveria district on the Bougainville mainland along the Keita-Buka highway. The first settlers comprised families from the Carteret Islands and another atoll, Nissan. Families from the atolls of Mortlock and Tasman atoll indicated that while they had initially been keen to resettle, they would now only consider coming later.[17]

A provincial data system survey conducted in December 1985 recorded 128 settlers had relocated to the Atolls Resettlement Area on the mainland, with over half from the Carteret Islands. Anthropology Professor Maeve O'Collins and her students visited the resettlement area in 1985 and made a number of recommendations to improve the livelihood options of the settlers. They noted that considerable progress had been made by the settlers, drawing particular attention to the fact that in the resettlement area, the settlers lived away from the sea and were dependent on gardening for their livelihood.[18] The major problems identified by Professor Collins related to relationship issues with the local population and access to fishing rights. Not long after relocation, two of the Carteret families left the resettlement site on account of the uncertainty surrounding long-term land rights and the need to maintain existing land rights on the Carteret Islands.

In the 1990s, Bougainville became embroiled in civil unrest known as the Bougainville crisis. No one factor was solely responsible for this crisis, which developed into a bloody civil conflict with roots in an independence movement from Papua New Guinea, ethnicity issues, and access to significant mining resources. In the midst of this conflict, all atoll settlers left the resettlement site and returned either to their atoll or elsewhere in Bougainville. Once again the increased population on the atolls resulted in food insecurity.

No one factor ever explains why people leave their land. In this small case study thus far, overpopulation and food insecurity are the elements identified necessitating a resettlement program. The food insecurity is attributed to crop failure and too many mouths to feed given the livelihood options on the atolls. The population pressure was temporarily eased by relocation, but instability in the resettlement site, insufficient guarantees relating to entitlements for livelihoods (in this instance fishing rights), and uncertainty surrounding future stability resulted in some returning early and all returning eventually in the light of a larger conflict focused on entitlements.

The Twenty-first Century

Fast forward to the twenty-first century; post-Bougainville crisis, the population on the atolls has continued to grow and food insecurity has become even more apparent. People are now surviving on the atolls because the Autonomous Bougainville Government is delivering rice to the atolls every three months or, more correctly, when the government has money for rice and when the ship is fit to sail and when families on the mainland are sending food supplies to their families on the atolls. The people on the atolls are experiencing crop failures, extreme weather events, insufficient rain, monsoon conditions, and land inundation with salt water at increasing levels, and formerly known weather patterns are changing. They are starting to understand all of these events through the paradigm of climate change.

In 2007, in light of the increased crowding and deteriorating weather patterns, the Autonomous Bougainville Government reaffirmed an urgent need to resettle communities from the atolls northeast of Bougainville, as it was now very apparent that the population was growing too large for the islands even with the supplementary rice deliveries. Further, there has been limited success with alternative income-generating sources to sustain a viable economic livelihood for the island communities. Many of these initiatives had been short term and proved to be unsustainable for numerous reasons, including the limited financial resources of the government. The arable land for food crops on the islands has diminished, and now there is also a shortage of timber for traditional building materials due to sea water inundation and increasing levels of salt in the soil.[19]

In the light of this conclusion, the Planning Division of the Bougainville Administration adopted an Atolls Integrated Development Policy and requested two million Kina ($700,000 USD) from the National Papua New Guinea Government to assist with resettlement of communities from the atolls. It announced that by March 2009, forty families would be resettled on the Bougainville mainland.[20] The key job of the Bougainville Administration was now to secure suitable land for the resettlement of people from the atolls.

It is at this point that two resettlement schemes began to evolve, one led by the Autonomous Bougainville Government, the other by a nongovernment organization, Tulele Peisa, led by a Carteret Island woman, Ursula Rakova. In 2009, Ms. Rakova also announced, with a significantly smaller amount of money, that her organization, Tulele Peisa, would relocate five families to the mainland on land donated by the Catholic Church.[21] Why two resettlement schemes?

In the last decade, both the Autonomous Bougainville Government and Tulele Peisa have conducted social surveys of the Carteret Islands. Both social surveys have concluded that there is a worsening situation on the islands. The government has then proceeded with caution. A resettlement site has been identified at Karoola, on the Bougainville mainland. Mindful of past relocation failures, the government has conducted extensive consultations with landowners and neighboring communities of Karoola. However, in spite of these efforts, the site has not yet been secured, and no one has been relocated. Frustrated by the slowness of government, perceived broken promises, and concern over the use of the relocation funds, the Carteret Islanders have at the same time made decisions of their own. Believing that they needed to take their own steps, the elders of the Carteret Islands have supported the establishment of an indigenous organization Tulele Peisa tasked with organizing a well-planned, staged program of moving Carteret Island people from their home atolls to the Bougainville mainland, "where they could be safe and secure with access to economic opportunities as well as health and education services."[22] The Catholic Church of Bougainville has donated more than seventy-one hectares of land, private funds have been raised, and five families have been relocated. The group's leaders realize that their relocation process will be slow. The Tinputz land can only accommodate twenty families, but the Catholic Church has offered four more locations.[23]

In essence, over fifty years on from the early documentation of their plight, the Carteret Islands people are more at risk than ever. Daily the factors of environmental degradation, changes in climate, food insecurity, overcrowding, and poverty impact their lifestyle, and yet even with international media attention, no durable solution to their situation has been found.

When asked about their plight, the Carteret Islands people who have expressed interest in relocating to the Autonomous Bougainville Government listed food, shelter, and fresh water as their three top priorities.[24] Their knowledge of the natural world has been passed to them through their elders, their traditions, and their own experience. Some have had formal education in mainstream science, but these are few. When interviewed, they are very clear about the immediate changes that are happening to their environment and the acceleration of these changes especially in relation to the climate, weather events, and their crops. In recent times, government officials from relevant departments on the mainland have come to speak with them about climate change and the need for adaptation. Some have even seen Al Gore's video on climate change: *An Inconvenient Truth*. What they do know is that measures put in place on the Carteret Islands to adapt to rising sea levels and extreme weather events, primarily sea walls, are insufficient to combat the rising tides and resulting salt inundation. Ironically, these people are among the world's lowest carbon emitters, yet they believe that they are experiencing a disproportionate amount of impact from human interference with the climate system.

Discussions about climate change and climate adaptation can also be confusing for these islanders. Well versed in Scripture, many strongly believe that God has made a covenant that will protect their land from sinking or being overwhelmed with water. The covenant that many Islanders put their faith in is from Genesis 9:8 through 9:17, when God promised Noah that he would not destroy the earth any more: Then God said to Noah and to his sons with him (v. 8), "As for me, I am establishing my covenant with you, and your descendants after you (v. 9), and with every living creature that is with you, the birds, the domestic animals, and every animal of the earth with you, as many as came out of the ark" (v. 10). "I establish my covenant with you, that never again shall all flesh be cut off by the waters of a flood, and never again shall there be a flood to destroy the earth" (v. 11). God said, "This is the sign of the covenant that I make between me and you and every living creature that is with you, for all future generations" (v. 12). "I have set my bow in the clouds, and it shall be for a sign of a covenant between me and the earth"(v. 13). "When I bring clouds over the earth, and the bow is seen in the clouds" (v. 14), "I will remember my covenant that is between me and you and every living creature of all flesh; and the waters shall never again become a flood to destroy all flesh" (v. 15). When the bow is in the clouds, I will see it and remember the everlasting covenant between God and every living creature of all flesh that is on the earth" (v. 16). God said to Noah, "This is the sign of the covenant which I have established between me and all flesh that is on the earth" (v. 17). These strong religious beliefs are not enough to explain or address the issues that they face now and into the future, but it will be difficult to overcome this reliance on religious assurance without leadership and sensitive education.

Christians are increasingly becoming aware of the harm they are doing to the earth and are responding with a new way of being on earth.[25] Australian theologian Denis Edwards calls this new way of being a conversion as people come to know that creation is a precious gift. For Christians this process of conversion results from us "seeing the Earth and all its creatures as God's good creation, the creation that God radically embraces in the incarnation of the Word made flesh."[26]

Most Pacific Islanders are Christians, but most have not been introduced to a formal Christian approach to ecology. It would seem that the challenge to the Carteret Islanders impels Christians to embrace the challenges of our natural world within a theological framework of conversion. We also need to be mindful that the presentation of the challenges of our natural world will not always be so obvious. They will be found in slow onset land degradation, food insecurity, and poverty.

A further challenge for us is how we should best conceptualize these affected people and their plight. What are their rights and entitlements in our globalized world and how can we best advocate with them for these entitlements? As mentioned earlier, the Catholic Church has always looked beyond the 1951 UN definition of refugees and referred to a category of people, including disaster-affected people, as de facto refugees. Is this an adequate conceptualization of these island people on the move, and does it afford them the protection and supports they need?

What is becoming clearer is that people displaced by environmental degradation and climate change are not considered to meet the UN definition of a refugee, preventing affected people seeking protection from the effects of climate change in signatory states. Presently there is also much discussion about whether the UN definition of a refugee needs to be revisited to reflect current realities of forced displacement, but there is concern that such a process could result in a narrower rather than a more expansive definition, and much effort is being put into ensuring that states' responses to climate change are consistent with their human rights obligations under domestic and international law. Catholic social teaching and Christian ecological theology are some of the means by which we can come to understand how best to respond to one of the most pressing issues of the twenty-first century. Our pastoral work facilitates our encounter with these challenges, and like the Diocese of Bougainville, the Catholic Church may respond with immediate and practical support. We are also called to ensure that those most affected are not left to sail the waves on their own due to our indifference, but rather are embraced and offered full inclusion in society.[27]

Notes

1. Pontifical Council 'Cor Unum' and Pontifical Council for the Pastoral Care of Migrants and Itinerant People, *Refugees: A Challenge to Solidarity* (1992), http://www.vatican.va.

2. Convention Relating to the Status of Refugees, opened for signature July 28, 1951, 189 UNTS 150 (entered into force April 22, 1954).

3. Debarati Guha-Sapir, Phillipe Hoyois, and Regina Below, *Annual Disaster Statistical Review 2012* (Brussels: Centre for Research on the Epidemiology of Disasters [CRED], Universite Catholique de Louvain-la Neuve, 2013).

4. Norman Myers, "Environmental Refugees: A Growing Phenomenon of the 21st Century," *Philosophical Transactions: Biological Science* 357, no. 1420 (2002): 609–13.

5. Organization for Economic Cooperation and Development, *Poverty and Climate Change. Reducing the Vulnerability of the Poor through Adaptation* (Paris: OECD, 2003).

6. Pope Francis, *Evangelii gaudium* (Vatican City: Liberia Editrice Vaticana, 2013), no. 2.

7. Ibid., no. 210.

8. Homily of Pope Francis, July 8, 2013, http://en.radiovaticana.va.

9. Ibid.

10. Intergovernmental Panel on Climate Change, *Fifth Assessment Report, Working Group II, AR5, Summary for Policy Makers*, http://www.ipcc-wg2.gov/AR5/.

11. Intergovernmental Panel on Climate Change, *Mitigation of Climate Change* (IPCC (2014).

12. Rabab Fatima, Anita Jawaadurova Wadud, and Sabira Coelho, *Human Rights, Climate Change, Environmental Degradation and Migration: A New Paradigm* (Bangkok: International Organization for Migration and Migration Policy Institute, 2014).

13. IRIN, *Papua New Guinea; The World's First Climate Change Refugees* (June 8, 2008), http://www.irinnews.org/report/78630/papua-new-guinea-the-world-s-first-climate-change-refugees.

14. Nobuo Mimura et al., "Small Islands. Climate Change 2007: Impacts, Adaptation and Vulnerability," in *Contribution of Working Group II to the Fourth Assessment Report of the Intergovernmental Panel on Climate Change,* ed. M. L. Parry et al. (Cambridge: Cambridge University Press, 2007), 687–716.

15. Tsiroge (1963).[Letter to P Mollison]. Photocopy in possession of Maryanne Loughry.

16. Clancy (1963). [Letter to the Secretary, Department of the Administrator, Port Moresby]. Photocopy in possession of Maryanne Loughry.

17. Maeve O'Collins, "Carteret Islanders at the Atolls Resettlement Scheme: A Response to Land Loss and Population Growth," in *Implications of Expected Climate Change in the South Pacific Region: An Overview, UNEP Regional Sea Reports and Studies 128*, ed. J. C. Pernetta & P. J. Hughes (Nairobi: United Nations Environment Program, 1990), 247–69.

18. Maeve O'Collins et al., "Carteret Islanders at the Atolls Resettlement Scheme: Adapting to a New Way of Life" (1986), unpublished manuscript.

19. Autonomous Government of Bougainville, "Bougainville Atolls Resettlement: An Exploration of Key Social and Cultural Impacts" (2009), unpublished manuscript.

20. "Carteret Islanders to be Resettled to Bougainville," *Solomon Times*, November 5, 2008, http://www.solomontimes.com/news/carteret-islanders-to-be-resettled-to-bougainville/2971.

21. *Carteret Islanders-First Climate Refugees*, *Solomon Times*, May 6, 2009, http://www.solomontimes.com/news/carteret-islanders--first-climate-refugees/3964.

22. Tulele Peisa, http://www.tulele-peisa.org/.

23. Julie B. Edwards, "The Logistics of Climate-Induced Resettlement; Lessons from the Carteret Islands, Papua New Guinea." *Refugee Survey Quarterly* 32, no.3 (2013): 52–78.

24. Bougainville Atolls Program Coordination Unit, "Quantitative and Qualitative Assessment of Resettlement-affected Communities of Carterets & Karoola" (2012), unpublished manuscript.

25. Denis Edwards, *Jesus and the Natural World: Exploring a Christian Approach to Ecology* (Melbourne: Garratt Publishing, 2012).

26. Ibid, 4.

27. Pope Francis, *Evangelii gaudium*, http://w2.vatican.va.

Partaking in "Foreignness" as Consolation

The Work of Centro Astalli with Refugees in Rome[1]

Diego Alonso-Lasheras, SJ

As the *capital* of the Catholic Church, Rome is usually associated with solemn ceremonies and beautiful Renaissance and Baroque churches filled with magnificent works of art. Yet, there is much more to it. In the heart of the city, the Centro Astalli welcomes more than five hundred refugees from all over the world every day. It is located on Via degli Astalli, a small street that separates Palazzo Venezia from the Church of the Gesù, where Saint Ignatius Loyola is buried. Centro Astalli began in 1981 as the Italian branch of the Jesuit Refugee Service (JRS).

This case study shows how the defense of human rights of refugees is at the heart of the church by presenting how Centro Astalli serves, advocates for, and accompanies the poorest of the poor. Pedro Arrupe, in the letter in which he instituted JRS, affirmed, "God is calling us through these helpless people. We should consider the chance of being able to assist them a privilege that will, in turn, bring great blessings to ourselves and our Society."[2] By accompanying refugees, and partaking in their struggle, they extend this blessing also to the heart of the church.

The Origins of JRS and Centro Astalli

JRS was founded by Pedro Arrupe, then superior general of the Society of Jesus, on November 14, 1980.[3] In the letter with which he created JRS, he narrated how, around Christmas of 1979, "struck and shocked by the plight of thousands of boat people and refugees,"[4] he had felt it his duty to send cables to twenty major superiors of the Society of Jesus around the world, asking them what they could do in their own countries and what the global Society of Jesus could do to alleviate such a dramatic situation. Subsequently, Arrupe called a consultation in September of 1980 to examine what could be the response of the Society of Jesus to the increasingly serious problem of refugees. During the consultation, Arrupe affirmed that he considered the work with refugees "a new modern apostolate for the Society [of Jesus] as a whole, of great importance for today and the future, and of much spiritual benefit for the Society [of Jesus]."[5] As a result of the consultation, JRS was created as an extension of the social secretariat at the Jesuit General Curia in Rome.[6]

Among the aims and objectives of JRS are establishing a network of already-existing work for refugees in order to better coordinate and plan aid, collect information to understand new opportunities of service to refugees, mediate between the offers of help coming from the provinces and the needs of international organizations and agencies, raise the level of conscience among Jesuits of the importance of this apostolate, and encourage Jesuit institutions to research and publish about refugee issues.[7] JRS was not to become a big operation; rather, it was to become a loving response by the Society of Jesus toward helpless people.

Arrupe had witnessed the plight of the Vietnamese boat people who were soon followed by their Cambodian and Laotian neighbors, but he was also moved by the extreme need of the Ethiopian refugees in Rome who were fleeing from Menghistu's regime.[8] Soon after Arrupe's letter, in the basement of the Jesuit community of via degli Astalli, 14/A, a first response to the Ethiopian refugees was given.

Arrupe had asked Michael Campbell-Johnston, head of the Jesuits' social secretariat, to run JRS in its first steps,[9] and Campbell-Johnston was directly involved in setting up Centro Astalli. He was keen on making Centro Astalli a work of the Church of Rome. To guarantee that this would happen, Campbell-Johnston tried to involve as many institutions and people as possible. Seminarians from the Pontificio Collegio Pio Brasileiro and the Pontifical North American College (PNAC), as well as scholars from the Collegio Internazionale del Gesù, where Jesuits in formation from all over the world study, were part of the team. Many religious sisters also answered the call as well as religious men and young laymen and women belonging to the Christian Life Community (CLC) who met at the church of Sant'Andrea al Quirinale. For medical attention, refugees were welcomed at the Ospedale San Giovanni Calibita, run by the Hospitaller Order of Saint John of God. The Centro Astalli was born as a collaborative work of the Church of Rome to defend and serve the human rights of refugees.[10]

In the beginning, the operation was rather precarious. At first, sandwiches were distributed; soon afterward hot meals were cooked on a stove that someone had found abandoned somewhere. The kitchen was coordinated by a religious sister and staffed by the young men and women of the CLC. In the summer of 1983 some building work was done, industrial stoves and refrigerators were installed, and a pantry set up. Toilets and showers were also built.[11] As Chiara Peri recalls, soon, without any governmental support, hundreds of people were being fed every day in the very center of Rome.[12] Centro Astalli opened at 5 p.m., with supper at 6:30 p.m.

Some refugees were received in a Roman parish; some were received at the PNAC and others in different religious houses. Beyond food, refugees found in Centro Astalli a place where they could stay and be with others. American seminarians would teach them English, and young CLC members would teach them Italian. They received help with bureaucratic paperwork. They could read the newspaper or just chat with each other and with many of the volunteers who worked there. It was the embodiment of Campbell-Johnston's emphasis on making Centro Astalli a work of the whole Church of Rome.

Centro Astalli is an initiative that resounds with the experience of St. Ignatius of Loyola and his first companions shortly after they arrived in Rome.[13] Fr. Peter Hans Kolvenbach, general of the Society of Jesus following Arrupe, recalls how the first Jesuits looked after many of the impoverished people who were drawn to Rome in the winter of 1538 after a year of a poor harvest. Many people slept in the streets, and some met death while they slept. In response to that tragic situation, the first Jesuits would beg during the day through the streets of Rome for food or firewood. At night, they collected some of the homeless from the streets in the house where they lived. There they washed and fed them, and they all gathered after supper around a big fire.[14] Kolvenbach also describes how JRS had grown and developed in ten years. Among the different initiatives that were mentioned, he wrote, "Here in Rome, some 140 Ethiopian refugees meet every night at the *Centro Astalli.*"[15] Arrupe had affirmed that JRS should not become a big operation, but the growing number of refugees was taking JRS—and Centro Astalli—in a different direction.

The Plight of Refugees and Centro Astalli Today

According to the United Nations, migrations worldwide are a growing phenomenon in quantity, complexity, and impact.[16] The plight of the refugees is particularly dramatic. On April 19, 2015, the question of refugees was dramatically brought to the attention of Italian public opinion when more than seven hundred people died trying to reach Lampedusa, Italy's southernmost island and territory.[17]

The number of refugees in the world grew from around ten million people in the early 1980s when Centro Astalli was founded, to around sixteen million between 1990 and 1992. After 2007, the number of refugees in the world started growing again. These numbers almost triple if internally displaced people are taken into account.[18]

In 2012, there was a 20 percent increase from the previous year in the number of people applying for asylum in the European Union, reaching a total of 335,380. By 2014, the asylum seekers to the European Union reached 626,000.[19] Italy's geographical position, at the center of the Mediterranean, looking toward the Middle East and North Africa, makes it especially sensitive to conflicts. Good weather conditions, together with certain political circumstances, encourage the transit of asylum seekers on dinghies to the southern coasts of Italy. In the last few years, there has also been a qualitative transformation of the asylum seekers, with an increase of families and vulnerable minors. Although the Italian law of asylum, the Bosi-Fini Law, is restrictive, Italy ranks as one of the countries in Europe with the highest asylum-granting percentage, 80.7 percent, over a European average of 31.1 percent. In 2012, the total number of asylum seekers in Italy was 64,779.[20] By the end of May 2015, 46,500 refugees had arrived in Italy.[21]

Centro Astalli has been accompanying, serving, and defending the human rights of refugees since it was founded. It has tried to become not just a place where room and board is offered but also a place in which "education and medical assistance, and the possibility of assuming responsibility for their own lives, cultivating their own cultures and traditions, and freely expressing their own faith"[22] becomes possible, a place where cultural rights are taken into account. It has grown from a place that offered sandwiches and good company to around thirty people to a structure that encounters every year around 37,000 asylum seekers, helping them to heal the deep wounds that have been inflicted on them in their flight, recognizing their human dignity, and giving them the possibility of regaining control of their lives.[23]

The people who arrive in Rome after an exhausting trip discover that one of the first things they need in order to be able to apply for asylum is a domicile in which they can be reached. Therefore, for many of the people who live in the streets, via degli Astalli, 14/A, becomes a domicile in which they can receive mail. In this way, this reception service becomes the first step in the long bureaucratic process to get some type of legal protection. In 2013, more than six thousand people asked to have their domicile in via degli Astalli, 14/A. Everyday dozens of refugees arrive at the reception desk of Centro Astalli to check if they have any mail.[24]

The *mensa*, Centro Astalli's soup kitchen, was the seed from which the entire operation grew, and it is still today the heart of the organization. It is a crossroads of languages and cultures. Everyday around 3:00 p.m. a long line forms in via degli Astalli at the very center of Rome. Refugees, who are usually rendered invisible, become visible in the midst of tourists who flock to the center of the Eternal City. The *mensa* serves a simple meal to 350 to 400 people a day. The service operates five days a week from Monday to Friday.[25]

The premises of via degli Astalli, 14/A, though, are open from 9:00 a.m. to welcome anyone seeking information or just a place in which to stay warm or take a shower. Beyond these services at the site, refugees are offered legal and medical services. Italian law recognizes the right to medical assistance for forced migrants upon their arrival on Italian territory.[26] Making this right a reality requires the constant work of accompaniment done at Centro Astalli. Volunteer doctors offer first aid consultation for minor health problems and provide referrals for people who are in need of more important medical help. This service depends on volunteers who do cultural and linguistic mediation and help patients to register in the Servizio Sanitario Nazionale—Italy's public health service—and assist them in using it. Some of the patients are first-timers, but others are old-timers who come back because they particularly trust the doctor who first saw them or because they find themselves culturally and linguistically understood at Centro Astalli, and not just medically helped.[27]

Asylum seekers in Italy struggle to understand the bureaucratic procedures and long waiting times they have to go through. To accompany the asylum seeker in these trials is the task of the Centro di Ascolto e Orientamento Socio-Legale, a counseling center where asylum seekers are helped to prepare their application and the hearing in front of the Territorial Commission for Asylum Seekers but also to navigate all the legal and bureaucratic procedures they have to go through.[28]

Over thirty years, the work of Centro Astalli has overflowed beyond its original premises. JRS conceives the accompaniment of refugees as "an encounter of endless mutual learning."[29] The men and women working and volunteering at Centro Astalli have learned that food and warmth are good, but not enough, and slowly but surely—*piano piano* as the Italians like to say—the organization has extended its premises throughout the Eternal City. It now provides housing for sixty men at San Saba, using an old parish cinema that has been turned into a dormitory. Seventy women are housed at Casa di Giorgia. More than two hundred men have been able to use Il Faro, a dormitory that was opened in 2006 to host the Afghani asylum seekers who, until then, slept at Ostiense train station. Sixty-three families and eighteen vulnerable minors enjoy housing at the Centro per Famiglie e Minori Pedro Arrupe, Centro Astalli's bigger and more complex facility. Besides housing, all these places help refugees through the Italian language school that Centro Astalli runs and through many initiatives that foster the development of capabilities that allow refugees to integrate themselves in Italian society, to be able to find a job, and to relinquish the help that they receive, in order to take back full command of their lives.[30]

In extending its services beyond the original premises of via degli Astalli, the organization has remained faithful to Campbell-Johnston's original intention of making Centro Astalli a work of the Church of Rome. Many religious women and men are part of the more than 450 volunteers who make Centro Astalli's activities possible. Bishops send seminarians for internships, which sometimes requires that they live in one of the housing facilities with the refugees. After their internships or volunteer work, seminarians are offered the opportunity to reflect on the meaning of the commitment to justice for a diocesan priest.[31]

As it grows, Centro Astalli has learned to collaborate with other church associations and has particularly developed a number of projects with Caritas Rome. These projects include teaching Italian, actions oriented to promote social integration, and providing psychological treatment for asylum seekers.[32] Pope Francis's visit to via degli Astalli, 14/A, has further developed the implication of other church groups in welcoming refugees into the heart of the church.

Refugees at the Heart of the Church

Pope Francis's visit to Centro Astalli's soup kitchen on September 10, 2013, rendered decidedly visible the men and women who are usually invisible in the very center of Rome, where the most conspicuous phenomena are the city's beautiful monuments, the throngs of tourists and pilgrims, and the presence of the church's headquarters. Pope Francis is particularly sensitive to the plight of refugees, as he proved in his visit to Lampedusa in July of 2013. In his visit to one of the most important points of entry into the European Union for migrants and refugees, Pope Francis celebrated Mass at the site of what is called the graveyard of wrecks and alerted during his homily against "the globalization of indifference."

Pope Francis has restated his concern for refugees in his Apostolic Exhortation *Evangelii gaudium*, in which he calls the church to draw near to the new ways of poverty and vulnerability, among which he cites refugees. He affirms that "Migrants present a particular challenge for me, since I am the pastor of a Church without frontiers, a Church which considers herself mother to all."[33] John Paul II had affirmed that the plight of refugees was "perhaps the greatest tragedy of all the human tragedies of our time."[34] Benedict XVI expressed himself in a similar way in February 2008, when he referred to JRS as the development of "one of Fr. Arrupe's last far-sighted intuitions" and affirmed that the Society of Jesus "continues to do praiseworthy work in the service for refugees, who are often the poorest of the poor."[35]

Pope Francis's visit to Lampedusa was certainly a surprise, as was his visit to the *mensa* of Centro Astalli two months later. Upon his arrival, he greeted the people waiting in line to get in, and then he went inside the building and with simplicity and warmth greeted and chatted with refugees and the people working at the *mensa*. The pope then proceeded to the Church of the Gesù, where he met with 350 refugees and 300 volunteers of Centro Astalli. In his speech, he highlighted that in working with refugees, one does not just give something or some time, but rather tries "to enter into a relationship with asylum seekers and refugees, recognizing them as people, committed to finding concrete responses to their needs."[36]

Toward the end of his speech, he stated that "it is important for the whole Church that welcoming the poor and promoting justice not be entrusted solely to 'experts' but be a focus of all pastoral care, of the formation of future priests and religious, and of the ordinary work of all parishes, movements and ecclesial groups."[37] The pope's words have certainly had an effect. Some Roman parishes have started to open up to welcome refugees, and a number of religious communities have offered some spare housing space in convents and religious houses.[38]

Foreignness:
An Essential Dimension of Christian Faith[39]

Kevin O'Brien has argued that the work of JRS can be conceived as consolation in action.[40] In the work of JRS, and particularly in Centro Astalli, consolation is not just experienced by refugees but also by the women and men involved in all of the organization's activities. In defending the human rights of refugees, Christians are able to deepen their faith.

Consolation, in Ignatian vocabulary, is a very technical word, for all of Ignatian discernment is based in the interpretation and judgment of consolations and desolations. Saint Ignatius defined consolation as "an interior movement in the soul which leads her to become inflamed with the love of its Creator and Lord [. . .]; lastly, [. . .] consolation [is] every increase of hope, faith and charity, and all interior joy which calls and attracts to heavenly things."[41] Serving the refugees, a person of faith is consoled because he or she grows in hope, faith and charity.

The history of the Christian faith begins with Abraham hearing God's call: "Go from your country, your people and your father's household to the land I will show you" (Gen. 12:1). According to Rabbi Mark-Alain Ouaknin, the story of Abraham teaches us that the identity of the human being is not linked to a land or to a lineage. Abraham is the one who leaves father, land, stock. Abraham leaves his father's household, under God's promise. And again in the land of Canaan, Abraham was forced to go down to Egypt in search of food because of a famine. From Abraham on, the Bible becomes—according to Ouaknin—a school of foreignness, where one learns that personal identity is not about the land, but rather, it is about an ethos, a way of living, that is learned by being a member of a new people, the People of God. This is suggested again in the narratives of the children of Israel going down to Egypt (Gen. 42–50), in Exodus, and in all the narratives around the Babylonian exile, after Judah went into captivity, away from her land (2 Kings 25:21).

This school of foreignness continues in the New Testament. Joseph took Jesus and Mary down to Egypt to escape from Herod's persecution, and they remained there until the death of Herod (Matt. 2:13–15). The story of Jesus's disciples puts forward again the idea of foreignness. After the stoning of Stephen "a great persecution broke out against the church in Jerusalem, and all except the apostles were scattered throughout Judea and Samaria" (Acts 8:1). The early church also experienced the Christian faith as about foreignness, as attested by the *Epistle to Diognetus* when it declares that Christians "live in their own countries, but only as aliens. They have a share in everything as citizens, and endure everything as foreigners. Every foreign land is their fatherland, and yet for them every fatherland is a foreign land" (v. 5).

What is striking in all these narratives is that persecution and flight are not presented as malediction, as pure evil, but as the occasion for Abraham to become a great people, for the children of Israel to save their lives from famine and become a numerous people in Egypt, for the Israelites to be guided by God in the desert and become God's people, for the deported Jews in Babylon to find time of penance and reconciliation with God. In the case of the church, persecution is presented as the *kairos* for the propagation of the Christian faith (Acts 8:4). This *kairos* has repeated itself in history.

Arrupe had himself been a refugee when the Society of Jesus was expelled from Spain by the Republican Government in 1932.[42] Arrupe must have heard also the stories of Jesuits who had been expelled before from many countries, expulsions that contributed (as John O'Malley points out) to the propagation of Jesuit missions around the world.[43] The story of Jesus and his disciples, and the story of faith in Jesus Christ, is also the story of persecution and fleeing. The work with refugees forces workers and volunteers to, somehow, leave their land, if they want "to enter into a relationship with asylum seekers and refugees," if they want to serve, accompany, and defend them, if they commit themselves "to finding concrete responses to their needs," as Pope Francis asked.[44] To accompany, serve, and defend the human rights of refugees is to experience foreignness, and in doing so one experiences consolation in the way Saint Ignatius describes it: as an increase in faith, hope, and charity. At Centro Astalli one experiences "that God is present in human history, even in its most tragic episodes."[45]

Arrupe's prophetic words to the end of his letter founding JRS, "we should consider the chance of being able to assist them a privilege that will, in turn, bring great blessings to ourselves and our Society," have become true not just for the Society of Jesus. Through Centro Astalli, the great blessings reach the heart of the church, in Rome.

Notes

1. By the term foreignness, I mean the quality of being, appearing, or being perceived as foreign. This article affirms that foreignness is an important dimension of the Christian faith. I dedicate this case study to all the refugees that I have encountered, with whom I have experienced that "where sin increased, grace increased all the more" (Rom. 5:20). In particular, I dedicate it to my grandparents who were refugees in France during the Spanish Civil War, and to my mother who, because of the same war, was born as an internally displaced child.

2. Pedro Arrupe, "The Society of Jesus and the Refugee Problem," *Acta Romana Societatis Jesu* (November 14, 1980): 321.

3. Ibid., 319–21.

4. Ibid., 319.

5. Ibid., 320.

6. A detailed version of the consultation can be found in Michael Campbell-Johnston, "Arrupe y el servicio a los refugiados," in *Pedro Arrupe, general de la Compañía de Jesús: nuevas aportaciones a su biografía*, ed. di Gianni La Bella (Bilbao, Spain: Mensajero, 2007), 793–804.

7. Arrupe, "The Society of Jesus and the Refugee Problem," 320–21.

8. Kevin O'Brien, *Consolation in Action : the Jesuit Refugee Service and the Ministry of Accompaniment*, (Saint Louis, MO:Seminar on Jesuit Spirituality, 2005), 4.

9. Ibid., 15.

10. For much of the data of the very beginning of Centro Astalli I rely on an e-mail questionnaire, of May 15, 2014, with Fr. Antolín de la Muñoza, then a young Jesuit scholastic studying in Rome (1982–86) who collaborated with Centro Astalli during all his years in Rome. Fr. De la Muñoza is now missioned in Badajoz, Spain.

11. Interview with Antolín de la Muñoza SJ.

12. Chiara Peri, "Venticinque anni di storie. L'intuizione di padre Arrupe: 'aiutare i rifugiati un privilegio per tutti noi,'" *Servir: Centro Astalli* (February 2007): 2.

13. O'Brien, *Consolation in Action* , 10–15.

14. Peter-Hans Kolvenbach, "Review of the Jesuit Refugee Service," *Acta Romana Societatis Jesu* (1991): 316.

15. Ibid., 315.

16. Antonio Ricci, "Popolazione, migrazione e sviluppo: lo scenario mondiale nel 2012," in *Immigrazione: Dossier statistico 2013* (Rome: Ufficio Nazionale Antidiscriminazione Razziali, 2013), 26.

17. "Strage migranti, i morti sono tra 700 e 900," *Il Messaggero* (June 20, 2015).

18. Antonio Ricci, "Popolazione, migrazione e sviluppo: Lo scenario mondiale nel 2012," in *Immigrazione: Dossier statistico 2013* (Rome: Ufficio Nazionale Antidiscriminazione Razziali, 2013), 64.

19. "Eurostat: 44 Percent Hike in Asylum Applications in EU," *D.W.* (March 20, 2015), http://www.dw.com/en/eurostat-44-percent-hike-in-asylum-applications-in-eu/a-18330905.

20. Ricci, "Popolazione, migrazione e sviluppo," 65–70.

21. "Sea Arrivals to Italy," UNHCR, http://data.unhcr.org/mediterranean/country.php?id=105.

22. Pontifical Council for the Pastoral Care of Migrants and Refugees, Cor Unum, "Refugees: A Challenge to Solidarity," (1992), 12.

23. *Rapporto Annuale 2014. Attività e servizi del Centro Astalli* (Rome: Centro Astalli, 2014), 3–6.

24. Ibid., 10–11.

25. Ibid., 12–13.

26. Centro Astalli, "Il diritto d'asilo in Italia," s.d., http://centroastalli.it.

27. *Rapporto annuale 2014. Attività e servizi del Centro Astalli*, 28–29.

28. Ibid., 34–35.

29. *Side by Side. Learning What Accompaniment Is All About* (Rome: JRS, 2013), 24.

30. *Rapporto annuale 2014. Attività e servizi del Centro Astalli*, 14–39.

31. The statistics that Centro Astalli offers in its *Rapporto Annuale* do not take into account religious affiliation or state of life of volunteers. I owe this information to an interview with Fr. Camillo Ripamonti, SJ, Director of Projects at Centro Astalli, May 27, 2014, in which I asked him about some qualitative issues of the service of Centro Astalli, that statistics are not able to reflect.

32. *Rapporto annuale 2014. Attività e servizi del Centro Astalli*, 47–50.

33. Francis, *Evangelii gaudium*, 210.

34. John Paul II, "Address to Refugees in Exile at Morong," (Philippines, February 21, 1981), *Acta apostolica sedis* 73 (1981): 390.

35. Benedict XVI, *Address of His Holiness Benedict XVI to the Fathers of the General Congregation of th Society of Jesus* (February 2008).

36. Pope Francis, "Visit to the Astalli Center," Jesuit Refugee Service in Rome (September 10, 2013).

37. Ibid.

38. Information coming from the interview with Fr. Camillo Ripamonti, SJ.

39. This theological reflection is, of course, based on the sources that I quote, but it is also based in my experience, my prayer, and my reflection on my work with JRS in Bosnia in the summer of 1999, with Centro Astalli from 2002 to 2004 and from 2008 to 2011, and with Salvadorian people who suffered a terrible civil war and fled to the United States in Saint Benedict's parish from 2004 to 2007. My reflection is also indebted to conversations and discussions with Jesuits and non-Jesuits working with refugees. Of all these, my interview with Camillo Ripamonti, SJ, has been particularly helpful.

40. O'Brien, *Consolation in Action*.

41. Ignatius de Loyola e Michael Ivens, *The Spiritual Exercises of Saint Ignatius of Loyola* (Herefordshire, UK: Gracewing, 2004), 95.

42. José María Margenat, "De Bilbao a Japón (1907–1938)," in *Pedro Arrupe, general de la compañía de Jesús: nuevas aportaciones a su biografía*, ed. Gianni La Bella (Bilbao, Spain: Mensajero, 2007), 793–804.

43. John W. O'Malley, *Gesuiti: una storia da Ignazio a Bergoglio* (Milan, Italy: Vita e pensiero, 2014), 115–16.

44. Pope Francis, "Visit to the "Astalli Center."

45. "JRS Charter," in Danielle Vella, ed., *Everybody's Challenge. Essential Documents of Jesuit Refugee Service 1980–2000* (Rome: JRS, 2000), 16.

Immigration Policy between Selective Recruitment and Restriction

Ethical Questions Concerning Third-Country Migrants in the Czech Republic

Peter Štica

The countries of the former Communist Bloc of Eastern Europe were rightly perceived in the second half of the twentieth century as emigration countries.[1] The collapse of the Communist regimes and the fall of the Iron Curtain altered the situation. The ability to cross borders freely constituted an important sign of regained freedom. At the same time, this implied that following these political changes, some of these countries—among them the Czech Republic—gradually became immigration countries themselves and confronted a new *challenge of immigration*.

The Czech Republic, which is one of the *young* immigration countries of Eastern Europe, will be the direct focus of this essay. First, I will briefly outline the evolution of migration and migration policy in the Czech Republic. Second, I will highlight some current Czech legislation and political practice, which impose ethical questions when seen from a theological and human rights perspective. In view of the limited scope of this essay, my reflections focus merely on one particular group of migrants: the citizens of non-EU countries who immigrate to the Czech Republic predominantly for socioeconomic reasons in search of work and better opportunities for themselves and their families. This includes not only legal residents with a regular employment contract but also those categorized for any reason as irregular.[2]

Immigration to the Czech Republic: Contemporary Developments

As indicated above, the political and economic changes that occurred in 1989 significantly affected the development of migration. While migration balance[3] had always been negative in Czechoslovakia before World War II and at the time of the Communist regime, the situation changed considerably after the Velvet Revolution. The Czech Republic, a country that has only limited experience with immigration, turned into a country with a positive migration rate that has steadily risen in recent years. From 2005 to 2008, there was a positive balance of about 225,000.[4]

By the beginning of the 1990s, immigration in Czechoslovakia was "highly regulated from the center."[5] The Communist state basically allowed only the citizens of the Soviet bloc countries or other *friendly socialist states* to immigrate. These included, for example, citizens from Vietnam, Poland, Hungary, or Mongolia who immigrated to Czechoslovakia for the purpose of study or work.[6] In the mid-1990s, Czechoslovakia became a transit country for the migration from East to West, but "as time went by, it evolved into a destination country."[7] While the number of foreigners with either permanent or long-term residence status amounted to approximately 77,700 in 1993 (that is, 0.75 percent of the entire population), their number increased almost constantly in the following years— in 1997, for instance, there were approximately 210,000 (2 percent) and then by 2007 around 394,100 (3.8 percent) registered foreigners.[8] Current figures for the year 2012 speak of nearly 438,000 foreigners, constituting 4.2 percent of the entire Czech population.[9] The existence of irregular migrants is admittedly established; however, they are not gathered in the conventional statistics.[10] The estimated number of irregular migrants ranges between 17,000 and 300,000.[11] Recent studies claim that the real number rather lies at the upper limit.[12] With regard to the proportion of migrants in the population, the Czech Republic, together with Slovenia, constitutes a special case among the new EU states of Eastern and Central Europe. The Czech Republic is therefore denoted as a "Goliath of immigration" in this region.[13]

The presented figures demonstrate clearly that "the dynamic of the growth of immigration is very high."[14] This dynamic is comparatively remarkable even within the European Union. In 2008, the Czech Republic had the fourth largest annual increase of migrants among all EU countries.[15] The number of migrants increases steadily; however, the makeup of foreigners residing in the Czech Republic remains stable. Since 1996, most migrants have come from Ukraine, followed by Slovakia, Vietnam, Russia, and Poland. By December 31, 2012, there were 112,500 migrants registered from Ukraine, 85,800 from Slovakia, and 57,300 from Vietnam.[16]

Similar to other economically developed countries, there is a polarization of the employment of migrants in the Czech Republic who work either in highly qualified jobs, or perform unqualified or socially marginalized and insecure works.[17] One of the typical characteristics of socially marginalized work is lack of permanency. Equally typical is the case where migrants remain forever in one work sector because they have very little chance to get out of it.[18]

The Czech labor market is dependent on foreign workers. This is illustrated by the so-called green card, which was paradoxically initiated at the time of the latest economic crisis (2008). The purpose of this project consisted initially of lessening the bureaucratic burden of obtaining approval of migrants from selected countries[19] and in fostering a circular, temporary labor migration that could be readily regulated by the state.[20]

Immigration Policy of the Czech Republic

The development of the Czech immigration policy is often designated on a restrictive–liberal scale.[21] The Czech immigration policy from 1990 to 1996 can be characterized as liberal and poorly coordinated. The issues linked to immigration were not among the priorities of the first Czechoslovakian and later Czech governments after the political change.[22] The liberal immigration policy contributed to the fact that economic migrants, ever since the 1990s, considered the Czech Republic as an attractive transit and destination country. Along with the rapid economic development of the country in the 1990s, this provided the basis for the transformation of the Czech Republic from an emigration country to an immigration country. At the same time, the first law that regulated the sojourn of foreigners entailed neither integration policy measures nor the possibility of permanent residence and naturalization.[23]

The period between 1996 and 1999 can be characterized as restrictive. On the one hand, it is influenced by the worsening economic situation, and, on the other hand, it mirrors the effort to harmonize legislation for foreign migration and asylum with the EU legislative policy.

The following period (2000–2004) can be described as a time of consolidation that was characterized by an in-depth institutionalization and harmonization with EU policy.[24] The short *neoliberal period* (2005–2007), which is characterized by economic growth and increasing demand for workforce, was replaced by a *neorestrictive time* in 2008.

This suggests that Czech immigration policy can be considered as an "ad hoc designed immigration policy," although in very recent years a tendency toward a more systematic approach can be observed.[25] In addition to other features of the Czech immigration policy are the strong influence of EU policy and "a bureaucratic approach."[26] The bureaucratic approach means, on the one hand, that the topic of migration does not play a key role in political debates and, on the other hand, that a huge decision-making power with respect to these issues rests with officials.

Despite the fact that individual departments of immigration policy were earlier divided under various ministries, the regulation of migration is now almost exclusively concentrated on the interior ministry.[27] For this reason, security aspects are predominantly emphasized in dealing with immigration. This raises the question if such an approach does justice to the complexity of migration. It tends to sidetrack other important aspects, such as human rights of migrants, and to concentrate merely on security risks.[28] With regard to the political practice of the United States, Kristin Heyer rightly indicates the danger that such a one-sided emphasis on security aspects—which gradually was established in the immigration policies in the United States and Europe after September 11, 2001[29]—can lead to a *de-personalization of immigrants*. This implies that migrants are primarily understood and depicted as a threat to the social or economic security of the host society, or even as lawbreakers.[30] However, an approach like this hardly does justice to an ethically sensitive and responsible immigration policy and to a Christian conception of the human person.

The arrangement of access by migrants to the Czech job market divides foreigners into two groups.[31] The first group includes EU citizens and their family members, all foreigners who acquired permanent residence, and those who are granted asylum or international protection. They do not require any special work permit for their access to the labor market. All the others enjoy only limited access to the labor market. Third-country foreigners who do not hold a permit for permanent residence are the second group of migrants.

Ethical Reflections on the Regulation of Access of Third-Country Migrants

In this section, I will deal—from an ethical point of view—with selected topics of legislation and political practice that need to be discussed in relation to third-country migrants.[32]

Preference for Temporary and Circular Migration

The Czech immigration policy is marked by a clear preference for temporary labor migration.[33] Michal Nekorjak and Ondřej Hofírek accurately formulate it:

> The Czech Republic has clearly long preferred the model of a temporary or circular labor migration, where migrants are primarily considered as labor power, who "cover" a chronic, short-term or seasonal shortage of workers in certain employment sectors. Due to this rationale, the migrants enjoy only very limited rights and limited control over their own mobility in the labor market. If they are no more required in the labor market, they are to return immediately to their homeland, regardless of their life situation or of a transitional period of a short time of unemployment . . . between two labor contracts. In the world of a temporary migration, migrants live in a permanent state of uncertainty about their own future and they are also thus easily vulnerable.[34]

The preference for circular migration, which can be found in other European migration countries as well,[35] is reflected in the Czech immigration policy, among others, in the attachment of the residence permit to a specific occupation and thus to a particular job. A problem arises when the migrant loses his or her job. Since the residence permit is attached to a concrete occupation, he or she, therefore, immediately loses the residence permit as well. Consequently, he or she is virtually forced to emigrate. This is often the moment in which the immigrant moves into the category of *irregular*. In recent years, a new strategy to obtain further residence permits was established: the change of the purpose of residence from employee (employment) to independent entrepreneur. This, however, does not necessarily mean that the affected migrants themselves are or will become independent entrepreneurs. They could be *employed* through the use of a trade license (quasi–self-employment). Nevertheless, this status implies several disadvantages for the migrants—for instance, they cannot hold public health insurance and need to provide private health insurance, which differs largely from public health insurance. Furthermore, the process of an application for a work permit is accompanied by bureaucratic constraints.[36] This uncertain situation should be modified in favor of the migrants. It could, for instance, be relaxed by implementation of a brief protection period during the time of their search for a new job.[37]

However, it is not realistic to think that all the migrant workers immigrate merely for the short period of time of their employment. An active and ethically responsible migrant worker recruitment strategy should, therefore, not only be transparent but also be accompanied by a prointegration policy that targets migrants who plan to settle down.[38]

Irregular Migration and Problems with the Client System

A system of private employment agencies, which procure jobs for migrants from non-EU countries, has been established in the Czech Republic. This is, to some extent, welcomed also by employers in certain employment sectors (e.g., building industry), as they can obtain flexible and cheap labor quickly and in an uncomplicated way through these structures. This process is for convenience (employers need not get involved in the elaborate procedures for the hiring of a third-country national). It furthermore does not carry with it any risk (they are not responsible for potential infringements of Aliens or Labor Law), and the process accompanied by only minimal costs (social and health insurances are undertaken by the employment agencies). Employers externalize their risks and their expenses as well.[39]

In the immigration from the countries of the former Soviet Union (above all from Ukraine), a specific mediation structure took root, for which now a special concept became established—the so-called client system. *Client*, in this case, does not stand for a customer who uses a specific product or service; on the contrary, the term describes mediators who arranges for expensive "labor power from post-Soviet countries and provides them to the Czech labor market for the sake of one's own earnings."[40] Some clients offer migrants a complete service—not only do they mediate a job, but they also arrange all necessary permissions, accommodation, food etc. The extent and prevalence of this system constitute a special case in view of the European, respectively the global, situation.[41] This *client system* could be allied with organized crime, and in certain cases, it resembles traits of human trafficking.[42] This system operates generally at two different and separate levels: (1) between clients and migrants and (2) between clients and the mafia who demands payments from them for various services, for instance, for the "protection of the client."[43]

This system has a direct impact on the living and working conditions of migrants: Their wages are not directly paid by the employer but are mediated through the client. The clients thereby retain about 20–45 percent of wages for "the necessary costs."[44] Moreover, the danger of this system consists in the fact that it opens up ways for migrants to slip into irregularity. It may happen that

> the mediator, who obtains all documents for an immigrant, does not convey to him at all that his visa has expired. The foreigner discovers only later that he is actually living illegally in the country. The fact that the residence visa, because of its employment purpose, is always bound to a certain employer makes the foreigner dependent on his employer. The latter can basically terminate the employment contract at any time and report him to immigration police.[45]

Besides, clients can make affected migrants dependent on them by other means and lead them into further irregularities. They can, for instance, take away the foreigner's passport immediately after their entry. The passport is required to apply for all other important documents in the new country.[46] The situation is all the more complicated if an immigrant drifts into irregularity, because he or she has, de facto, only little chance to get a legal residence permit again. This phenomenon, thus, is not a marginal problem. It is estimated that about 40 percent of the migrants from Ukraine have this experience with the client system.[47]

The restrictive and bureaucratically complex immigration policy also implicitly contributes to the success of the client system.[48] One peculiarity of clients lies, namely, in the fact that they—contrary to the newly immigrated foreigners from the countries of the former Soviet Union—not only have acquired language skills but also have good contacts with Czech employers, officials, and people who are specialized in overcoming bureaucratic hurdles. Admittedly, the system can also help the migrants to get an initial orientation into the labor market and administrative obstacles. However, it is obvious that it can also place the migrants in a position where their rights and legal certainties are restricted and their standard of living harmed.

It belongs to the priorities of an ethically responsible immigration policy to minimize the possibilities of migrants getting into irregularity. This implies not only measures against potential exploitation on the part of the job mediator or employer, but also for a transparent immigration policy that allows legal labor migration. It can be assumed that "through the opening up of legal ways into labor markets for differently qualified labor power, it would pre-emptively be prevented that people attempt irregularly to satisfy the European countries' demand for labor power."[49] Regulation of labor migration can be considered an essential and indispensable means for the diminution of irregular migration and irregular employment relationships, as well as for the protection of the migrants' rights.

Migrants' Access to Health Insurance

Several questions arise with regard to the provision of access to health insurance.[50] The Czech health insurance system divides insured people into two groups: The majority of the population holds public (state) health insurance. Foreigners who are employed or possessing a permanent residence permit also have access to this public health insurance. The others can only make use of private (commercial) health insurance. This concerns foreigners without a permanent residence permit who are self-employed or entrepreneurs, students, or others who do not work (e.g., family members).[51] This system raises several ethically relevant problems.

First, foreigners are indeed obliged to get health insurance; the private insurance providers, however, are not reciprocally obliged to admit them to their insurance, which generates an asymmetry. Second, the scope of benefits financed by private health insurance differs largely from services provided by public health insurance. Private health insurance categorically excludes some diseases from benefits (e.g., hereditary diseases, sexually transmitted diseases), and likewise, support is excluded if the cause of the illness existed before the entry into the Czech Republic or if the insured person personally caused or contributed to it. Health insurance providers can refuse insurance benefits for various reasons. Third, the costs for specific care are, de facto, higher, in some cases, for private health insurance customers than those receiving public health insurance.[52] Fourth, the level of costs of health insurance is determined on the basis of age and gender, meaning that children, potential mothers, and also elderly people mostly have to pay more and are thus disadvantaged. Fifth, health insurance providers obligate the insured people to pay the entire insurance premium in advance and if they—for instance, in the case of attaining employment—switch to the system of public health insurance, the residual premium payments of the private providers are withheld from them.[53]

These examples make clear the difficulties encountered by third-country labor migrants who do not possess permanent residence permit. Among them are also those who are *forced* to be *self-employed*, although their jobs really correspond with the common labor contract between employers and employees. From an ethical perspective, it is obvious that the arrangement of private insurance needs to be changed and should be fashioned more justly in favor of the migrants. For instance, the services that are guaranteed and financed by commercial health insurance should be extended and legally stipulated.

Conclusion

After the political change of the 1990s, the Czech Republic became an immigration country. Its current immigration policy is shaped by numerous changes that respond flexibly to the trends of the labor market as well as the demands and requirements of the national economy. Distinctive in this case is an oscillation between the liberal and restrictive poles, which is also perceptible in the current policy concerning the regulation of labor migration. Regulations for self-employed migrants are rather liberal, whereas the rules concerning third-country foreigners, who do not possess a permanent residence permit and work as employees (or those who are not economically active), can be described as restrictive. On the one side, it is clear that the Czech labor market, at least in some sectors, is dependent on foreign labor. On the other side, it is obvious that the state evidently favors temporary labor migration and wants to control it to great extent.

In view of specific regulations concerning third-country foreigners, the following desiderata seem to be particularly important. First, immigration policy should be accompanied by an appropriate integration policy. Second, it must be assumed by the regulations that the fight against irregular migration not only includes the effort to eliminate illegal employment circumstances and possible criminal practices but also presupposes a transparent and equitable arrangement of legal labor migration. The extension of the possibility of legal immigration is indeed—as Petra Bendel claims—"no panacea for 'illegal migration.' It would, however, allow more control of migration and help to establish a genuine migration management."[54] It implies a challenge for the immigration policy of the European Union to be more proactive (not only reactive), coherent, and more coordinated.[55] It is equally important for a functioning management of labor migration that immigration is not only perceived from the perspective of security. Rather, aside from the protection of the host society, other aspects of migration, as well, are to be considered such as the demand for workers, the demographic development of the society, and—not least—the protection of human rights of migrants.

It poses a great challenge for Christians and theologians to indicate the complexity of immigration and to engage oneself for a just immigration policy that is guided by the principles of human rights. This challenge implies, among others, that immigration policy be so patterned, that it is not understood merely as an abstract, pragmatic admission/exclusion policy that is exclusively oriented toward economic interests or security aspects of the host country. A responsible immigration policy should both be aware of the complex social realities of the globalized world and be people oriented in every aspect.

Notes

1. The essay was first published in German under the title: "Ethische fragen zur aktuellen regelung des zugangs von immigranten aus drittstaaten zum arbeitsmarkt in der tschechischen republik," *Ethik und gesellschaft* 2 (2013): *Arbeit und migration*, http://www.ethik-und-gesellschaft.de. The essay was revised for republication in this volume. I am thankful to Jiji Philip Karikoottathil, VC, for the translation and Sherrey Murphy, OSF, for the careful reading of the text.

2. Political refugees and asylum seekers as well as immigrants from EU countries who are subject to different legal framework, thus remain unconsidered.

3. The migration balance (*migrationssaldo*) expresses the figure one gets if the immigration (number +) and emigration (number −) are added up within a certain period of time.

4. Cf. Dušan Drbohlav et al., *Migrace a (i)migranti v Česku: kdo jsme, odkud přicházíme, kam jdeme?* (Prague: Sociologické nakladatelství, 2010), 18–31.

5. Miroslava Rákoczyová, "Přistěhovalectví v České republice aneb co vyčteme ze statistic," in *Sociální integrace přistěhovalců v České republice*, ed. Miroslava Rákoczyová and Robert Trbola (Prague: Sociologické nakladatelství, 2009), 16.

6. Cf. Dušan Drbohlav, "Mezinárodní migrace v Česku s důrazem na legální pracovní migraci," in *Nelegální ekonomické aktivity migrantů*, ed. Dušan Drbohlav (Prague: Karolinum, 2008), 57–58.

7. Drbohlav et al., *Migrace a (i)migranti v Česku*, 31.

8. Cf. ibid., 39.

9. Cf. Czech Statistical Office, *Foreigners in the Czech Republic 2013*, http://www.czso.cz.

10. Cf. Heike Wagner and Elisabeth Petzl, "Konstruktion von Migration in Statistik, Diskurs und Praxis," in *Ethik und Migration: Gesellschaftliche gerausforderungen und sozialethische reflexion*, ed. Michelle Becka and Albert-Peter Rethmann (Paderborn, Germany: Schöningh, 2010), 28–31.

11. Cf. Drbohlav et al., *Migrace a (i)migranti v Česku*, 46.

12. Cf. Ondřej Hofírek and Michal Nekorjak, "Neregulérní práce imigrantů v České republice," *Sociální práce* 6, no. 2 (2007): 84; Dušan Drbohlav, "Imigrace a integrace cizinců v Česku: Několik zastavení na cestě země v její migrační proměně z Davida na téměř Goliáše," *Geomigrace: sborník ČGS* 116 (2011): 408; Dušan Drbohlav and Lenka Medová, "Estimating the Size of the Irregular Migrant Population in Prague—An Alternative Approach," *Tijdschrift voor Economische en Sociale Geografie* 104 (2012): 75–89.

13. Drbohlav, "Imigrace a integrace cizinců v Česku," 416.

14. Rákoczyová, "Přistěhovalectví v České republice," 16.

15. Cf. Dušan Drbohlav and Lenka Medová, "Czech Republic: Irregular Migration—'Old Wine in New Bottles,'" in *Irregular Migration in Europe: Myths and Realities*, ed. Anna Triandafyllidou (Farnham, UK: Ashgate, 2010), 71–92.

16. Cf. Czech Statistical Office, *Foreigners in the Czech Republic 2013*, http://www.czso.cz.

17. Cf. Miroslava Rákoczyová, "Místo dole, místo nahoře: cizinci ze třetích zemí na českém trhu práce,"in *Institucionální podmínky sociální integrace cizinců v ČR II. Role zaměstnání a vybraných institucí v procesu integrace* ed. Robert Trbola and Miroslava Rákoczyová (Brno, Czech Republic: Barrister & Principal, 2011), 13–16; Stephen Castles, Hein de Haas, and Mark J. Miller, *The Age of Migration: International Population Movements in the Modern World*, 5th ed. (New York: Palgrave Macmillan, 2014), 244–45.

18. Cf. Rákoczyová, "Místo dole, místo nahoře," 23.

19. In 2008, this referred to Australia, Montenegro, Croatia, Japan, Canada, Korea, New Zealand, Bosnia and Herzegovina, Macedonia, the United States, Serbia, and even the Ukraine.

20. Cf. Pavel Čižinský et al., *Cizinecké právo* (Prague: Linde, 2012), 110–12.

21. Cf. Tereza Kušniráková and Pavel Čižinský, "Dvacet let české migrační politiky: Liberální, restriktivní, anebo ještě jiná?" *Geomigrace: sborník ČGS* 116 (2011): 498–99; Drbohlav et al., *Migrace a (i)migranti v Česku*, 71–85; Andrea Baršová and Pavel Barša, *Přistěhovalectví a liberální stát. Imigrační a integrační politiky v USA, západní Evropě a Česku* (Brno, Czech Republic: Masarykova Univerzita v Brně, 2005), 221–26.

22. Cf. Čižinský et al., *Cizinecké právo*, 34.

23. Cf. Drbohlav et al., *Migrace a (i)migranti v Česku*, 72.

24. Cf. Kušniráková and Čižinský, "Dvacet let české migrační politiky," 498.

25. This proves that the Aliens Law has been amended altogether thirty-three times (!) since 2000. Cf. Čižinský et al., *Cizinecké právo*, 36.

26. Drbohlav et al., *Migrace a (i)migranti v Česku*, 70.

27. Cf. Pavel Čižinský, "Kdo má řídit migraci? Stručná analýza kompetencí úřadů" (2009), http://aa.ecn.cz/img_upload/224c0704b7b7746e8a07df9a8b20c098/PCizinsky_Kdomariditmigraci.pdf; Yana Leontiyeva, "Imigranti v ČR—žádaní a nechtění. Současné migrační a integrační politiky v ČR," in *Institucionální podmínky sociální integrace cizinců v ČR I. Integrační politika*, ed. Robert Trbola and Miroslava Rákoczyová (Brno, Czech Republic: Barrister & Principal, 2011), 32; Drbohlav et al., *Migrace a (i)migranti v Česku*, 69.

28. Cf. Michal Nekorjak and Ondřej Hofírek, "Program výběru kvalifikovaných zahraničních pracovníků–stále ještě nevyužitá šance?" in *Institucionální podmínky sociální integrace cizinců v ČR I. Integrační politika*, ed. Robert Trbola and Miroslava Rákoczyová (Brno, Czech Republic: Barrister & Principal, 2011), 54.

29. Cf. Petra Bendel, "Neue Chancen für die EU-Migrationspolitik? Die Europäische Union im Spagat zwischen Sicherheits-, Entwicklungs- und Außenpolitik," in *Zuwanderung im Zeichen der Globalisierung. Migrations-, Integrations- und Minderheitspolitik*, ed. Christoph Butterwegge and Gudrun Hentges (Wiesbaden, Germany: VS Verlag für Sozialwissenschaften, 2006), 125.

30. See Kristin E. Heyer, *Kinship across Borders. A Christian Ethic of Immigration* (Washington DC: Georgetown University Press, 2012), 14.

31. Pavel Čižinský, "Analýza legislativního rámce sociální integrace cizinců v České republice," in *Institucionální podmínky sociální integrace cizinců v ČR I. Integrační politika*, ed. Robert Trbola and Miroslava Rákoczyová (Brno, Czech Republic: Barrister & Principal, 2011), 135–40.

32. The problem areas that are listed here naturally do not constitute an exhaustive, list but rather provide an incentive for further reflections from an ethical point of view.

33. Cf. Čižinský, "Analýza legislativního rámce," 161; Kušniráková and Čižinský, "Dvacet let české migrační politiky," 504–5.

34. Nekorjak and Hofírek, "Program výběru kvalifikovaných zahraničních pracovníků," 56.

35. Cf. Andreas Fisch, "Über arbeitsmigration zur entwicklung. Sozialethische analyse des konzepts, zirkuläre migration," in *Christentum und solidarität. Bestandsaufnahme zu Sozialethik und religionssoziologie*, ed. Hermann-Josef Große Kracht and Christian Spieß (Paderborn, Germany: Schöningh, 2008), 534–44.

36. Cf. Čižinský et al., *Cizinecké právo*, 213–15.

37. Cf. Karolína Babická, "Pracovní migrace do České republiky," in *Migrace a kulturní konflikty*, ed. Harald Christian Scheu (Prague: Auditorium, 2011), 190. These difficulties disappear as soon as immigrants obtain permanent residence permit.

38. Cf. Marianne Heimbach-Steins, "Zauberformel, integration'? Sozialethische sondierungen zur migrationspolitik," *Amosinternational* 1, no. 3 (2007): 3–9; Andreas Fisch, "Durch zuwanderung dem arbeitskräftemangel begegnen. Gesellschaftspolitische und ethische erwägungen," *Amosinternational* 4, no. 4 (2010): 49.

39. Cf. Hofírek and Nekorjak, "Neregulérní práce imigrantů v České republice," 86.

40. Michal Nekorjak, "Klientský systém a ukrajinská pracovní migrace do České republiky," *Sociální studia* 3, no. 1 (2006): 90.

41. Cf. Dita Čermáková, "Klientský system a jeho specifika," in *Nelegální ekonomické aktivity migrantů*, ed. Dušan Drbohlav (Prague: Karolinum, 2008), 168–69.

42. Cf. Drbohlav, "Imigrace a integrace cizinců v Česku," 409.

43. Cf. Nekorjak, "Klientský systém a ukrajinská pracovní migrace do České republiky," 90.

44. Cf. Čermáková, "Klientský system a jeho specifika," 169.

45. Babická, "Pracovní migrace do České republiky," 187.

46. Cf. Nekorjak, "Klientský systém a ukrajinská pracovní migrace do České republiky," 96–99. The scope of exploitation is diverse: while some clients are passive and act as relatively normal job providers (and pay enforced fees to the mafia), other clients are an inherent part of the mafia network with all their mechanisms. (Cf. ibid., 105–6).

47. Cf. ibid., 92.

48. Cf. ibid., 92–99.

49. Andreas Fisch, "Irreguläre migranten zwischen grenzsicherung und legalisierung. ethische ansprüche an das zugangsregime der europäischen union," *Ethica* 17 (2009): 168.

50. Cf. Čižinský, "Analýza legislativního rámce," 144–57.

51. Cf. ibid., 151.

52. Cf. ibid., 152–53.

53. Cf. ibid., 154.

54. Bendel, "Neue vhancen für die EU-migrationspolitik?," 133.

55. Cf. Petra Bendel, "Wohin bewegt sich die Europäische einwanderungspolitik? Perspektiven nach dem Lissabon-vertrag und dem Stockholm-programm," in *Europa–Quo vadis? Ausgewählte Problemfelder der europäischen Integrationspolitik*, ed. Gundrun Hentges and Hans-Wolfgang Platzer (Wiesbaden, Germany: VS Verlag, 2011), 200–201.

THE PLACE OF DISPLACEMENT

The Ethics of Migration in the United States

William O'Neill, SJ

"Has any one of us wept because of this situation and others like it?" Has any one of us grieved for the death of these brothers and sisters? Has any one of us wept for these people who were on the boat? For the young mothers carrying their babies? For these men who were looking for a means of supporting their families?[1]

—Pope Francis

Life, says Camus, is not tragic merely because it is wretched.[2] Pope Francis's lament for the drowned migrants at Lampedusa reminds us that tragedy is never simply given. So much depends on how we see the young mothers, the fathers looking for a means of supporting their families. And how we see the displaced is itself a function of place—the rhetorical loci (*topoi*) of our common sense. In these pages, I will first consider the *commonplace* views of migration in the United States: the communitarian locus of *member and stranger*, and the liberal–philosophical locus of *citizen and alien*. I will then explore, as a rhetorical via media, the Christian commonplace of *near and distant neighbor* rooted in Scripture and the heritage of Catholic social teaching. Finally, I will look to the surplus of Christian meaning, as displacement itself becomes a privileged place (locus) of revelation.

Common Sense

What do we see when we look at migration today? In the new millennium, all the world's a market—a complex, globalized network of economic, social, and cultural interdependence. And yet the millennial promise of a global household (*oikoumenē*) remains elusive. From Syria to Sudan, the recurrence of intrastate ethnic strife and regional instability has riven our global village. Today, more of our sisters and brothers, c. 45.2 million, are "displaced than at any time since 1994." Children constitute "46 per cent of the refugee population."[3] Already victims of ethnic cleansing and mass expulsion, many of those fleeing persecution subsist in camps where basic human rights remain unfulfilled after years in exile.[4] With little prospect of a durable solution to their plight, such refugees are increasingly perceived, not as victims but as perpetrators of insecurity.[5]

Similar fears beset our domestic migration policies in the United States. As at Lampedusa, barriers against migration leave our borders, in the words of Gloria Anzaldua, "*una herida abierta* [an open wound] where the third world grates against the first and bleeds."[6] Since the militarization of the US–Mexican border in the mid-1990s, "deaths of border crossers have occurred at a rate of at least one every twenty-four hours." Kristin Heyer reports that "almost half of total unauthorized migrants to the United States are female, and women are nearly three times more likely to die from exposure" in our southern deserts "than men, with the vast majority falling victim to sexual assault."[7] In fiscal year 2014, the US government estimates that some ninety thousand unaccompanied migrant children, mostly fleeing endemic violence in Central America, will seek refuge in the United States. Human Rights Watch reports that, contrary to international law, many of these children have been detained for long periods in unsafe facilities and deported without adequate legal counsel or representation.[8]

The threat of further displacement persists for those who succeed in crossing. Some 11.1 million undocumented men, women, and children are subject to summary apprehension, detention, and deportation.[9] Despite promises of reform, "the overwhelming majority of detained asylum seekers and other civil immigration law detainees are held in jails or jail-like facilities—almost 400,000 detainees each year, at a cost of over $2 billion.[10] Here, too, we must single out the enduring tragedy of the 14,500–17,500 victims trafficked into the United States annually—a modern form of slavery. The US Conference of Catholic Bishops/Migration and Refugee Services estimates conservatively that "about one-third of foreign born victims trafficked into the country are children."[11]

Yet as I noted above, what Walter Benjamin called "the suffering and passion of the world" is never simply given.[12] For how we see migrants depends on our "moral squint": the rhetorical loci (*topoi*) comprising "storehouses for arguments" regarding "values and hierarchies."[13] *Citizenship* and *membership* are words to conjure with, even beyond their original, theoretical backing. Indeed, we shall see, a politics of exclusion draws on communitarian and liberal loci, while a biblical hermeneutics of hospitality offers a more inclusive, secular idiom for US policy.

Rival Commonplaces

For communitarians, ethics begins at home. Knit together by shared history and sentiments, we have, says Edmund Burke, "given to our frame of polity the image of a relation in blood," embedding us by birthright in particular moral communities. Our cherished liberty, says Burke, "has a pedigree and illustrating ancestors. It has its bearings and its ensigns armorial" sharply distinguishing members from stranger.[14] And so it is, rights become the patrimony of positive law—an "entailed inheritance" resting on the "politics of the [particular] common good"[15]—the "latent wisdom" and "prejudice" of our distinctive communities.[16]

Recognizing the bonds of membership in our particular polity or subgroup is thus decisive. In Michael Walzer's words, "The primary good that we distribute to one another is membership in some human community. And what we do with regard to membership structures all our other distributive choices: it determines with whom we make those choices, from whom we require obedience and collect taxes, to whom we allocate goods and services."[17] The rhetorically circumscribed "we" of the body politic need not be xenophobic or racist, though popular anti-immigrant polemics often betray such prejudice.

Our liberal philosophical heritage, conversely, ascribes natural or human rights to sovereign selves, emancipated, says Hannah Arendt, from "all tutelage" of traditional mores.[18] Unbridled by "the despotism of custom," in John Stuart Mill's memorable words, "the only freedom which deserves the name is that of pursuing our own good in our own way."[19] Liberty, in turn, is specified in our several immunities or negative rights, limited principally by (negative) duties of forbearance. Under the banner of negative freedom, positive delimitations of liberty (e.g., migrants' claim rights to adequate nutrition or health care) are relegated to an inferior sphere, if not dismissed as mere rhetorical license. In such closed social systems, noncitizens are owed the duty of forbearance; but as *aliens*, they lack legal title to the primary good of citizenship and the protections it confers.

We see, here, the perplexities of modern human rights. For as Arendt remarks of the forcibly displaced at the end of World War II, the "world found nothing sacred in the abstract nakedness of being human."[20] In the new millennium, as in the old, our very *right to have rights* typically depends on citizenship in a particular state. Even with the partial eclipse of the Westphalian nation-state system, enjoying, asserting, or enforcing claim-rights seems ineluctably bound to citizenship, so that the "loss of home and political status" is tantamount to "expulsion from humanity altogether": The "alien" becomes, not the exemplar of the generalized other, but "a frightening symbol of difference as such." We speak of illegal aliens, whose very bodies, rather than their behavior, become "illegal." Deprived, in Arendt's words, "of their place in the world," such migrants are rhetorically effaced, divested of legal and even moral standing.[21] We see at play a perverse dialectic—that in detaining forced migrants and asylees, we fear and punish difference, and in so doing, reproduce the very differences we fear.

We come full circle; for if communitarian recognition of bonds to the *concrete other* restricts rights to membership in a particular policy, so liberal respect for the *generalized other* fails to generate positive moral obligations to forced migrants: the exclusionary economy of ascribing rights through a putative social contract belies the concrete conditions of their redemption. And where cosmopolitan liberalism favors global citizenship, it does so at the expense of recognizing the concrete bonds of membership—the losses of family and home suffered by forced migrants and refugees.

A Christian Commonplace

What do we owe to the forcibly displaced—those "unencumbered" of "home and political status"?[22] Linking the virtue of respect for the *generalized other* with the virtue of recognition of the *concrete other*, the biblical locus of neighbor, I will argue, provides the rudiments of a response. And biblical hermeneutics begins with migration. For the great biblical themes of love, justice, and hospitality unfold against the backdrop of exile and redemption. Again and again, God bids Israel to remember her saving history. In the Book of Exodus, the Decalogue is itself a deed of memory: "You shall also love the stranger for you were strangers in the land of Egypt." (Deut. 10:16–19; Exod. 20:2). Save for worship of the one God, no command is repeated more often in the Hebrew Bible.[23] Yet for the children of Exile, the *golden rule* of Leviticus 19:18 is no mere abstraction: neighbor-love is epitomized by the migrant.

Such lived remembrance proves Israel's covenant fidelity (*sedaqah*) in deeds of justice (*mispat*).[24] For a people born of exile, freedom is always "bonded," in Walzer's words, proven true in the redemption of the anawim.[25] In times of prosperity, Israel is thus summoned to remember that the land "was a gift not a birthright."[26] And so it is, in gracious hospitality to the widow, orphan, and stranger—those most vulnerable in kinship societies—Israel realizes her distinctive covenant identity.[27] Cultivating the virtue of hospitality to the stranger or alien is thus no mere supererogatory act of "charity."[28] Hospitality is the measure of righteousness, *our* token of belonging.

Now for Christians too, memory speaks. In Luke's Gospel, Jesus inaugurates his prophetic ministry, his Exodus to Jerusalem, by recalling the words of Isaiah, "to bring good news to the poor (Luke 4: 18–19). "Today," says Jesus, "this scripture has been fulfilled in your hearing" (Luke 4: 21). Luke's Koine Greek speaks of a fulfillment that persists in history, at once an invitation and a demand.[29] For at the heart of Christian ethics is the law of love (Luke 10:27; cf. Lev. 19:18, 33; Deut. 6:4ff., Mark 12:30f., Matt. 22:37ff.); and for Jesus's disciple in Luke's Gospel, it is the stranger, and not the scribe or religious expert, who reveals its meaning (Luke 10:29–37). Jesus's disciples are called to "go and do likewise" (i.e., to love the nameless, half-dead stranger as themselves).

In what Walter Benjamin calls "anamnestic solidarity" (the solidarity of remembrance) with the stranger[30]—like the man fallen among thieves, stripped of title, status, and role—disciples "prove themselves" faithful to the covenantal demands of agape (Luke 10:36). Citizens of faith "see and have compassion" (*esplanchnisthe* signifies being moved in one's inmost heart), even as compassion (literally, a "suffering with") becomes a way of seeing the stranger "in all her truth"—the stranger, says Simone Weil, is "exactly like me," albeit "stamped with a special mark by affliction."[31]

Not surprisingly, Christian hospitality to "strangers and aliens" (*xenoi kai parokioi*) shaped the earliest understanding of disciples as fellow "citizens with the saints" in the "household of God" (*oikeioi tou theou*) (Eph. 2:19). Indeed, hospitality (*philoxenia*: love of the stranger) is at the very heart of Christian discipleship. In Donald Senior's words, "Jesus begins his earthly journey as a migrant and a displaced person—Jesus who in this same gospel would radically identify with the 'least' and make hospitality to the stranger a criterion of judgment (Mt. 25:35)."[32] And for Luke, we have seen "seeing and having compassion" for these least (e.g., the naked, half-dead stranger, marks the "way" of eternal life). Luke's narrative reveals the boundless, universal scope of love precisely in demanding a moral solidarity with those who suffer—my "neighbor, the masses."[33] The trope, "neighbor," in Luke's parable thus serves as a metaphorical "bridge" between identity and difference (*xenos* came to signify both guest and host):[34] a hermeneutics of hospitality enjoins anamnestic solidarity where care is offered, not to the alien or stranger, but rather to my neighbor, "stamped with a special mark by affliction."

Again and again, in the image of the eschatological feast (Amos 9:13–15; Joel 3:18; Isa. 25:6–8), hospitality is offered not to kin and kind, but to those whose only claim is vulnerability and need (Matt. 8:11; 22:1–14; Luke 14:12–24).

The Task of Translation

As the token of covenant fidelity in neighbor love, hospitality forms the moral squint of citizens of faith. But how are these biblical imperatives to be fulfilled today, in our hearing? To be sure, no simple or complete translation is possible— there is, as we shall see in our final section, always a surplus of biblical meaning. Yet the central themes of love, covenant fidelity, and hospitality permit a partial translation for a religiously pluralist polity like our own.

The primacy of the love command, for instance, enjoins more than mere respect for people's dignity as bearing the image of God (*imago dei*). But as we have seen, in biblical wisdom, agape is never less than just. People possess worth, not price, so that we may speak of a generalized respect, yet always for the *concrete other*—dignity is always in local garb.

Inspired by the great biblical injunctions of justice or righteousness (*sedaqah*) and right judgment (*misphat*) in the reign of God, Catholic social teaching specifies such generalized respect for the concrete other in the modern idiom of human rights. In respecting people *as* agents, we necessarily recognize their basic human rights (as the conditions or capabilities of exercising agency) and correlative duties. And just as such basic rights comprise not only *negative* liberties, but *positive* claims to security and subsistence/welfare; so duties correlative to rights prescribe more than forbearance. For even the most negative of liberties, of freedoms of speech, assembly, or religion, impose positive duties of provision and protection. And these duties give rise to structural or institutional imperatives, constituting the political common good.

As Catholic social teaching integrates the civic virtues of liberal respect and communitarian recognition, so *thickening* rights talk gives rise to a *thinner* or analogical interpretation of the common good. In *Pacem in terris*, the earlier comprehensive conception of the good teleology is now glossed in deontological terms as "the sum total of those conditions of social living" which protect and promote the dignity and rights of every person, including, a fortiori, their rights of effective participation in civil society and the state.[35] In a similar vein, the principle of subsidiarity underscores the distinctive role of the mediating institutions of civil society (e.g., the family, churches, unions, and other voluntary associations).[36]

In providing for a rights-based conception of the common good, the Roman Catholic tradition charts a via media between the collectivist subordination of individuals to a suprapersonal entity (e.g., the state or ethnic group, and the reductive individualism of modern liberalism). Where the common good is violated, conversely, we may speak of systemic deprivation (social sin). And it is the enduring threat of systemic deprivation that warrants our translating the biblical ideal of hospitality to the widow, orphan, and stranger into the ethical *option for the poor*, where the *poor* signify all those vulnerable to such deprivation.

As a political virtue, hospitality thus enjoins solidarity where care is offered, not to the *illegal alien* or stranger but to my neighbor, especially my neighbor in need. Christianly, the Samaritan's hospitality tutors our imagination; the virtue of hospitality, in the words of Jean-Marc Éla, becomes a "pedagogy of seeing" our neighbor's basic human rights.[37] As in the parable, our very moral entitlement to equal respect or consideration justifies preferential treatment for those whose basic rights are most imperiled—in Camus's phrase, our taking "the victim's side."[38] In social ethics, such an "option for the poor" finds expression in the graduated moral urgency of differing human rights (i.e., the priority of my neighbor's basic rights to adequate nutrition, health care, education, employment and "effective participation") over other, less exigent claims (e.g., property rights), and in the differing material conditions presumed for realizing the same human rights (i.e., culturally fitting ways of fulfilling correlative duties of provision and protection).[39] In public policy, then, we must ask the following: Whose equal human dignity and equal human rights are unequally threatened or denied? Who is missing from the table of policy? Whose rights to effective participation are systematically denied?

Immigration Policy

Our translation of the biblical motifs of love, justice, and hospitality leaves many questions unresolved. Yet the ethical ideal of a rights-based common good (underwriting an option for my neighbor in need) reveals the lineaments of an equitable immigration policy. For just as the legitimate sovereignty of states in regulating immigration serves the global common good, so states are morally bound to respect the basic human rights of citizen and alien alike. A just policy will recognize the moral priority of relative need: the gravity and imminence of harm and particular vulnerabilities (e.g., of women and children). Here, the claims of the most vulnerable—for example, children at US borders forced to migrate because of generalized violence, hunger, lack of health care, etc.—are especially exigent. Further criteria for a just immigration policy include recognizing familial relationships; complicity of the host country in generating migratory flows; historical or cultural affiliations, for example, historic patterns of migration; and a fair distribution of burdens, for example, which countries should offer asylum.[40]

Catholic social teaching, accordingly, recognizes not open, but rather porous borders, respecting a person's right to change nationality for social and economic as well as political reasons. For in view of the "common purpose of created things" (and the mutually implicative character of basic rights), "where a state which suffers from poverty combined with great population cannot supply such use of goods to its inhabitants . . . people possess a right to emigrate, to select a new home in foreign lands and to seek conditions of life worthy" of their common humanity.[41]

Pope Paul VI and his successors urge acceptance of "a charter which will assure [people's] right to emigrate, favor their integration, facilitate their professional advancement and give them access to decent housing where, if such is the case, their families can join them."[42] As we saw above, among the most exigent duties enshrined in such a charter is the preservation and protection of families and, of these, the most vulnerable (e.g., victims of trafficking). Citizens of faith, conversely, can never accept detention of undocumented children, or threats of massive deportation separating families, many of whom are of *mixed status*. Such policies, as immigrants' stories attest, undermine the very rule of law, imperiling people's most basic human rights.

In conjunction with the bishops of Mexico, the US bishops favor comprehensive and equitable immigration reform: reforms addressing both the *push* and *pull* factors underlying immigration, lest we forget the first right of forced migrants is not to become one.[43] The bishops seek to redress the massive poverty and global inequities spurring migration. So, too, our bishops support expanded family reunification opportunities, a restoration of due process for migrants and asylum seekers, "earned legalization," and an equitable temporary worker program: one including a path to permanent residency which is achievable/verifiable; family unity which allows immediate family members to join the working kin; job portability which allows workers to change employers; labor protections which apply to US workers; mechanisms and resources to enforce worker's rights; wages and benefits which do not undercut domestic workers; mobility between the United States and homeland and within US; a labor-market test to ensure US workers are not harmed.[44]

Conclusions:
A Religious Surplus

A hermeneutics of hospitality for my neighbor in need binds citizen and disciple alike. Still, there remains a surplus of religious meaning. Agape is never less than just. Yet if the Christian "justices" in her moral deliberations, so justice bears the mark of "loving tenderly, compassionately" (Luke 10:37). As we saw, the

Samaritan in Luke's parable not only "sees and has compassion" but, in becoming neighbor, enters the world of the *anawîm*. Here, compassion, Francis reminds us, itself becomes the disciple's way of seeing, of learning to weep.

In anamnestic solidarity with the half-dead stranger, those "broken and oppressed in spirit," the disciple must "go and do likewise": not merely taking the victim's side (the essential requirement of ethics) but taking the victim's side as our own (in Karl Rahner's terms, the formal, existential demand of love).[45] For "to be a Christian," says Gustavo Gutiérrez, "is to draw near, to make oneself a neighbor, not the one I encounter in my journey but the one in whose journey I place myself."[46] And the journey is our story, the gospel in which we are finally strangers no longer but fellow "citizens with the saints" in the "household of God."

For disciples, then, the migrant is never the object of a policy of assimilation but a source of blessing. Indeed both guest and host are transformed as the "alien who resides with you" is treated "as the citizen among you" (Lev. 19:33). Like Israel of exile, the church must "become what it has never been before"—a "new creation."[47] "Strangers and foreigners on earth," Christians, says Donald Senior, seek "a better homeland," the world-affirming reign of God (Heb. 11:12–15; cf. Rom. 15:7).[48]

For "beloved aliens and exiles" (1 Pet. 2:11–12), displacement thus becomes itself the place (rhetorical locus) of revelation. Hebrews recalls the revelatory hospitality of Sarah and Abraham at Mamre in Genesis 18: "Do not neglect to show hospitality to strangers, for by doing that some have entertained angels without knowing it" (Heb. 13:2). And in the Synoptic Gospels, the image of a feast "for all peoples" (Isa. 25:6), reveals God "powerfully and eschatologically as Israel's host." In the parable of the final judgment (Matt. 25:31–46), the disciple thus passes over from being *host* to Christ's *guest* at the eschatological fiesta—the very borders of the self becoming porous for migrant and citizen alike: In loving, one comes to see oneself—one *is* revealed—in the beloved community; the command of love being, finally, love's command. And so grace does what seems to outstrip human possibility: we *pass over* to the Crucified and Risen One—who first *passed over* to us: Christ who, as Augustine wrote, is our Good Samaritan, coming to the aid of our wounded humanity.[49]

Notes

1. Pope Francis, "Pope on Lampedusa: 'the Globalization of Indifference,'" Homily (July 8, 2013), http://www.news.va/.

2. Albert Camus, *Lyrical and Critical Essays*, trans. Ellen Conroy Kennedy (New York: Alfred A. Knopf, 1968), 201.

3. UN High Commissioner for Human Rights (UNHCR), *Statistical Yearbook 2012*, "Introduction," http://www.unhcr.org/.

4. Gil Loescher and James Milner, *Protracted Refugee Situations: Domestic and International Security Implications* (London: International Institute for Strategic Studies, 2005), 7.

5. UNHCR, *The State of the World's Refugees 2012*, http://www.unhcr.org. Cf. Loescher and Milner, *Protracted Refugee Situations*, 23–34.

6. Gloria Anzaldua, *Borderlands La Frontera: The New Mestiza,* 3rd ed. (San Francisco: Aunt Lute Books, 2007), 25.

7. Kristin Heyer, *Kinship across Borders: A Christian Ethic of Immigration* (Washington, DC: Georgetown University Press, 2012), 8–9.

8. Human Rights Watch, "U.S.: Surge in Detention of Child Migrants" (June 25, 2014), http://www.hrw.org.

9. Jeffrey S. Passel and D'Vera Cohn, Pew Research Hispanic Trends Project, "Unauthorized Immigrants: 11.1 Million in 2011," http://www.pewhispanic.org/.

10. Human Rights First, *Jails and Jumpsuits: Transforming the U.S. Immigration Detention System—A Two-Year Review* (New York: Human Rights First, 2011), i.

11. United States Conference of Catholic Bishops, http://www.usccb.org/.

12. Walter Benjamin, *The Origin of German Tragic Drama,* trans. John Osborne (London: Verso, 1998), 166.

13. Chaim Perelman and L. Olbrechts-Tyteca, *The New Rhetoric: A Treatise on Argumentation,* trans. John Wilkinson and Purcell Weaver (Notre Dame, IN: University of Notre Dame Press, 1969), 83–84. Membership and citizenship specify qualitative or essential loci in the sphere of the preferable.

14. Edmund Burke, *Reflections on the Revolution in France* (New York: Liberal Arts, 1955), 38–39.

15. See Michael Sandel, "Introduction," in *Liberalism and Its Critics,* ed. Michael Sandel (New York: New York University Press, 1984), 4, 6, 10.

16. Burke, *Reflections on the Revolution in France,* 83, 85.

17. Michael Walzer, *Spheres of Justice: A Defense of Pluralism and Equality* (New York: Basic Books, 1983), 31. Cf. Michael Walzer, "The Moral Standing of States," *Philosophy and Public Affairs* 9 (1980); Michael Walzer, "Nation and Universe," *The Tanner Lectures on Human Values XI* (Salt Lake City: University of Utah, 1990).

18. Hannah Arendt, "The Perplexities of the Rights of Man," in *The Origins of Totalitarianism* (New York: Harcourt, Brace, &World, 1966), 290.

19. John Stuart Mill, *On Liberty,* ed. Gertrude Himmelfarb (New York: Penguin Books, 1974), 72, 200.

20. Arendt, 295.

21. Ibid. 299, 297, 301.

22. Michael Sandel, *Liberalism and the Limits of Justice* (Cambridge: Cambridge University Press, 1982), 54, 94. Cf. Michael Walzer, *Thick and Thin: Moral Argument at Home and Abroad* (Notre Dame, IN: University of Notre Dame Press, 1994), 21–25.

23. See W. Gunther Plaut, "Jewish Ethics and International Migrations," *International Migration Review: Ethics, Migration and Global Stewardship* 30 (Spring 1996): 20–21.

24. See John R. Donahue, "The Bible and Catholic Social Teaching: Will This Engagement Lead to Marriage?" in *Modern Catholic Social Teaching: Commentaries and Interpretations,* ed. Kenneth R. Himes (Washington, DC: Georgetown University Press, 2004), 9–40.

25. Michael Walzer, *Exodus and Revolution* (New York: Basic Books, 1985), 53, 73–90.

26. Donald Senior, "Beloved Aliens and Exiles: New Testament Perspectives on Migration," in *A Promised Land, A Perilous Journey: Theological Perspectives on Migration,* ed. Daniel G. Groody and Gioacchino Campese (Notre Dame, IN; University of Notre Dame Press, 2008), 21.

27. For a consideration of Israel's *Sabbath* obligation to treat the landless poor as "brothers and sisters," see Walter Brueggemann, *The Land*, 2nd ed. (Minneapolis: Fortress Press, 1977), 56–65.

28. See Christine D. Pohl, *Making Room: Recovering Hospitality as a Christian Tradition* (Grand Rapids, MI: William B. Eerdmans, 1999).

29. Robert J. Karris, "The Gospel According to Luke," in *The New Jerome Biblical Commentary*, ed. Raymond Brown, Joseph Fitzmyer, and Roland Murphy (Englewood Cliffs, NJ: Prentice Hall, 1990), 690.

30. Walter Benjamin, *Illuminations: Essays and Reflections*, ed. Hannah Arendt, trans. Harry Zohn (Orlando, FL: Harcourt Brace Jovanovich, 1968), 253ff. Cf. Thomas McCarthy, *Ideals and Illusions: On Reconstruction and Deconstruction in Contemporary Critical Theory* (Cambridge, MA: MIT Press, 1991), 205–10. Cf. Helmut Peukert, *Wissenschaftstheorie, handlungstheorie, fundamentale theologie* (Dusseldorf, Germany: Patmos, 1976), 278ff.

31. Simone Weil, "Reflections on the Right Use of School Studies with a View to the Love of God," in *Waiting for God*, trans. Emma Craufurd (New York: G. P. Putnam's Sons, 1951), 115.

32. Senior, "Beloved Aliens and Exiles," 23.

33. M. D. Chenu, "*Les masses pauvres,*" in G. Cottier et al. *Eglise et pauvreté* (Paris: Cerf, 1965), 169–76, at 169.

34. See John Koenig, "Hospitality," in *The Anchor Bible Dictionary*, vol. 3, ed. David Noel Freedman (New York: Doubleday, 1992), 299–301. As Koenig observes, "The Jesus movement was itself both guest and host of the kingdom." Ibid., 301. I am especially grateful to Victor Adangba, S.J., for his wisdom in developing this insight.

35. John XXIII, *Mater et magistra*, no. 65, in *Catholic Social Thought: The Documentary Heritage,* ed. David J. O'Brien and Thomas A. Shannon, expanded edition (Maryknoll, NY: Orbis Books, 2010), 94; cf. also *Pacem in terris*, nos. 55–61, at 140–41; and *Gaudium et spes*, no. 26, in *Catholic Social Thought*, 26.

36. Pius XII, *Quadragesimo anno*, nos. 79–80, in *Catholic Social Thought*, 60.

37. Jean-Marc Éla, "Christianity and Liberation in Africa," in *Paths of African Theology*, 143 (Maryknoll, NY: Orbis Books, 1994).

38. Albert Camus, *The Plague* (New York: Alfred A. Knopf, 1960), 230.

39. See Henry Shue, *Basic Rights: Subsistence, Affluence, and U.S. Foreign Policy* (Princeton: Princeton University Press, 1980), 71–77.

40. See Seyla Benhabib, *The Rights of Others: Aliens, Residents and Citizens* (Cambridge: Cambridge University Press, 2004).

41. Sacred Congregation of Bishops, *Instruction on the Pastoral Care of People Who Migrate*, 7, no.14.

42. Paul VI, *Octogesima adveniens*, no. 17, in *Catholic Social Thought*, 289, 271.

43. United States Conference of Catholic Bishops and *Conferencia del Episcopado Mexicano, Strangers No Longer: Together on the Journey of Hope* (Washington, DC: USCCB, 2003).

44. See United States Conference of Catholic Bishops, "Catholic Church's Position on Immigration Reform" (August 2013), http://usccb.org/. Cf. *"On Strangers No Longer": Perspectives on the Historic U.S.–Mexican Catholic Bishops' Pastoral Letter on Migration*, ed. Todd Scribner and J. Kevin Appleby (New York: Paulist Press, 2013).

45. Karl Rahner, "On the Question of a Formal Existential Ethics," in *Theological Investigations*, vol. 2, trans. Karl H. Kruger (Baltimore: Helicon, 1963), 217–34.

46. Gustavo Gutiérrez, "Toward a Theology of Liberation" (July 1968), in *Liberation Theology: A Documentary History*, ed. Alfred T. Hennelly (Maryknoll, NY: Orbis Books, 1990), 74.

47. Brueggemann, *The Land*, 43. With the crossing of the Jordan, "Israel does indeed become a new creation, a slave becomes an heir, a helpless child becomes a mature inheritor (see Ezek 16:1–14)."

48. See Senior, "Beloved Aliens and Exiles," 28.

49. Augustine, *Quaestiones evangeliorum* 2.19; cf. also *De natura et gratia* 43, 50.

Part III

Gendered and Embodied Borders

Sex Trafficking and Feminicide along the Border

Re-Membering Our Daughters

Nancy Pineda-Madrid

Along the US–Mexico border region of El Paso, Texas, and Ciudad Juárez, Chihuahua, sex trafficking and feminicide have taken hold and continue to metastasize at an alarming rate at the dawn of the twenty-first century. Paradoxically, at the same time that women have greater access to higher education and professional positions, poor women find themselves under an escalating and ever more severe, violent assault unto death. For many today, these tragedies may seem unimaginable to the point of incredulity; in the wake of such responses, these horrors get dismissed as the troubled invention of a warped mind but certainly not real happenings in our time and place. In addition, these horrors may seem so transfixing as to invite a voyeuristic gaze held in place by every emerging detail and account, leaving one unable to think through and move toward a just and merciful response. Sex trafficking and feminicide take on a particular hue in the El Paso–Ciudad Juárez borderlands. These borderlands are increasingly a kind of denationalized place when it comes to the bodies of the poor, particularly poor, brown women. Forced and unforced migrations in both directions across this border heighten the horrors transpiring here. The impact is tragic. The bodies of poor women victimized by sex trafficking and feminicide must command the attention of those who claim to follow Christ if the Christian faith is to be credible today.

Alejandra García Andrade's story is one repeated thousands of times. She was a seventeen-year-old who had been working on an assembly line at a downtown Ciudad Juárez *maquila* (factory) for over a year when she was kidnapped, February 14, 2001. After she was a few hours late in arriving home from work, her family suspected that something was seriously wrong. They went to the police to report her missing. The police refused to respond, insisting that the family had to wait at least a day. The police authorities then proceeded to speculate that she probably ran off with her boyfriend or that she was likely leading a double life as a prostitute, both speculations being different versions of a *blame the victim* strategy. Her family became frantic trying to find her. One week later, her naked body was found wrapped in a blanket and left in front of the plastics plant where she worked. Alejandra had been dead a matter of hours. Her capturers severely beat her, raped her, cut off parts of her breasts, and choked her to death. While Alejandra's story exemplifies the stories of many feminicide victims, as well as of many victim of sex trafficking, her story is an all too common one.[1]

Considering sex trafficking and feminicide alongside one another in the El Paso–Ciudad Juárez region clarifies the ways in which each of these brute realities reflects and reinforces the emergent rhetoric and instantiation of *mujeres desechables* (disposable women). These two assaults on women, singly and together, stand as examples of the bodily crucifixion of women as women. Only in recognizing the ongoing crucifixions of women in varied forms, and only in re-membering the daughters who have been assassinated, can the broken body of Christ be re-membered.

Sex Trafficking

Human trafficking is a term for modern slavery. When trafficked, human beings become objects of commerce, taken against their will, held in circumstances that exacerbate their vulnerability, and sold for material profit. Sex trafficking, in particular, almost always targets poor women and children who are kidnapped, forced into prostitution, and then their bodies are sold repeatedly, with utterly destructive consequences for their lives. It is a form of slavery unto death in many cases. After the death of the trafficked person, the perpetrators seek out new bodies with the intention of their enslavement. And so the cycle continues. It frequently begins with a young woman of a very poor family who is seemingly wooed by a man of some means. He convinces her that he is in love with her, entices her to travel with him to another location, often a foreign country, where they will marry and have a better life. He takes her to a location where she has no connections, perhaps a country where she does not speak the language, and instead of marrying her, he along with other men repeatedly rape her, often violently abuse her until she feels completely demoralized and beaten down. Having been broken, in a situation fully designed to exacerbate her vulnerabilities and to deepen her sense of shame, her captors force her into prostitution so as to keep them well heeled.[2]

While those victimized by sex trafficking are often lured by any number of false pretenses, along the US–Mexico border, these take on a particular character. Indeed, sex trafficking here must be understood within the context of the daily ebb and flow of people and vehicles across the four international bridges connecting these two cities.[3] Daily migration in both directions, legal and illegal, has always been a way of life in this region. Accordingly, a woman's captor may steal and use identification documents to menace her, or, they may threaten to notify immigration authorities of her immigration status. Transgender Mexicans and Mexican children are particularly vulnerable in the El Paso–Ciudad Juárez region given the number of US tourists seeking easy access to sexual gratification without the risk of legal consequences. Further, according to the US State Department's *Trafficking in Persons Report 2014*, prosecutors report that many judges in Mexico do not adequately understand "the dynamics of human trafficking including the trauma experienced by victims, often leading to the acquittal of traffickers."[4] Dominant gender ideologies in Mexico have contributed to sex workers accepting physical and verbal violence from clients, co-workers, and police as part of their job. To resist abuse or to fail to go along with what is demanded could have serious consequences. For poor women, a climate of insecurity and fear lingers across this border region. Drug traffickers and drug violence have made their mark here as well.

Notwithstanding that sex trafficking is horrific in every instance; the highly volatile context of the border region amplifies its horrors. In this region, with its sociopolitical and economic vicissitudes, the poor, and especially women, find their vulnerabilities exacerbated. The geographical proximity of El Paso and Ciudad Juárez matters greatly as together they function as a single transnational space. In this context, sex traffickers operate with relative ease since movement across the border can be done inexpensively and quickly. In the largely Latino/a culture of this region with its honor-shame culture, sex work for women is decidedly stigmatized. Female *purity* carries a high value. Moreover, the general climate of heighted violence (mostly related to drug traffic) has given rise to sex work with a higher proportion of it linking sadistic practices (biting, slapping, and inflicting pain), and the sex act. Clients view this connection as enhancing their sexual gratification. Women caught in the web of sexual trafficking here more often find themselves subject to violent encounters.[5] As Cepeda and Nowtny note, much more research needs to be done concerning violence experienced by female sex workers along the US–Mexican border.

Furthermore, the border itself creates a zone of greater complexity with regard to crimes committed. Two different international jurisdictions, civil authorities, languages, and cultures, come together in El Paso and Ciudad Juárez. Not only are the legal systems distinct, but, consequently, apprehending a criminal becomes a much delayed, more complicated, or, even impossible, endeavor. Without a single legal jurisdiction, those who are most vulnerable are even more so. International conventions are not binding. If after committing a crime, the perpetrator crosses the border, he or she, in fact, almost always enjoys impunity. While this reality distinguishes most instances of international sexual trafficking, the convenience associated with this region can hardly be overstated. Relatedly, money generated from crime in this region is more difficult to trace and much more easily laundered. As Julia Monárrez Fragoso observes, organized crime has created a denationalization of space, which means that justice here is being disarticulated.[6] And according to the US State Department's *Trafficking in Persons Report 2014*, "There were no comprehensive statistics available on the number of trafficking victims identified during the year,"[7] which means that the Mexican government does not have a sense of the scope and depth of this problem or a clear picture of its particular characteristics. This makes it difficult to clarify the need for psychological, legal, medical, and social resources for those who have been victimized. All of this has led to a context of a lack of trust in local, state, and federal authorities.

Feminicide

Feminicide identifies the most extreme form of gender-based violence against women, namely, the assassination of women because they are women. *Feminicide* is one of two terms scholars commonly use to name this kind of violence. The other term, *femicide*, is synonymous with homicide except that it refers to the killing of women exclusively. Similar to homicide, it may be used to refer to a single murder. In contrast, feminicide (or *feminicidio*) is genocide against women. It not only refers to the killing of women by men but also, and more importantly, it specifies a large number of assassinations, distinguishes the killings as particularly brutal, and refers to a system of impunity for the perpetrators. Feminicide presumes a system of gender inequalities and is the term increasingly preferred by scholars and activists. When the character of a society deteriorates, resulting in the violation of women's health, well-being, and freedom, then these violations contribute to "the assumption that women are usable, abusable, dispensable, and disposable,"[8] and, over time, contribute to a climate in which feminicide can erupt and develop.

Feminicide is most often associated with Ciudad Juárez, where it began in 1993 when journalists and others began to pick up on a growing pattern of gendered assassinations.[9] The victims of these killings were poor brown women and girls typically between the ages of ten and twenty-nine. They were often raped, beaten, and then brutally murdered. Many were sexually mutilated. It is nearly impossible to obtain an accurate count of the number of victims of this feminicide. There are, of course, different variables that distinguish this kind of tragedy. Sociologist and leading authority, Julia E. Monárrez Fregoso, reports that 382 girls and women were assassinated between 1993 and 2004.[10] However, she and other scholars readily acknowledge that the number of victims is likely much higher, particularly since the number of the disappeared girls and women has sharply increased in the latter half of the first decade of the twenty-first century. *El Paso Times* journalist and feminicide investigator, Diana Washington Valdez, reported that as of April 2009 more than six hunderd women and girls had been raped, tortured, and murdered.[11] *Al Jazeera* journalist Chris Arsenault reported that 878 women and girls have been killed in Ciudad Juárez between 1993 and early 2011.[12]

The growth of feminicide can no longer be seen as localized only in Ciudad Juárez. Patterns similar to those seen there have emerged across the Paso del Norte region, leading scholars, such as Monárrez Fregoso, to name this as *cross-border feminicides* and argue that these patterns suggest an element of *convenientia*, in the Foucaultian sense of the term. In November of 2001, a young El Pasoan, five-year-old Alejandra Flores, was kidnapped, strangled, burned, and killed. Her body was found naked suggesting that the act of killing her was eroticized by her murderer. Her murder took place just a couple of weeks after the now infamous cotton field murders in Ciudad Juárez.[13] Roughly four years later, four young women's bodies were found dumped in the desert just beyond the city limit of Las Cruces, New Mexico, located some forty-five miles west of El Paso, Texas. Similar to others, these bodies also revealed the murderers' eroticization of the killing of women. Part of the border reality is that it can often function as a safe harbor for those who would be criminals. A crime can be committed in one country, and the perpetrators can escape to the other country without fear of being apprehended for their crimes.[14]

Feminicide has not only proliferated geographically but also intensified in its horror. This form of "violence against women has ultimately focused on their genital organs—symbols of their sexuality and their femininity—which are then raped, tortured, and abused."[15] When violence and sex are conflated in a given act, then it expresses irrationality. Often in feminicide what is eroticized is the act of killing, of murder. A severe, base incongruity asserts itself at the time a male killer finds it erotic to brutally mutilate, rape, and kill the object of his desire. In some cases, the men who perpetrate this violence are well known to their victims, and in other cases they are complete strangers.[16]

Along the Border

The emergence and escalation of this kind of violence does not happen without cause. Economic power in this region, the result of neoliberal economics, has brought about in Mexico the disarticulation of the state and the disarticulation of justice. The power brokers of neoliberal economics have reorganized political power so that it carries a minimal risk to global market economics. Organized crime has taken advantage of the globalized economic world and further advanced the denationalization of Mexico and forged a transnational unity between Mexico and the United States. Organized crime quite effectively manipulates political power on both sides of the border so as to advance its own particular interests in a globalized world economy. This reorganization has increasingly generated the disposability of labor, particularly female labor. Women have become viewed socially as *low-valued individuals*, a term coined by Saskia Sassen, or as *ciudadanas x* of a denationalized city/region, as described by Alicia Schmidt Camacho.[17] The term, *ciudadanas x*, recognizes the absence of state and national power to act on behalf of the civil society.

The intensity of the violence against women can be mapped geographically. In this region, in the last decade of the twentieth century, two developing trajectories come into sharp relief: the deepening absence of the state and, concurrently, the sharply increasing brute force of neoliberal economics, accelerated through the implementation of the North American Free Trade Agreement. What this means is that the state invests less in schools, health care, roads, and other forms of public works, and so the state itself becomes increasingly attenuated and porous, failing to exercise its power as would be typically expected. Unauthorized forces step in to fill this vacuum: drug cartels, organized crime, and guerilla gangs. Violence and public insecurity escalate as confidence in civil authority—municipal, state, or federal—declines.[18] These conditions make it imperative for nonstate actors to identify and advocate for justice in this context.

This tristate, international region forms a magnet for the very poor, most often migrants, who, as outsiders, experience an exacerbated vulnerability and discrimination. It is predominantly women who have migrated to these cities in search of a way out of extreme poverty who end up suffering sex trafficking and/or feminicide, and not women who grew up in either Ciudad Juárez, El Paso, or Las Cruces. The degree to which many of the assassinated women are brought into the region as the work of sexual trafficking organizations remains an open question.[19]

Mexican authorities and hegemonic groups claim that "feminicide is a 'myth' [which serves to] reinstate the impunity of feminicide and the tolerance for gender violence in service of the city's image as an attractive destination for international investment based on low wages and poor jobs in order to exploit marginal people."[20] Tensions have deepened. The business leaders of these border cities argue that their cities' images are damaged by the publicity of these murders. These leaders exert powerful pressure on political authorities to keep these murders quiet and under wraps for the sake of the cities' and region's economic vitality. In the process, women's lives, the pursuit of justice for victims, the transformation of the region's culture into one of greater freedom for all residents—all these values are set aside, sacrificed on the altar of economic growth and greed. As Monárrez Fragoso observes,

> Even though the Paso del Notre region is celebrated as a tristate region where sociocultural and economic borders evaporate, questions of sovereignty and political power are invariably used as an excuse to avoid creating binational and bilateral initiatives to investigate, identify, and address violence against women; nation-states on both sides of the line are guilty of this.[21]

Mujeres Desechables

The crucifixion of women in this region not only expresses itself bodily but also is furthered through the proliferation of the myth of *mujeres desechables*, "disposable women," a notion reflective of the ways in which global capitalism treats and disposes of women. Identifying and naming this operative myth of disposability are the first steps toward dismantling its venomous effects.

> The myth of the disposable third world woman revolves around the trials and tribulations of its central protagonist—a young woman from a third world locale—who, through the passage of time, comes to personify the meaning of human disposability: someone who eventually evolves into a living state of worthlessness. The myth explains that this waiting process occurs within the factories that employ her as she, within a relatively short period of time and at a young age, loses the physical and mental faculties

for which she was initially employed, until she is worth no more than the cost of her dismissal and substitute. In other words, over time, this woman turns into a form of industrial waste, at which point she is discarded and replaced. The myth explains this unlucky fate as a factual outcome of natural and cultural processes that are immune to external tampering. In short, there is nothing, says the myth, that can be done to save its unfortunate protagonist from her sad destiny.[22]

One of the paradoxes present, as Melissa Wright observes, is that just as the third-world woman is transformed to personify human disposability, a commodity to be used and discarded, she is simultaneously producing products of value in the market.[23] Although Wright names this disposability myth in relation to global factory work—in this case the *maquilas* of Ciudad Juárez—it applies as well to women who suffer slavery unto death in sexual trafficking, and to women who are the victims of feminicide, whose death the state overlooks. This myth, like many myths, is advanced to obscure the political relationships that have formed and to foreclose any *discussions of politics*. This myth attempts to make the situation of third-world women appear to be natural, to make this situation appear to be a preordained *fait accompli* that is beyond any political purview and critique. Arguably, the condition of dispossession, as Judith Butler develops it, rightly names what is transpiring for third-world women; it is "precisely what happens when populations lose their land, their citizenship, their means of livelihood, and become subject to military and legal violence."[24] In theological language, it is the making of a crucified people at the hands of the state beholden to economic power brokers.

In popular discourse, the myth of *mujeres desechables* finds expression in multiple forms and venues. Within the border region, a climate of fear, lurking misogyny, as well as the threat of violence and murder, have all contributed to a strategy of controlling women. For example, local leaders in Las Cruces, who track the phenomenon of abuse there, have reported various accounts of men who threaten to take a woman to Juárez to kill her if she does not comply with the man's wishes. Men in these situations argue that if Mexican police are led to believe that a woman killed in Juárez is a local feminicide victim, the assassination may never be investigated nor the body discovered, given the institutionalized impunity that blankets civil authorities in Juárez. It is not difficult for a man to force a US woman to travel south of the border where he can kill her and enter back into the United States or to kill a woman in the United States and run her body across the border to dump it there without any fear of recourse.[25] Indeed, the feminicides in Juárez have been used, over time, to incite violence against women in West Texas and southern New Mexico, contributing to what has become a zone of impunity on both sides of the border. There is an erosion of justice along the border where the politics of misogyny bolsters the confidence of any would-be assassins.

On the Need to Re-Member

What enables us to see the broken body of Christ in the bodies of victims of sex trafficking and feminicide? This case study has focused on a spatial vortex that consumes women—consumes their spirit; soul; freedom; agency; subjectivity; most of all, their humanity; and then, in most cases, their lives. This horrific vortex feeds off of and furthers the myth of *mujeres desechables*. These two assaults, sex trafficking and feminicide, singly and together stand as examples of the bodily crucifixion of women as women.

> What is meant by "crucified people" here is that collective body, which as the majority of humankind owes its situation of crucifixion to the way society is organized and maintained by a minority that exercises its dominion through a series of factors, which taken together and given their concrete impact within history, must be regarded as sin.[26]

Thus, "a crucified people" is not simply people who know suffering but a particular group who suffer because of their shared historical reality, their collective vulnerability. The victims exemplify a group "from whom the sin of the world continues to take away all human form, and whom the powers of this world dispossess of everything, seizing even their lives, above all their lives."[27] There is no more apt theological description of the victims of feminicide. Only in recognizing those who suffer sex trafficking and feminicide as a crucified people can the broken body of Christ be seen for what it is today.

The Christian faithful affirm belief in the mystical body of Christ.

> Metaphorically, the mystical body of Christ is a compact way of speaking about the role of the supernatural in healing, unifying, and transforming our body of broken bones. The mystical body is a rich and multivalent way of signifying the concrete oneness of humanity, Christ's identification with the one human race in his own body, New Testament language about the body, and the sacrament of the Eucharist.[28]

The bodies of many women who are assassinated carry a political message, namely, that they are too insignificant to be seen by the state, their bodies dumped like garbage outside the city limits, referred to by some as the residue of an absent state.[29] Slowly these dead cease to have ever existed. Forgotten. Are they, too, the residue of an absent church? Do the disciples of Christ also regard these dead as existing beyond our understanding of the mystical body of Christ? How are disciples of Christ today to re-member the mystical body of Christ so as to include these dead? To re-member the mystical body of Christ such that it is transformed by those who have suffered sex trafficking and feminicide? In other words, how are Christians to remember these dead as constituting the oneness of the humanity of us all?

Notes

1. Nancy Pineda-Madrid, *Suffering and Salvation in Ciudad Juarez* (Minneapolis: Fortress, 2011), 97–121; Diana Washington Valdez, *The Killing Fields: Harvest of Women* (Burbank, CA: Peace at the Border, 2006), 206; Teresa Rodríguez, Diana Montané, and Lisa Pulitzer, *The Daughters of Juárez: A True Story of Serial Murder South of the Border* (New York: Atria Books, 2007), 159–167, 178.

2. I thank Danielle Heitmann for providing research assistance for sexual trafficking.

3. In the month of June 2014, for example, well over half a million vehicles crossed from El Paso, Texas, into Ciudad Juárez, Chihuahua. See: https://www.elpasotexas.gov, and http://www.txdot.gov/.

4. United States Department of State, Office to Monitor and Combat Trafficking in Persons, "Country Narratives: J-M." *Trafficking in Persons Report 2014* (Washington, DC: Global Publishing Solutions, 2014), 272, http://www.state.gov [hereafter United States Department of State, *Trafficking in Persons Report 2014*].

5. Alice Cepeda and Kathryn M. Nowotny, "A Border Context of Violence: Mexican Female Sex Workers on the U.S.–Mexico Border," *Violence Against Women* 20, no. 12 (2014): 1506–31.

6. Julia E. Monárrez Fragoso, "Death in a Transnational Metropolitan Region," in *Cities and Citizenship at the U.S.–México Border: The Paso Del Notre Metropolitan Region*, ed. Kathleen Staudt, César M. Fuentes, and Julia E. Monárrez Fragoso (New York: Palgrave Macmillan, 2010), 36–37.

7. United States Department of State, *Trafficking in Persons Report 2014*, 273.

8. Pascha Bueno-Hansen, "Feminicidio: Making the Most of an 'Empowered Term,'" in *Terrorizing Women: Feminicide in the Américas*, ed. Rosa-Linda Fregoso and Cynthia Bejarano (Durham, NC: Duke University Press, 2010), 293.

9. For a thorough discussion, see Nancy Pineda-Madrid, *Suffering and Salvation in Ciudad Juárez* (Minneapolis: Fortress Press, 2011).

10. Julia Estela Monárrez Fragoso, *Trama de Una Injusticia: Feminicidio Sexual Sistémico en Ciudad Juárez* (Tijuana, B. C., México: El Colegio de la Frontera Norte, 2009), 9, 105.

11. Diana Washington Valdez, "Mexico on Trial in Murders of Women," *El Paso Times* (April 30, 2009), http://www.elpasotimes.com.

12. C. Arsenault, "In Juárez, Women Just Disappear," *Al Jazeera* (March 8, 2011), http://www.aljazeera.com.

13. Pineda-Madrid, *Suffering and Salvation*, chap. 4.

14. Julia E. Monárrez Fragoso and Cynthia Bejarano, "The Disarticulation of Justice: Precarious Life and Cross-Border Feminicides in the Paso Del Norte Region," in *Cities and Citizenship*, 51, 53, 55–56.

15. Ibid., 45.

16. Ibid.

17. Ibid., 63; Alicia Schmidt Camacho, "La ciudadana X reglamentando los derechos de las mujeres en la frontera México-Estados Unidosm" in *Bordeando la violencia contra las jujeres en la frontera norte de México*, ed. Julia E. Monárrez Fragoso and María Socorro Tabuenca Córdova (Tijuana, B. C., México: El Colegio de la Frontera Norte, 2007).

18. Julia E. Monárrez Fragoso, "Death in a Transnational Metropolitan Region" in *Cities and Citizenship*, 28–29.

19. Monárrez Fragoso and Bejarano, "Disarticulation of Justice," 60–63.

20. Ibid., 64.

21. Ibid.

22. Melissa W. Wright, *Disposable Women and Other Myths of Global Capitalism* (New York: Routledge, 2006): 2.

23. Wright, Disposable Women, 2.

24. Judith Butler and Athena Athanasiou, *Dispossession: The Performative in the Political* (Cambridge: Polity Press, 2013), 3.

25. Monárrez Fragoso and Bejarano, "Disarticulation of Justice," 54–59.

26. Ignacio Ellacuría, "Discernir 'el signo' de los tiempos," in *Escritos teológicos, tomo II, primera* (San Salvador, El Salvador: UCA Editores, 2000), 133–35. English translation is from Kevin F. Burke, "The Crucified People as 'Light for the Nations': A Reflection on Ignacio Ellacuría," in *Rethinking Martyrdom*, ed. Teresa Okure, Jon Sobrino, and Felix Wilfred, in *Concilium* no. 1 (2003): 124.

27. Ibid.

28. M. Shawn Copeland, *Enfleshing Freedom: Body, Race, and Being* (Minneapolis: Fortress Press, 2010), 102.

29. Monárrez Fragoso, "Death in a Transnational Metropolitan Region," 38.

Immigration and Vulnerable Bodies

Migrants and Health Risks in Brazil

Alexandre Andrade Martins, MI

"I was a stranger and you received me in your homes (. . .) I was sick and you took care of me" (Matt. 25:35–36). There is no way to deny that caring for the foreigner and the sick belongs to the mission of Jesus's disciples. This mission comes from the heart of the gospel. After narrating the parable of the Good Samaritan, Jesus said to a teacher of the Law, "You go, then, and do the same" (Luke 10:37). Two people, a priest and a Levite, were indifferent to the situation of a man who was suffering after he was robbed and hurt. A third person was moved by compassion. How many suffering faces do we see on streets that move us to compassion?

Pope Francis, in a prophetic homily in Lampedusa on July 8, 2013, affirmed,

> the culture of comfort, which makes us think only of ourselves, makes us insensitive to the cries of other people, makes us live in soap bubbles which, however lovely, are unsubstantial; they offer a fleeting and empty illusion which results in indifference to others; indeed, it even leads to the globalization of indifference. In this globalized world, we have fallen into globalized indifference.[1]

In the documents of Aparecida, the Latin American bishops critiqued the model of globalization based in neoliberal principles, because it resulted in a concentration of power and wealth in the hands of a few people. Consequently, an immense population is exploited and excluded from access to the essential goods they need to live with dignity.[2] The bishops made an appeal to all disciples–missionaries: "Before this form of globalization, we feel a strong call for promoting a different globalization that is marked by solidarity, justice, and respect of human rights in a way that will make Latin America and Caribbean not only a continent of hope, but also the continent of love."[3]

This essay will focus on health risks and access to health care of migrants in Brazil, particularly of two major groups: Bolivians, which is the largest migrant population, and Haitians who have recently arrived in Brazil. I argue in defense of inclusive policies and actions in health care that can integrate migrants into Brazilian society and are grounded in human dignity, solidarity, and health care as a human right. These must address social injustice and health inequalities that affect the Brazilian society, especially vulnerable groups such as migrants.

This essay will approach this issue of migrants and health risks from a liberationist–theological perspective. I will use the pastoral method of Latin American Christian Communities: *see—judge—act*. First, I will present the social conditions of migrants in Brazil and the health risks they face, and will employ the social sciences in order to understand the structural mechanisms that render groups of migrants vulnerable. Second, I will look at this reality from a theological perspective based on some elements of Catholic social tradition from the perspective of the preferential option for the poor. Third, I will present and evaluate some pastoral actions that address migrant situations and struggle for rights, as well as suggest new ones.

Immigration and Health Risks

Regardless of social conditions, the mere reality of being a migrant has a radical impact on a life. In a new land, migrants begin a life of much uncertainty and insecurity, especially those who are undocumented. However, the challenge of living in a strange land becomes harder in a context of social vulnerability, without social security, and without rights to social benefits such as health care.

In general, two factors directly affect the migrant's health: social determinants of health and access to health care services. In street language, the first makes migrants sick, and the second leaves them hopeless with no treatment.

Grounded in Catholic social teaching principles, such as social justice, the common good, and solidarity,[4] and supported by the World Health Organization's (WHO's) advocacy of *health for all*, health and health care must be considered as human right for all human beings, regardless of color, ethnicity, gender, religion, political belief, and socioeconomic status.

The right to health is an inclusive and extensive right.[5] By inclusive I mean that the health care needs of all must be met, including those of migrants, especially the undocumented, and the poor. By extensive I mean the health sector must act in collaboration with other institutions to address social determinants of health that render migrants vulnerable to health risks.

According to the WHO report *Health of Migrants*, most migrants are healthy and young. However, conditions surrounding the migration process increase health risks. This is especially true among migrants who are fleeing from natural or human-made disasters and human rights violations, those who migrate through clandestine means, and those who are victims of exploitation or human trafficking. Health risks also increase due to "poverty, stigma, discrimination, social exclusion, language and cultural differences."[6] Lack of social security and protection, and terrible living and working conditions pose significant health risks to migrants.

In countries such as Brazil, an inclusive and extensive right to health must immediately address seven social areas that affect migrant health: (1) access to fresh water and basic sanitation; (2) access to healthy and fresh food; (3) access to adequate food; (4) working conditions and exploitation; (5) education/information, in general, and for health, in particular; (6) gender inequalities; and (7) transportation facilities.[7]

A public health system that is sensitive to migrants' health has the following features. First, it is grounded in an anthropological perspective that regards migrants as possessing the same dignity as the citizens and overcomes the concept that they are a threat to the security of the country. Second, it sees migrants as people who can contribute to social and economic development through their work. Enjoying good health is essential for being partners in development.

WHO's report suggests four strategies in public health care for migrants: "ensure migrant health rights, avoid disparities in health status and access, reduce excess mortality and morbidity, and minimize negative impact of the migration process."[8]

Moreover, the cultural aspect and habits of all migrant groups should be considered in responding to their health needs. This requires health profiles from the countries of origin and health profiles of migrants in the host country by different groups, areas, and networks. Health care structures and providers must be able to handle cultural health specificities and the particular needs of migrants.

Bolivian and Haitian Migrants in Brazil

While all the challenges presented above about immigration and migrant health are present in Brazil, it has one reason to celebrate: its universal health system offers services to all migrants, legal residents or undocumented, without exclusion. All migrants have the same constitutional right to health care as Brazilian citizens, and the Brazilian health system (known as *Sistema Único de Saúde*—SUS) is based on a concept of human dignity and health as a human right. On the other hand, SUS has many limitations and challenges to address.

Migrants suffer the same problems in accessing health care as Brazilian citizens in vulnerable situations. Migrants may be worse off, however, because they suffer from language barriers, lack of access of information, fear of being deported, health profiles from a different country, and the lack of preparation among health workers to deal with foreigners.

Basically, the deficiencies of SUS can be grouped into four areas: access to health care services, management of resources, financing, and external factors that affect all health care structures and viability.[9] While the Brazilian public health system is universal, there are also private health systems that provide supplementary care. Eighty percent of people are SUS *dependentes*, that is, they are dependents of the public health system and are not able to afford any supplementary health plan.[10] Among Bolivian migrants, about 96 percent are SUS *dependentes*,[11] and, despite the fact that there is no data about the Haitian population of SUS *dependentes*, it is likely that close to 100 percent depend exclusively on SUS for any health care services.

The Brazilian Health Ministry offers data about the services that SUS provides and the demographic profile of all those who use these services. One can find information by gender, age, city, state, region, kind of health care service, and so forth.[12] However, there is no classification that allows identification of migrants among those who have used public health care services. Therefore, the lack of differentiation between citizens and noncitizens (which prevents migrants from suffering disadvantages and prejudices in their health care) has the negative consequence of preventing the system from meeting specific health needs of migrants.

Two specific groups are examples of this structural problem: Bolivians living in São Paulo and Haitians who have migrated to Brazil in large numbers in recent years. Brazil has approximately 1.4 million international migrants,[13] of which about 200,000 are undocumented.[14] Among undocumented migrants, 40 percent come from Bolivia, the poorest country in South America. Almost half of Bolivian migrants are in São Paulo, living and working in poverty conditions, especially as workers in the textile industry.

A study of Bolivians living in downtown São Paulo shows that 97.3 percent are employed, but only 3.8 percent have signed work papers that guarantee social protection for employers.[15] Most do not have a formal job. Only 3.2 percent have private insurance, and 98.8 percent are SUS *dependentes*.[16] This study also shows that 66.1 percent of Bolivians use primary care when they are sick. Most health issues of Bolivian migrants are related to living and working conditions that put them at a high level of vulnerability. In addition, the Brazilian health system is not ready to meet migrant health needs. The researchers affirm that "The health care supply should be guaranteed for immigrants in structured services that allow access and reception of groups with health concepts and practices that are usually different from the social-cultural context in the country of destination."[17]

Another study of Bolivians living in São Paulo City studies the incidence of tuberculosis (TB) among Bolivians and access to TB treatment. TB cases among Bolivians in downtown São Paulo increased 260 percent in ten years, while among Brazilians in the same area, it decreased 40.5 percent.[18] The reason for this growth is the deterioration of living conditions in this locale. Also, many Bolivians bring TB from their home country, and there is no efficient screening control on Brazilian borders. Nevertheless, this study also shows that all Bolivians with TB who went to public health received treatment, and the rate of treatment outcomes was better than among Brazilians (71.6 percent cures and 1.2 percent deaths among Bolivians, and 63.2 percent and 5 percent among Brazilians).[19] The conclusion of this study is that there is no difference in access to health care and in quality of the treatment provided to Bolivians and Brazilians.[20] The big difference is in terms of vulnerability; Bolivians are more vulnerable because they live and work in precarious conditions.

The second example is migrants from Haiti. Since 2011, many Haitians have come to Brazil via Peru or Bolivia. They arrive in two cities—Tabatinga (AM) and Brasiléia (AC)—without anything but with much hope of getting a job and beginning a new life. However, things are not easy for them. Despite the Brazilian government's creation of a special visa for them (the Humanitarian Visa), and provision of all needed documents to live and work in the country, they are living in precarious conditions, and there are no policies for social inclusion. Human rights groups have denounced the inhumane situation of Haitians in Brasiléia where approximately forty migrants arrive each day.[21]

Though the local government created a lodging facility designed for the Haitians while they wait for their documents, it has an average of 2,500 people living there in terrible conditions (it is designed to hold 300 people).[22] It does not meet minimal conditions of hygiene, healthy food, or clothing, and the local hospital does not have structures to provide efficient health care services. In addition, residents have to wait for a long time before getting Brazilian documents because of government inefficiency.[23] Brasiléia and Tabatinga are small cities without amenities or other resources to address Haitian needs. They wait there only until they get their documents, and then they go to cities such as São Paulo and Rio de Janeiro. While the federal government provided documents for them to have legal work status, it has not come up with policies toward cultural, professional, and social inclusion. According to a study for the Universidade Federal da Amazônia, the Catholic Church Pastoral of Migrants and nongovernmental organizations are trying to help them in this process of social inclusion.[24]

Because usually only healthy people take the risk of leaving their homeland, Haitians are fairly healthy. However, their health becomes fragile because of the long arduous journey crossing the Brazilian borders as well as the living conditions they find in Brazil. They are vulnerable, and the public health system does not have a structure to address their health needs.

Human Beings with Dignity and Vulnerable Bodies

In Lampedusa, Pope Francis denounced what he called the globalization of indifference. In his Apostolic Exhortation *Evangelii gaudium*, he affirmed that "an authentic faith—which is never comfortable or completely personal—always involves a deep desire to change the world, to transmit values, to leave this earth somehow better that we found it. (. . .) The earth is our common home and all of us are brothers and sisters."[25] There is no doubt that these words of the pope are grounded in the God of Exodus, who heard the cry of an oppressed people, and of Jesus Christ, who set free prisoners and proclaimed the good news to the poor (Luke 16:18). Jesus and his Father, who are united by the Holy Spirit, is a God who is sensitive to the suffering of people. All who believe in this liberator God have a mission to hear the cry of those brothers and sisters who are prevented from a life with freedom, dignity, and peace.

An authentic faith leads us to see the face of those who are suffering, which a globalization of indifference fails to see. It moves us toward a preferential option for the poor that is engaged in transforming structures responsible for making billions of people suffer as poor, hungry, thirsty, sick, and stranger. Where these least ones are, Jesus is with them, and the liberation will start from there (Matt. 25:34–36).

The Aparecida documents affirm that globalization raises "new poor faces" that we are invited to contemplate—those of migrants, refugees, and victims of human trafficking.[26] Aparecida recognizes the social evil that forces people to leave their land to seek better conditions.[27] Latin American and Caribbean bishops encourage the Catholic Church to feel herself as a church without borders, engaged in a pastoral care of migrants: churches that welcome migrants; help them in their needs; and, at the same time, support their advocacies by giving them a voice; and by struggling for social structures and policies that promote social inclusion and opportunities.[28]

The Christian tradition presents an integral anthropology that is grounded in the universality of human dignity. This Christian anthropology is founded on two theological principles. The first comes from the Old Testament: human beings are made in the image and likeness of God (Gen. 1:26–27); the second comes from the New Testament: God through the Son has made all people God's children. These two theological principles imply that all humans possess dignity and should live harmoniously as brothers and sisters among cultural, ethnic, and religious diversity.[29]

Human dignity is not an attributive value. Nobody gives dignity to another. It is recognized, respected, and promoted. Human dignity does not depend on citizenship, documents, health conditions, social status, personal qualities and capacities, and neither individual nor collective behaviors. Dignity belongs to human nature, and one does not have the right to deny it to another.[30] Unfortunately, the dignity of most migrants, especially the undocumented ones, is violated.

Based on the principle of human dignity and freedom, Pope John XXIII affirmed as much in 1963:

> Every human being had the right to freedom of movement and of residence within the confines of his own country; and, when there are just reasons for it, the right to emigrate to other countries and take up residence there. The fact that one is a citizen of a particular state does not detract in any way from his membership in the human family as a whole, nor from his citizenship in the world community.[31]

As vulnerable bodies, migrants need special attention in order to meet their needs and be given an opportunity to build a life with dignity. They are poor who are worthy of a preferential option. The preferential option for the poor presents those who must be the first recipients of social actions to address social injustice and health inequalities. This is not only a theological or Catholic social principle, but it is a guide that promotes a worthy life for those who are excluded and also empowers the poor to participate in the common good.

Migrants want to participate in the common good and collaborate in its growth. But excluded from rights, they cannot be integrated into a social structure in which they access the common good and make it grow. As WHO has noted, "Addressing the health needs of migrants can improve their health status, avoid stigma and long term health and social costs, protects global public health, facilities integration, and contributes to social and economic development." The preferential option for the poor leads us to address health needs of migrants from their perspective, cultural specificities, particular needs, and health profiles.

Migrants are not the enemies of host countries. Host countries and their citizens must move from a view of the migrant as competition for jobs or as cheap labor to be exploited, toward collaboration and solidarity with migrants so they can more effectively contribute to the common good. Globalization may be good if it is marked by solidarity that leads to justice and respect for human rights.[32] Pope John Paul II presented solidarity as a social virtue that makes us responsible for all and overcomes any egoist attitude.[33] This principle can break the globalized indifference, and help us to see and care for the vulnerable bodies of migrants as the Good Samaritan did.

Compassion, Courage, and Transformation

"You go, then, and do the same" (Luke 10:37). With these words of encouragement, Jesus concluded this conversation with the teacher of the Law after telling the story of the Good Samaritan who, moved by compassion, left his comfort zone to help a vulnerable body.

In Brazil, the Catholic Church and her communities have done many things for migrant health through the well-known *Pastorais Sociais*[34] (that is, social ministry of the Catholic communities) whose contributions have been recognized by secular groups and the Brazilian government.[35] I present three examples of commissions in Brazil that help migrants: the Pastoral of the Migrant, Pastoral of Human Mobility, and Pastoral of Health.

The Pastoral of the Migrant[36] is one of few groups that has helped Haitian migrants in Brasiléia and Tabatinga. It also welcomes Haitians when they move to São Paulo City through the action of *Casa do Migrante* situated in downtown São Paulo. The Pastoral of the Migrant is spread throughout the country, but it is focused in big centers with large concentrations of migrants. In Brasiléia and Tabatinga, it provides food, clothing, health care, hygiene, and orientations about getting documents and a job. In São Paulo, *Casa do Migrante* has welcomed international migrants from more than sixty-five different countries who come there to find a place to sleep and eat. It addresses five areas of concern: (1) Culture: migrants are taught about Brazilian culture and ways for a cultural and social integration without denying their mother culture; (2) Education: they receive Portuguese classes and some professional courses; (3) Health: *Casa do Migrante* provides basic care for immediate health needs and orientation on the public health system, how migrants can use it, and where they can find health care services; (4) Legal: it helps migrants get Brazilian documents and a legal status; and (5) Labor: *Casa do Migrante* tries to help them get their first job. It works in partnership with companies and employers from all over the country who want to hire migrants. *Casa do Migrante* has ecumenical, interreligious, and humanitarian actions based on Christian principles. Basically, all people who work at *Casa do Migrante* and in all *Pastorais Sociais* are volunteers who are there only because of their faith in Jesus and their love for the neighbor.

The Pastoral of Human Mobility[37] promotes policies to support international and national migrants. In some places, it works in partnership with other Pastorals, such as the Pastoral of the Migrant and CPT (the Pastoral Land Commission, which focuses on rural workers, against exploitation, and advocacy for agrarian reformation), and the Pastoral of Marginalized Women. The Pastoral of Human Mobility has developed innumerous activities against human trafficking and forced labor, such as conferences, studies, denunciations, rescue of victims of trafficking, counseling, and social inclusion of victims of trafficking and forced labor, advocacy for public policies, for social security, and for inclusion of migrants.

The Pastoral of Health[38] focuses on support for migrants who are sick and for public policies that address migrant health. The Pastoral of Health is organized along three lines—a *solidarity dimension*, *communal dimension*, and *political social dimension*. The first dimension directly caters to those who are sick providing counseling, sacraments, and care in health institutions. The second dimension engages the local communities; the Pastoral of Health provides health education, basic medical services and medications, orientation about the public health system, and support for sick people in their houses. The third one advocates for public health care policies and for improving the quality of the public health system. It has people present in many public health care institutions and governmental environments of decision making in health care, advocating for the poor and vulnerable groups.

These three examples show Christian communities responding to help vulnerable bodies. Grounded in the Catholic social tradition, they act from a preferential option for the poor and vulnerable. They have the support of the National Conference of Bishops of Brazil (CNBB) that encourages all dioceses and parishes to establish a *Pastoral Sociais* according to their social context. From its side, every year, CNBB engages in a *Fraternity Campaign,* which invites all Catholic communities and the whole society to reflect about one social issue and address it. The last Fraternity Campaign (2014) was about human trafficking. CNBB distinguished migration from human trafficking, but emphasized that migrants, especially undocumented ones, are the most vulnerable group to trafficking, sexual exploitation, and forced labor.[39] During this campaign, the Brazilian bishops published a document about a social issue, employing the pastoral method *see—judge—act*. This document is written in a simple language and is distributed to all Catholic communities around the country who study it. These communities are encouraged to do something to address the issue and strengthen programs that already exist.

All these effective initiatives can lead to a false impression that the Catholic Church is doing a great deal in its social ministry to support migrants and other vulnerable bodies. Unfortunately, these ministries are not enough. There remains a huge silence about migrant conditions in Brazil. It is an underground problem, and nobody sees (or wants to see). More research is needed on migrants in Brazil to show who they are, where they are, what their living and working conditions are, and their social and health needs.

Christian responses to migrant needs should occur at the local, national, and international levels. Christian communities must open their doors to welcome migrants and help them with their immediate needs, as Pastoral of the Migrant is doing. Christian social ministry and public policies must address the five areas of concern identified by *Casa do Migrante*—culture, education, health, legal, and labor.

"I was a stranger and you received me in your homes (. . .) I was sick and you took care of me" (Matt. 25:35–36). Migrants, national or international, documented or undocumented, are endowed with dignity and are our brothers and sisters in Christ, whose suffering and vulnerability we Christians are called to address.

Notes

1. Pope Francis, *Visit to Lampedusa: Homily of Holy Father Francis* (Monday, July 8, 2013), http://w2.vatican.va/.

2. Cf. CELAM, *Documento de aparecida: Texto conclusivo da vV conferência geral do episcopado Latino-Americano e do Caribe* (São Paulo: Paulus/Paulinas; Brasília: Edições CNBB, 2007), nos. 61–62.

3. Ibid., no. 39.

4. Pontifical Council for Justice and Peace, *Compendium of the Social Doctrine of the Church* (Washington, DC: Libreria Editrice Vaticana, 2004), nos. 160–203.

5. The argument of the right to health as an inclusive right is supported by the WHO. I added the adjective "extensive" to underline that health is not something isolated from other factors of society. Cf. Organisation Mondiale de La Santé, *Le droit à la santé: Fiche d'information no. 31* (Geneva: United Nations, 2009), 3.

6. World Health Organization, *Health of Migrants—The Way Forward: Report of a Global Consultation* 8 (2010), http://www.who.int/hac/events/3_5march2010/en/.

7. This short framework was based on the WHO's list of social determinants of health. Cf. Organisation Mondiale de La Santé, *Le droit à la santé*, 3. In order to complete this list, but with factors directly connected to migrant and health risks, WHO presents an index of eight difficulties that exclude migrants from health rights. Cf. Organisation Mondiale de La Santé, *Le droit à la santé*, 24. English version available at http://www.who.int/.

8. Cf. World Health Organization, *Health of Migrants*, 10–12.

9. Cf. Conferência Nacional dos Bispos do Brasil, *Campanha da fraternidade 2012: Texto base* (Brasília: Edições CNBB, 2011), no. 147.

10. Cf. Ministério da Saúde, http://portalsaude.saude.gov.br/.

11. Cf. Cásio Silveira et al., "Living Conditions and Access to Health Services by Bolivian Immigrants in the City of São Paulo, Brazil," *Cadernos de Saúde Pública* 29, no. 10 (2013): 2021.

12. Cf. Ministério da Saúde, *Indicadores e dados básicos*, http://tabnet.datasus.gov.br.

13. Cf. Ministério da Justiça, http://portal.mj.gov.br/estrangeiros.

14. Cf. *Instituto migrantes and direitos humanos, migrações internacionais no brasil: Realidade e desafios contemporâneos*, 2010, http://www.cnbb.org.br.

15. Cf. Silveira et al., "Living Conditions and Access to Health Services by Bolivian Immigrants in the City of São Paulo, Brazil," 2020.

16. Cf. ibid., 2021.

17. Ibid., 2023–24.

18. Cf. Vanessa N. Martinez et al. "Equity in Health: Tuberculosis in the Bolivian Immigrant Community of São Paulo, Brazil," *Tropical Medicine and International Health* 17, no. 11 (2012): 1419.

19. Cf. ibid., 1421.

20. Cf. ibid., 1422–23.

21. Cf. Conectas, *Brasil esconde emergência humanitária no acre,* http://www.conectas.org.

22. Cf. Sidney Antonio da Silva, "Brazil, A New Eldorado for Immigrants?: The Case of Haitians and the Brazilian Immigration Policy," *Urbanities* 3, no. 2 (2013): 3–4.

23. Cf. ibid.

24. Cf. ibid., 4.

25. Pope Francis, *Apostolic exhortation: Evangelii gaudium*, no. 183.

26. Cf. CELAM, *Documento de aparecida*, no. 402.

27. Cf. ibid., no. 73.

28. Cf. ibid., nos. 411–14.

29. Cf. Alexandre A. Martins, "A Pastoral da Saúde e sua importância no Mundo da Saúde: Da presença solidária ao transcender a dor e o sofrimento," *O Mundo da Saúde* 34 (2010): 548–49.

30. Cf. CELAM, *Discípulos missionários no mundo da saúde: Guia para a pastoral da saúde na América Latina e no Caribe* (São Paulo: Centro Universitário São Camilo, 2010), no. 83.

31. Pope John XXIII, "Pacem in Terris: Peace on Earth," in *Catholic Social Thought: The Documentary Heritage*, ed. David J. O'Brien and Thomas A. Shannon (Maryknoll, NY, Orbis Books, 2012), no. 25 (hereafter *Catholic Social Thought*).

32. Cf. CELAM, *Documento de Aparecida*, no. 64.

33. Cf. Pope John Paul II, "Sollicitudo Rei Socialis: On Social Concern," in *Catholic Social Thought*, nos. 38–39.

34. You can see the list of *Pastorais Sociais* of the Catholic Church in the National Conference of Bishops of Brazil's website, http://www.cnbb.org.br. On this web page, there is a link to the web page of each Pastoral Social where you can see their mission and activities.

35. Cf. Sidney Antonio da Silva, "Brazil, A New Eldorado for Immigrants?: The Case of Haitians and the Brazilian Immigration Policy," *Urbanities* 3, no. 2 (2013): 7.

36. You can see the mission and all activities developed by *Casa do Migrante* at http://www.missaonspaz.org.

37. See Pastoral da Mobilização Humana, http://www.cnbb.org.br/da-mobilidade-humana.

38. See Pastoral da Saúde, http://pastoraldasaudenacional.com.br.

39. See Conferência Nacional dos Bispos do Brasil, *Campanha da fraternidade 2014: Texto-base* (Brasília: Edições CNBB, 2013).

Temporary Migrants, Their Bodies, and Families

Christine E. Gudorf

Historically and through the present day, Catholic sacramental care for migrants has taken the form of a pastor accompanying his parishioners in their collective migration or of members of missionary congregations doing the same. In the nineteenth and twentieth centuries in the United States and Canada, most Catholic immigrants settled in cities and formed urban parishes that were distinctively German, Irish, Polish, Greek, or another nationality. Integration has been a trial for newer migrant groups, with language, cultural, and class divisions. This makes it difficult to establish equilibrium between different groups, and parishioners with more choice of location often leave the parish.

Care for migrants within the church mostly ends at the local level. In many ways this is appropriate, because it is the local parish that must provide pastoral care. At the national level, the American bishops have, through both teaching statements and lobbying, also strongly supported national immigration reform, including providing a path to legal residence for undocumented workers and exempting children of undocumented immigrants who were brought here as young children from being deported to countries they do not know. The pastoral statement "Strangers No Longer: Together on the Journey of Hope"/"*Juntos en el camino de la esperanza ya no somos extranjeros*" (2003) described the current immigration system as badly in need of reform, offering a set of recommendations for creating a more just immigration system in the United States.[1]

Vatican documents on migrants, such as the 2004 *Erga migrantes caritas Christi* of the Pontifical Council on the Pastoral Care of Migrants and Itinerant People, have defended the right of people to migrate, while at the same time recognizing the right of nations to regulate migration.[2]

The Special Case of Temporary Migrants

It is not easy for the teaching arms of the church, the episcopacy and papacy, to know the situation of Catholic migrants in local Catholic parishes, but it is even more difficult to know the situation of Catholic migrants who are temporary workers in non-Catholic countries, or of non-Catholic migrants who are temporary domestic workers in Catholic homes or businesses. For such information, the hierarchy must rely on the many organizations that track migrants, represent

101

them in judicial hearings, record their complaints, and bring those complaints to the attention of both sending and receiving nations. Many of these migrant advocacy organizations are relatively new and are still in the process of creating global communication networks.

It is appropriate that most of the church documents on migrants, including the most recent, the 2004 *Erga migrantes*, are focused on the provision of pastoral care for migrants: seeing that they have full access to Mass and sacraments, to religious education for their children, and counseling in crisis. But pastoral care for temporary migrants presents special problems, beginning with locating them in a timely manner and providing services in their languages. The temporary migrant must also have freedom of movement to attend services, which is not often the case for female domestic workers and rarely for cruise ship crews. Recent documents, such as *Erga migrantes*, recognize the systemic abuses of migrants, and generally point out all those responsible for ending abuse as well as suggest remedies. John Paul II strongly lobbied many nations on the need to ratify the July 2003 International Convention on the Protection of Rights of All Migrant Workers and the Members of Their Families, which has been ratified by only about a quarter of the nations of the world.[3] The church, in, for example, *Erga migrantes*, has particularly pointed out that for economic migrants, the ideal answer would be economic development in their home countries, which could then offer them adequate work and prevent migration with all its risks and hardships. At the same time, *Erga migrantes* recognizes that even if development increases in the poor nations of the world, there will likely still be differences in wealth between some nations and others, offering enticing opportunities to those willing to migrate.[4]

Despite the right of nations to regulate migration, church teaching insists that nations should be open to a certain amount of migration. Currently, the two principal magnets for migrant workers are developed nations dealing with longstanding fertility deficits that leave their economies starved for workers and oil-rich nations in which much of the labor is furnished by foreigners.[5]

The Face of Temporary Migrants Is Female

Erga migrantes recognizes that the face of international migration is changing: it is becoming more female.[6] The preponderance of women in migration is almost completely limited to temporary migrants. Temporary migrants fall into two broad categories—those who migrate for education and those who migrate for work. Historically, both groups have been predominantly male, but over the last decade, temporary migrants seeking work have become predominantly female, and females have become a much larger proportion of those migrants seeking education abroad.

Given the sexism that characterizes virtually all cultures and societies in the world, the increasing number of poor women who leave their families and native land for work are put at even greater risk than their male compatriots. Some of these women are tricked or seduced into becoming sex workers, but most temporary female migrants are contracted as domestic workers. In both categories, however, female workers often find themselves in situations of virtual slavery.

In the Beginning

The problems of migrant workers often begin with recruiters, the middlemen who find workers in poor nations to fill an order from an employment agency in the prospective host nation. A common practice is for employers to advance a portion of the wages, from which the recruiter takes a significant fee per contract and from which the transportation costs of each worker are deducted. In some sending nations, while recruiters are contracting more workers, the workers who have already signed on are kept together and denied any freedom of movement for weeks and occasionally months, until a shipment of workers to a given country occurs. Some recruiters defend this practice as necessary quarantine to make sure that the workers who are sent are free of infectious diseases, but others admit that the purpose is to make it easy to collect contractees when the transportation is available and to prevent workers from changing their minds. For this time in *quarantine*, there is no payment, and workers are sometimes even charged for food and lodging during this time against their future wages. Needless to say, there is no medical examination or treatments to justify the *quarantine* label.

Thus, when workers arrive at their destination, they must work for varying periods of time without any wages, as their wages have already been spent on the recruiter and their transportation. One frequent tactic is to make contracts of relatively short duration, for example, six or eight months. In this way, the worker may only have two or three months' wages at the end of the contract. If a renewal of the contract is offered, the worker must again pay the recruiter fee, though not transportation. Workers also report that employers frequently refuse to pay wages or pay less than the contracted amount of wages.

Domestic workers, in particular, find it difficult to find justice in such situations. Their employers frequently take their passports and visas upon arrival. This makes it difficult for workers to report abuses to police or consulate, because they have no identity papers and are liable to deportation without having received either pay or documents. Besides wage violations of the contract, the most common abuses reported by temporary migrants are excessively long workdays, lack of days off, and physical abuse. Female domestic workers, in particular, report high rates of assault, both sexual and nonsexual, by both men and women householders.

One recent news story illustrates the utter defenselessness of many temporary migrant workers. In September 2013, the systematic abuse of Nepalese migrants working on the construction of stadiums for the 2022 soccer World Cup in Qatar was detailed in the British newspaper *The Guardian*, after forty-four of the migrants died. The Nepalese ambassador to Qatar was quoted in *The Guardian* story as saying that Qatar was an "open jail"; she was immediately recalled to Nepal, and Nepalese and Qatari officials then held a joint press conference at which they insisted that Nepalese workers in Qatar were "safe and fully respected."[7] There is general agreement that the Gulf States, Singapore, and Hong Kong have the worst records of treatment for temporary migrants, but most of the abuses found there can be found in other countries at lower levels of incidence.[8] The Nepali government failed to even demand investigation of the deaths of their citizens.

According to the research of Martin Ruhs of Oxford University, over 90 percent of national migrant programs in high-income nations are temporary migrant programs.[9] These are programs for attracting low-skilled workers. Permanent migrant programs, those that provide a path to permanent residency or citizenship, are almost always restricted to high-skilled workers and usually allow families to accompany the worker, which temporary migrant programs usually do not. In the Gulf States as a whole, 44 percent of the population is migrant, most of it temporary migrants. Only 15 percent of the North American population is migrant, a mix of temporary and permanent; 12 percent of the European population is migrant, also a mix of temporary and permanent.[10] According to a 2004 document of the International Labor Organization, over two million Asians leave their countries each year as temporary migrant workers.[11] The largest groups of these are from Indonesia and the Philippines. Major receiving nations include nearby Malaysia, Singapore, and Hong Kong, but also the Gulf States, Australia, Europe, and Canada and the United States. A significant number of the temporary migrants from Indonesia and the Philippines, as well as many temporary migrants from the Caribbean islands, also work on cruise ships that serve the United States and Europe, but are registered in the Bahamas, Liberia, and other nations with little regulation and low costs.

In virtually every nation, temporary workers lack the protections that permanent migrants receive. They are not only excluded from any possibility of earning residency in many nations but are also universally ineligible for political rights, such as voting, which might give them some influence with officials. Temporary migrants are also excluded from eligibility for economic assistance, such as retirement, or low-income housing, even free medical treatment/insurance and minimum-wage laws. But the primary foundation of the powerlessness of migrant workers, which leaves them so vulnerable to abuse, is the impressive contribution that their remittances make to the economy of their home countries. In many developing nations, the remittances of migrant workers constitute a quarter or more of the nation's gross national product. There is real fear that if nations like Nepal, or Indonesia or the Philippines, demanded worker protections for their migrants—such as criminal charges against those employers who cheat, beat or rape them, or fail to protect their safety—that the host nation would bypass their migrants in favor of those from other less demanding nations, and their nation would then lose this impressive piece of national income. Hence, the hurry with which the Nepalese ambassador was recalled from Qatar and the deaths ignored.

The Philippines has made some progress in protecting its workers by requiring proof of a high guaranteed wage in order for a Filipino to be allowed to leave for a foreign job, and by sending inspectors and envoys into the main receiving nations. Indonesia regularly passes laws regulating the foreign labor recruiters, but enforcement has thus far been lax. Amnesty International was as critical of Nepal's failure to regulate recruiters in Nepal as it was of Qatari employers. But no sending nation desires a nation-to-nation confrontation over the treatment of its migrants, preferring to deal with individual cases of maltreatment diplomatically, so as not to endanger the economic tie that binds the nations. When a major case of abuse hits the news at home, however, intense public pressure is put on the government to protest the violation of its citizens' rights.

Cruise Ship Crews

Cruise ship workers are a special case, because the laws that regulate them are those of the nation of the ship's registration, which are uniformly developing nations without any comprehensive regulation. Ships registered in the Bahamas, for example, fall under a code virtually unchanged since nineteenth-century British law of the sea, which allowed captains to jail, fine, and even physically punish crew for any verbal or bodily signal of disrespect of the authority of the captain. Cruise ships typically have a two-tiered crew—those who work with passengers, and those crew who are generally unseen below deck—the cooks, maids, engine crew, and other workers. They do not eat the same food as the passengers—common complaints concern the freshness and nutrition of the crew meals—nor on most lines are they allowed to use any of the entertainment facilities of the ship during any free time. They are typically crowded into dormitories with multiple others. But the principal issue for most migrant advocacy groups is the work hours of crew, which are typically many hours more than any developed nation allows, with pay at rates far below minimum wage in any developed nation; sometimes salaries and hours per month compute to barely $2 an hour. Maids, for example, often work ten- to fourteen-hour days, seven days a week, depending on the ship and the cruise line, and monthly wages of below-deck crew are often in the $500–650 range, even on cruise lines whose passengers are almost all Americans and Canadians.

As with temporary migrant workers on land, some of the most egregious cases of crew abuse involve safety violations and medical treatment for injuries that result. A number of cruise lines have been sued, for example, for not getting medical treatment for injured crew, even for attempting to dump sick or injured crew mid-cruise with no ongoing arrangements for medical care, for its cost, or for getting to the home port once treated.[12]

The Damages of Sexual Abuse

Victimization of temporary migrant workers, however, is not restricted to these items of unjust pay, long hours, poor accommodations, and lack of recourse in case of abuse or injury. Women migrant workers, who have become the majority recently, work primarily in domestic work in private homes, where abuse is shielded from public eyes; significant numbers also work as maids on cruise ships, where their supervisors are usually male. Sexual abuse is not uncommon in both situations, and there is little recourse. It is dangerous to report sexual abuse to the wife or mother of the abuser, who may not only be powerless to stop such abuse, but who may also blame the migrant worker, and have her fired and deported or denied the recommendation needed to get another position in migrant domestic work. On cruise ships, it is virtually impossible for maids abused by supervisors to have access to the captain or anyone over the level of her supervisor, even if such officers were willing to hear such charges and the maids were able to speak the language of the officers. In such cases, sexual abuse is often repeated. Needless to say, there are no counselors available to sexually abused women on cruise ships to help them deal with the trauma, much less to attempt to stop it.

Sexual abuse of domestic workers is so frequent that it is common knowledge in the villages and towns from which migrant workers come. Thus, married women, who make up an increasing number of temporary migrant workers, are likely to be suspected of adultery upon returning home by husbands and other townspeople, and unmarried women are suspected of loose morals—regardless of whether sexual activity occurred, or whether it was consensual or not. In many cultures it makes no difference that the sex may have been coerced, even violent—the woman is impure, guilty. Such attitudes may and do even result in ongoing domestic abuse after the woman returns home.

Nonsexual Problems in the Families of Temporary Migrants: Male and Female

Such burdens are in addition to those carried home by all temporary migrant workers, whether they be male or female. Spouses at home have carried the full burden of childcare and housework for months, even sometimes a year or more, often in addition to small-scale farming and market selling. The stay-at-home spouse imagines that the migrant, regardless of his/her tales of hardship, has been living in a kind of palace, eating like rich people. The stay-at-home spouse often expects the returning spouse to make their hardships up to them—but the returning spouse often feels the same. Both have endured hardships, but they are different. Both look for the reunion to lighten their burdens, but their expectations conflict.

Older children have missed their absent parent and either make extensive demands on them, or else have established new routines that do not involve the absent parent, which can be extremely painful to the returning worker. Younger children may not even remember the returning parent, which in itself is hurtful and demands efforts at reestablishing a relationship of trust. Partly as a way of dealing with these stresses and reestablishing relationships, many families want to reestablish unity and celebrate the end of separation and hardship, and often spend a significant portion of the migrants' wages, shortening the time until the migrants must again sign a contract to work abroad. Long absences make intimate marriages and involved parenting extremely difficult.

Some few families have adopted a rigid discipline that allows the absent spouse/parent to stay in touch, usually through regular Skype or mobile phone calls to individuals in the family. Not all migrants are aware of such possibilities; not all migrant families would be confident enough to explore the use of technology. Also, not all relationships are amenable to such verbal remedies; not all relationships can be kept alive through words alone.

Yet despite all the many problems involved in temporary migrant work, for many, the costs, even when understood, do not outweigh the benefits, which workers describe most often in terms of the possibility of building or buying a family home, and/or garnering better or longer education for their children, in the hope that home ownership and education will ensure economic security for the future for both parents and children.

Necessary Reforms

The most basic reforms necessary to protect temporary migrants are fairly obvious. The International Convention on the Protection of Rights of All Migrant Workers and Members of Their Families[13] includes provisions that would protect the basic human rights of temporary migrants but also include securing the same working conditions for migrants and nationals, sanctions against employers of undocumented workers, as well as against traffickers and those who use misleading information to lure migrants into working abroad. Since most temporary migrant workers leave poor nations to work in richer ones, the responsibility for their welfare should lie primarily with the rich nations. Yet the forty-seven nations that have ratified the convention are all sending nations—Mexico, Indonesia, Philippines, Morocco. None of the major receiving nations—United States, Canada, Western European nations, the Gulf States, and Australia—have ratified the convention or given any indication of intention to do so. Even the more advanced developing nations—China, India, Brazil, South Korea—are absent from the ranks of those who have ratified.

In the case of temporary migrants on cruise lines, the United States and the European Union need legislation that either requires all cruise lines serving their ports to be registered in the United States/European Union (which would make them subject to all US/EU law),[14] or requires that such liners meet US/EU minimum wage and maximum hour laws, and opens the justice system to noncitizen crews who have personal injury and assault grievances against cruise lines and their officers. Access to the police and courts in the United States can only help temporary migrants, however, if Homeland Security no longer allows itself to be used as the agent of offending employers, by deporting foreign workers, whether for cruise lines or other employers. Presently, migrant workers in the United States who attempt to protest their treatment are often fired and then reported to Homeland

Security for immediate deportation. Because their stay in the United States was dependent on working for a specific employer, once fired, the worker becomes an illegal alien. In the absence of a deported plaintiff, any case or investigation of the employer already begun is dropped.

But poor sending nations also benefit from temporary migrants, and though they have fewer resources to devote to protecting them, they, too, need to be involved in their protection. Much more could be done in the sending nations to regulate the flow of temporary migrants. Sending nations need to follow the lead of the Philippines and have agents working out of their consulates in the major receiving nations who monitor the welfare of their temporary migrants. This would mean that all migrant workers leaving a country be registered, so that the sending nation knows who is going to what specific employer, at what address, from when to when, on what contract. One excellent requirement would be to make regular interviews with such agents outside the place of employment a stipulation of the contracts of temporary migrants. Such interviews could be arranged near, but outside, the place of employment, so as not to inconvenience the worker, but still be beyond the supervision of the employer, in order to prevent coercion in reporting.

Licensing and supervision of migrant labor recruiters is also necessary in both sending and receiving nations, and should be paid for by a stiff license fee on such people and organizations. Fee rates of recruiter/agencies should be regulated, as should the conditions under which contracted workers live before traveling to the receiving nation. Regulation of recruiters would be a huge help in preventing recruiters from promising domestic or factory work to young people and then coercing them into becoming sex workers shifted around the globe. If recruiters were regulated, prospective migrants could be educated to check out offers that local recruiters make before signing on and showing up for transport. Contracts for migrant labor should at least meet the conditions for labor in the sending nations; wages should exceed the minimums in the sending nation and at least meet the minimums in the receiving nation.

Experts agree—and it is only common sense—that implementing many of these regulations can prevent many of the current abuses but will also inevitably drive some of the current recruiters into trafficking illegals in an attempt to continue high-profit revenue streams.

But many of these regulations, if implemented, especially registration of recruiters, regulation of contracts, and paying migrants prevailing minimum wages, will serve to make illegal transport more difficult and raise the risks of being caught. Especially at the sending end of the stream, nations must beware of corruption of their own officials charged with implementing newly imposed regulation of temporary migrants.

What responsibilities does the church have to temporary migrant workers? Church responsibilities for temporary migrants are, of necessity, different from responsibility for permanent migrants for whom the church has historically arranged pastoral care at the point of arrival. It would be virtually impossible for the church to arrange for the needs of the vast majority of Catholic temporary migrants in the Gulf States, Singapore, Hong Kong, or Malaysia, where the church is hardly present, much less on cruise ships. What the church can do is lobby for legislation in the rich countries where it is present and has significant influence (European Union, the United States, and Canada), and in sending countries where it has significant presence (Philippines, Caribbean islands). In religiously plural sending nations like Indonesia, the church can attempt alliances with other religions to lobby for migrant protection. This much the church owes to the poor and striving temporary workers everywhere. But more than this, in sending areas, the church needs to be involved in the migration process, as it often is, for example, in border areas between Mexico and the United States. It needs to counsel parishioners considering this option, check out the recruiters in the area, gather reports from other migrant workers who have returned, and keep in touch whenever possible with the migrants while they are gone.

For the church to make provision whenever possible for migrants to stay in touch with their families could be a huge aspect of pastoral care. Technical help in assisting prospective migrants to identify cell phones that will work in the receiving nation, providing one or more phones in the rectory or parish hall where phoneless families could receive calls, even educating families that can afford computers on how to use Skype or other online communication services could be a tremendous help in keeping families more intact and preventing some homecoming problems.

One Indonesian female migrant domestic worker in Saudi Arabia, whose family thought she lived the life of the rich, discovered her host family's Wi-Fi and sent pictures of the closet allotted to her, the bruises on her arms from her female employer, and the unappetizing dinner she was given. The family's expectations upon her return changed dramatically!

Counseling and support for the stay-at-home spouse and children should also be an important part of pastoral care. Too often church personnel in the sending nations treat migrant workers as people who have abandoned their families (as some few have), and understand migrant work as a near occasion of sin that should be avoided, with little compassion for the situation of the family involved. Workshops on migrant work that point out all the factors involved, and help families weigh the benefits and dangers, could be helpful, as could sessions on budgeting, especially how to budget so that families with a migrant worker can reach their goal, be it children's education, home ownership, or old age savings, while minimizing the number of migrant contracts a parent must sign.

In rich nations, it would not be out of place to have some sermons on social justice and tipping policy. Many people do not seem to know that maids in hotels and cruise ships depend for a significant part of wages on tips left by departing guests, just like taxi drivers, porters at airports, hairdressers who do not own the shop, waiters and waitresses in restaurants (the extent of worker dependence on tips varies from nation to nation). In some of these cases, including many temporary migrants, employees do not even earn the minimum wage without tips, and in other cases, where they do earn minimum wage, the schedule is arranged so that tips are the only thing that allow a minimum wage job to feed a family.

As *Erga migrantes* points out, so long as there is poverty in some regions and riches in others, poor people will migrate toward the riches to assure their welfare and the welfare of their families. Development is an ongoing but slow process in much of the world, and many of the most energetic and ambitious of the poor cannot wait for full-time work with decent wages to arrive in their region. They will accept the risks that accompany migrant work. It is the Christian obligation of the rest of us—especially those of us whose needs these migrants serve—to see that they are not abused and are treated with justice and dignity.

Notes

1. U.S. Conference of Catholic Bishops, "Strangers No Longer, Together on the Journey of Hope" (January 22, 2003), http://www.usccb.org.

2. Pontifical Council for the Pastoral Care of Migrants and Itinerants, *Erga migrantes caritas Christi* (May 3, 2004), no. 4, http://www.vatican.va (hereafter *Erga migrantes*).

3. Ibid., no. 6.

4. Ibid., no. 4.

5. See the reference to the needs of wealthy nations for manpower due to demographics in *Erga migrantes*, no. 4.

6. *Erga migrantes*, no. 5.

7. "And Still They Come: The Abuse of Migrants," *The Economist*, April 19, 2014, 54.

8. Ibid.

9. Martin Ruhs, *The Price of Rights: Regulating International Labor Migration* (Princeton, NJ: Princeton University Press, 2013).

10. Ibid.

11. International Labor Organization, "Towards a Fair Deal for Migrant Workers in the Global Economy" (2004), http://www.ilo.org.

12. Forrest Norman, "Screwed if by Sea: Cruise Lines Throw Workers Overboard When It Comes to Providing Urgent Medical Care," *Miami Herald*, November 11, 2004, http://www.miaminewtimes.com/.

13. General Assembly Resolution 45/158, *International Convention on the Protection of the Rights of All Migrant Workers and Members of Their Families*, adopted December 18, 1990, effective July 2003 on ratification by twenty nations, UN High Commissioner for Human Rights.

14. Such a bill has been languishing in Congress for a decade or more; cruise ship lines have much more influence on Congress than foreign cruise line workers.

Part IV

Cross-Border Marriages

and Migrant Families

Limiting Hope?
China's *Hukou* System and Its Impact on Internal Migration and Family Patterns

Regina Wentzel Wolfe

Most people are aware of the economic growth and development in China in recent years, the results of which seem to be changing the country at breathtaking speed. Great strides have been made in reducing poverty, even in rural China. With its rich history and newly found place in the global economy, China welcomed more than fifty-five million visitors in 2014. China's two most populous cities, Shanghai and Beijing, do not fail to impress visitors. They flock to Beijing, the home of the Forbidden City and the 2008 Summer Olympics, and the jumping off point for the Great Wall of China, as well as to Shanghai, with its famous Bund along the Huangpu River, the futuristic Pudong district, which is home to China's tallest buildings, and luxury shopping malls where visitors will find "the Chinese metropolis' most fashionable residents outspending their New York counterparts."[1]

It appears that for some, even many, of China's citizens, life is good; the future is bright and filled with hope. This cannot be said of all of China's citizens. Those who want to leave towns and villages that offer little or no hope of an improved lifestyle face significant challenges and barriers. Many of China's internal migrants are drawn to major cities, including Beijing and Shanghai, with hopes of improving their own standard of living as well as the standard of living of family members who are left behind. Those hopes, however, are seldom realized, in large part because of the manner in which movement of citizens is regulated.

China's *Hukou* System

The *hukou*, a registry system based on a person's place of birth, was established in the late 1950s as a means of assisting the social and economic reforms of Mao Zedong and the Communist Party. People were classified according to two categories: urban or rural and agricultural or nonagricultural.

Individuals registered under the agricultural category depended mainly on their own labor and the fluctuating harvests for survival; individuals registered under the non-agricultural category, on the other hand, were entitled to a "cradle-to-grave" welfare package provided by the government. As a result, urban residents were seen as superior to rural residents in terms of socio-economic status.[2]

People were required to live in the area in which they were registered; benefits, such as access to public education and health care, and the ability to purchase property are tied to a person's *hukou* status, which "is inherited from one's mother and thus is predetermined."[3]

Prior to the opening of the People's Republic of China in the late 1970s, the system made any form of internal migration extremely difficult. Given the levels of poverty in China at the time, however, differences in standards of living were not extreme, despite the supposed socioeconomic superiority of those with a nonagricultural urban *hukou*. Those living in rural areas did not necessarily view cities as providing better alternative lifestyles; there were not widespread attempts to circumvent the system. It was only after the Cultural Revolution, and the economic changes that followed, that significant differences in standards of living began to emerge between rural and urban Chinese. As these inequalities grew, hopes of finding a better life in China's cities led many to leave family and friends behind, despite difficulties posed by the *hukou* system. Given this internal migration, the two-tiered nature of the *hukou* system increasingly became a reality with those in possession of a *hukou* in the urban areas in which they lived and worked moving up the socioeconomic ladder. The majority of those in possession of rural *hukous* were left behind economically, even if they had migrated to an urban area. Despite recent attempts at reform, the structure of the *hukou* system does little to bridge the growing socioeconomic divide; in fact, it has created an underclass in many of China's largest cities. The magnitude of the problem cannot be ignored. According to the International Organization for Migration (IOM), 2014 data indicate that 230 million Chinese citizens are internal migrants; this represents approximately 16 percent of China's population.[4]

Looking for a Better Life

Among those looking for a better life is Liu Gang a consultant from Hunan Province who lives and works in Beijing.[5] Married with a young infant, he lives in a rental apartment, as he is unable to buy a residence in Beijing. In part, this is due to the exorbitant prices of real estate. "Based on the house price to wage ratio . . . China's large cities have the most expensive real estate in the world."[6] This is due to *hukou* restrictions that only allow him to purchase a home in the district in which he is registered. In order to get a foothold in the housing market, he has bought an apartment in his hometown even though he lives in rental housing in Beijing. In addition to concerns about the cost of housing, he and his family do not qualify for subsidized health care in Beijing. When his wife delivered a premature child, the family was responsible for all hospital bills, which were more than double his monthly income. "'Suddenly I am spending 110 per cent of my salary,' says Liu with frustration. 'Living expenses are getting higher. My savings are gone. That is a typical Chinese situation.'"[7]

Though Mr. Liu is not separated from his immediate family, he is not, it would seem, among the few fortunate people who have been able to transfer their registration to Beijing. According to *Bloomberg Businessweek* there are four ways to get a Beijing *hukou*.[8] The most common way of attaining an urban *hukou* is, as noted above, through inheritance. The second way is to be one of the very fortunate people who are hired by a state owned enterprise (SOE) that received an allotment of *hukous* from the government. SOEs able to give these *hukous* to select newly hired employees can hire the best and the brightest, thus gaining a competitive advantage. About six thousand of these *hukous* were given to Beijing SOEs in 2011.[9] However, instead of going to newly hired employees, many of these find their way on to the black market where they can fetch as much as US$25,000. This third way of acquiring an urban *hukou* is well out of reach of the average migrant coming to Beijing in search of a better life. The fourth way of getting an urban *hukou* is by marrying someone who holds one. *Hukous* obtained through employment or marriage are not without restrictions, however; people are required to relinquish rights of residency in their original home district.

For some, this is a deterrent because it precludes the possibility of returning home; among these is Deng Zongwei who wants to keep open the option of retiring to his hometown. He is among the many migrant workers whose families are split because of the inequities of a system that does not provide basic rights to all. His wife and son lived with him in Dongguan, an industrial city in Guangdong Province about fifty miles north of Hong Kong, until his son reached school age. Not eligible for free public education and the family unable to pay private tuition rates, his wife left her job to return with their son to their hometown where local children receive a free education. For his part, once a month Mr. Deng makes the 730-mile round-trip home to visit.[10]

While the education that Mr. Deng's son and the children of other migrants who are forced to return to their home districts for schooling might be free, these children are still disadvantaged. The quality of education in rural China is abysmal. The common hope of parents across the globe that an education can provide their children with a better life is being thwarted for many in China today. For example, the number of students from rural areas attending Beijing University dropped to 10 percent in 2011 "from more than 30 percent between 1978 and 1998."[11] Experts point "to the unequal distribution of educational resource" in China as one of the causes of this decline.[12]

Reform efforts have led to modifications of the national university examination system. Questions have been introduced that seem "to be more concerned with knowledge found outside textbooks, an advantage for teenagers who live in cities."[13] Other reforms attempt to shift the admissions processes away from a narrow focus based only on rank in the national entrance exams. An experimental program, begun in 2003 and now extended to eighty universities, enables universities "to use their own criteria to independently select 5 percent of their students from high schools around the country."[14] These focus "on students' creativity, imagination and learning skills. Students who are particularly talented in art, sport and literature can now enter these key universities despite their lower test scores."[15] More often than not, students in rural areas do not have access to music classes, travel opportunities, and other avenues by which to expand their horizons such as access to the Internet.

There are also China's so-called super schools. "These schools, usually based in provincial capitals or developed cities, take up more of the country's already uneven educational resources. Their influence is such that they can recommend their outstanding students to top universities without taking the national college entrance examination."[16] Admittance to these super schools is very competitive. Students from rural areas who manage to be accepted often must leave family behind and head to provincial capitals where the schools are located, thus creating another disruption to family life.

The inequities of access to education for children in rural areas, which includes the children sent home by families that have migrated to China's larger cities, are counter to the right of all to adequate education.[17] Moreover, the rights of parents to participate in the design and "functioning of schools and in the formulation and implementation of educational policies" are neither acknowledged nor protected.[18] Experts, such as Liu Yunshan of Beijing University believe that current policies are problematic. He noted, "Instead of offering opportunities to young people from rural areas to move up social classes through education, the tertiary education system is reinforcing the social divide in the country."[19]

The City Beckons

Young people from the countryside are leaving school and bypassing attempts to gain access to universities or vocational schools in favor of entering the labor market directly. Studies are clear that the labor market in large urban centers has expanded to meet the needs of the growing economy. However, there are insufficient numbers of urban residents to meet the demand for laborers. This is due in large measure to the decrease in the number of younger people inheriting urban *hukous*—a direct result of China's one-child policy.[20] As a result, migrant workers have entered the market to meet the demand.

Among these younger adults are millions of women. Their situations are often grim and the choices open to them difficult. For the most part they "find low-wage, low-skill jobs and . . . endure harsh working conditions."[21] However, "migration and urban work has been a liberating experience for many of them. Not only do they achieve some degree of economic independence through earning a cash income, but they also gain the opportunity to broaden their life horizon and to enhance their ability to negotiate more power and choice in their lives."[22] These gains are not necessarily permanent ones and can be greatly impacted by decisions about marriage. According to Hong Zhang, "marriage affects rural female migrants in two major ways. First of all, marriage often means an end to their labor mobility."[23] For many brides, marriage not only means a return to the countryside and giving up their wage-earning capacity, it also means acceptance of and adherence to the long-standing tradition of brides leaving their own families and moving to the villages and homes of their in-laws. While this traditional pattern has always presented challenges to brides, usually the bride and groom were from the same district or province, thus the bride was not living great distances from her own family. This is not the case for couples who meet in urban centers to which they migrated for work but come from different parts of China.

A second way in which marriage impacts young rural women is by what Zhang refers to as "long-distance marriages." These "marriages are characterized by a pattern in which the bride from a poor rural area marries a groom in an economically more advanced rural community or an urban center and settles there."[24] As noted above, such an arrangement is one of the ways a person can acquire an urban *hukou*. Zhang notes that for many, these are marriages of convenience. The bride is often seeking to enhance her social and economic status; often the husband has not been able to find a marriage partner, perhaps because of his age or some disability.[25]

Women who choose these long-distance marriages are far from home and often find themselves isolated in environments that are foreign to them. In some instances, they don't speak the local dialect or know the local customs. Often they are "viewed as outsiders by the locals in the new communities."[26] Rural migrant women who meet and marry migrant men and return to towns and villages far from their hometowns often share similar problems. They are left to negotiate relationships with husbands, in-laws, and neighbors with few support systems.

The Neolocal Marriage

There is a new pattern of marriage emerging for some younger rural migrant workers. Zhang, who did a study on young couples in Dongguan, the same industrial city in Guangdong Province where Mr. Deng is working, has dubbed it a neolocal marriage. "In this new marriage form, instead of returning to the countryside for marriage and family, the new brides set up their post-marital homes in Dongguan, and many continued to maintain their factory work after their marriage and childbirth."[27] The study seems to indicate that couples were unattached when they arrived in Dongguan and met either through work or were introduced by mutual friends, thus many of the marriages are cross-regional. The couples are also making their own decisions about marriage.

Most . . . interviewees indicated that they did consult with their parents in their marriage decision, but in most cases, their parents simply went along with their decision even though they might have reservations. One woman [said] that her parents insisted on her returning home to meet a man in her hometown that her parents had selected for her, but she refused to go home and told her parents that she was already dating someone in Dong-guan. Eventually, her parents accepted her choice.[28]

Other challenges to traditional marriage patterns are seen in the decreasing emphasis that seems to be place on the woman's role as daughter-in-law and the increased involvement of the wife's family, particularly in taking on childcare responsibilities. The ability for both spouses to continue to work, which this evolving marriage pattern enables, provides opportunities for couples to increase their savings. This is important given studies that "point out that the final goal of many migrant workers is to make enough money so that they can return back to their hometown to open their own business and become their own boss."[29] Finally, Zhang found that relationships between couples tend "to be equal and mutually dependent."[30] This should not be surprising given that they are starting married life together far from home and familial support systems.

The future for these young couples is uncertain since reforms to the *hukou* system are slow to be implemented. As they begin to have children, concerns about education arise. The lack of significant reforms means they encounter the same problem faced by Mr. Deng. Many make the same choice as the Dengs: the wife returns home to supervise the child's education. A few couples choose not to separate the family and try to find the financial wherewithal to pay the tuition fees. Others opt to send children back to the countryside where the education is free. These children live with family members and often see their parents only once a year.

Whether couples who have chosen this new pattern of marriage, with its new set of challenges, will be more stable in their commitment to one another remains to be seen. One thing that is certain is that they are in the minority. "Some 56 percent of all migrants working outside their home provinces are married, but such couples rarely live together. Elderly relatives and the farmland back home need to be cared for. So in most cases, husbands and wives see each other just annually, during the Chinese Lunar new year or February's Spring Festival."[31] Not surprisingly, divorce rates are rising. "Xu anqi, an expert in family relations from Shanghai Academy of Social Sciences argues that 'eclipsing family ties' in a period of social transformation is the principal reason. Among all rural divorce cases, local courts reported some 50 percent to 80 percent involved at least one migrant worker."[32] Change is essential if China's young migrant workers' expectations of a different life are to have any real chance of being met.

Glimmers of Hope

In February 2012, "the General Office of the State Council, China's cabinet, issued a national guideline on reform of the hukou system, pledging to provide equal access to public services for people living in urban areas without permanent residential permits."[33] This is in keeping with China's twelfth Five Year Plan (2011–2015), which included equal access by all citizens to public services. In addition, pilot programs aimed at reform have been under way in some regional cities for a few years. In April 2011, the Chengdu Municipal Government began providing nonurban workers with the same social benefits as urban workers. According to one official, the phrase *migrant worker* will no longer exist.[34] The changes are not sudden. "During the past eight years, the municipal government has spent a large amount of money on establishing an equal public service system for its rural and urban areas and providing them with equal social insurance benefits."[35] Other cities and provinces are also implementing reforms, though requirements for migrants to obtain a permanent *hukou* differ greatly and in some cases are quite difficult to meet, especially in Beijing, Shanghai, and China's large coastal cities. In addition, receipt of some urban *hukous* comes with conditions such as relinquishing all claims to land in the countryside.

Conclusion

While it would appear that change is coming, it is doing so at a painfully slow rate. The *hukou* system is still an obstacle to millions who are simply trying to live a dignified life, find employment, and provide for their families. These social goods are fundamental to the human dignity of all people as is the right to free movement in order to attain them.[36]

In a recent address to participants at the Seventh World Congress for the Pastoral Care of Migrants, Pope Francis noted that

> migration is still an aspiration to hope. Above all in areas of the world in difficulty, where the lack of work prevents individuals and their families from achieving a dignified life, there is a strong drive to seek a better future wherever that may be, even at the risk of disappointment and failure.[37]

The millions of migrant workers in China certainly have that drive. Each of their journeys can be called an aspiration of hope. The question remains whether there is a possibility that they might fulfill those aspirations.

Notes

1. Michelle Flor Cruz, "Shanghai Surpasses New York for Luxury Goods Buying, Despite Chinese Austerity Drive," *International Business Times*, January 30, 2015, http://www.ibtimes.com/shanghai-surpasses-new-york-luxury-goods-buying-despite-chinese-austerity-drive-1553742.

2. Kuang Lei and Liu Li. "Discrimination against Rural-to-Urban Migrants: The Role of the *Hukou* System in China," *Plos ONE* 7, no. 11 (November 2012): 1.

3. Ibid.

4. Ellen Wong, ed., "IOM Fact Sheet: Strengthening Capacity to Manage Mixed Migration Flows in China," 4 (June 16, 2014), http://www.iom.int/files/live/sites/iom/files/Country/docs/IOM-China-PRM-Fact-Sheet-EN.pdf.

5. Details about Mr. Liu are found in Clarissa Sebag-Montefiore, "Dreams Deferred," *New Internationalist* no. 461 (April 2013): 20–21.

6. Moran Zhang, "China Has the Priciest Housing on the Planet, and There's Nothing Beijing Can Do about It," *International Business Times*, July 3, 2013, http://www.ibtimes.com/china-has-priciest-housing-planet-theres-nothing-beijing-can-do-about-it-1333635.

7. Sebag-Montefiore, "Dreams Deferred," 20.

8. Dexter Roberts, "China May Finally Let Its People Go," *Bloomberg Businessweek* no. 4271 (March 19, 2012): 21–22.

9. Ibid., 21.

10. Ibid., 22.

11. Pumin Yin, "Rural Students Falling Behind," *Beijing Review* 54, no. 37 (September 15, 2011): 24–25.

12. Ibid., 25.

13. Ibid., 26.

14. Ibid.

15. Ibid.

16. Ibid., 27.

17. UN General Assembly, *Universal Declaration of Human Rights* (December 10, 1948), art. 26, http://www.un.org.

18. Pontifical Council on the Family, "Charter of the Rights of the Family," Vatican City (October 22, 1983), art. 5.e., http://www.vatican.va/.

19. Pumin Yin, "Rural Students Falling Behind," 27.

20. Xin Meng, "Labor Market Outcomes and Reforms in China," *Journal of Economic Perspectives* 26, no. 4 (Fall 2012): 94ff.

21. Hong Zhang, "Labor Migration, Gender, and the Rise of Neo-Local Marriages in the Economic Boomtown of Dongguan, South China," *Journal of Contemporary China* 18, no. 61 (September 2009): 639.

22. Ibid.

23. Ibid., 640.

24. Ibid.

25. Ibid., 640–41.

26. Ibid., 641.

27. Ibid.

28. Ibid., 643.

29. Ibid., 651.

30. Ibid., 652.

31. Angela Bao, "Endless Road in China," *World Policy Journal* 27, no. 4 (Winter 2010): 26.

32. Ibid.

33. Pumin Yin, "Breaking the Lock," *Beijing Review* 55, no. 12 (March 22, 2012): 26.

34. Ibid., 22.

35. Ibid., 23.

36. Pontifical Council for the Family, "Charter of the Rights of the Family." See also, Michael A. Blume, S.V.D., "Migration and the Social Doctrine of the Church" (December 2002), http://www.vatican.va.

37. Pope Francis, "Address to the Seventh World Congress for the Pastoral Care of Migrants" (November 21, 2014), http://cmsny.org.

Familismo across the Americas

En Route to a Liberating Christian Family Ethic

Kristin E. Heyer

Transnational migration is often framed as an economic or geopolitical matter, whereas families primarily channel the impact of immigration. Push factors propelling unaccompanied minors across borders and traumatic enforcement mechanisms endanger families' well-being with social consequences. Policies that prevent immigrant workers from maintaining family unity treat them as economic units rather than recognizing their full humanity as parents and children. Christian family ethics offers significant resources for contesting the overreach of market forces and enforcement tactics impacting transnational families such as the nature of familial relationships and the connections between family life and the common good. In turn, realities migrant family members endure contest idealized *family values*. This essay will consider the plight of transnational families across the Americas to (1) frame unjust immigration policies and practices in gendered and familial terms and (2) consider the challenges transnational families' experiences pose to dominant forms of Christian family ethics.[1]

Gendered Risks

Recent patterns of migration across the Americas reflect global feminization trends: Latin American immigrant women have increasingly joined the US labor force after a history of disproportionately male migration northward. Heightened US border enforcement since the mid-1990s has contributed to this trend; as it became more difficult to cross without documents or travel back and forth seasonally, male migrants extended their stays and arranged for their families to join them. Significantly more women are migrating on their own as well. With stagnating male wages in the lower sector and the growth of female-headed households, migrant women's employment wields increasing significance in determining families' economic well-being.[2]

Women on the move face particular threats, from sexual assault by smugglers and officials, to abuse on the job, to manipulation in detention facilities. Studies of Central Americans traveling to and through Mexico and Mexican and Central Americans traveling to the United States estimate from 60 to 90 percent are subject to sexual assault.[3] Exposure to exploitation persists for those who survive perilous journeys. Less likely to qualify for employment-based immigration than men, the majority of migrant women work in unregulated jobs in the informal sector. Whereas undocumented immigrants earn lower wages than citizens in the same jobs, women routinely earn less than their male counterparts. Undocumented women are often perceived by predators as *perfect victims* of sexual assault: they remain isolated, uninformed about their rights, and are presumed to lack credibility.[4] Women farm workers hide their gender with baggy clothing to deter assault: 80 percent of women of Mexican descent working in California's Central Valley report experiencing sexual harassment as compared to 50 percent of all women in the US workforce.[5] Beyond well-founded fears that reporting abuses will risk job loss and family separation via deportation, such women lack access to legal resources and face language barriers and cultural pressures.[6]

Widespread sexual abuse of women working at the Postville, Iowa (USA) meat-packing plant went unreported. Girls as young as fifteen who worked the plant's night shift were continually harassed by supervisors but noted they could not afford to speak up and lose their jobs, given debts to their coyotes (human smugglers). Because these women understood that immigration officials collaborate with law enforcement, they did not seek help from the latter. Even those women who pursue the U visa program, which protects victims of crime from being deported, often fail to see justice served. One hundred charges of sexual assault and harassment have been filed nationwide by farmworkers in the United States, yet no criminal prosecutions have been put forward in these cases. United Farmworkers' Association Cofounder Dolores Huerta characterizes the reality as "an epidemic in the fields."[7]

Mexican anthropologist Olivia Ruiz Marrujo's research on women in the Soconusco region reveals how gender relations heighten susceptibility to sexual misconduct on the move. She writes, "in daily conversation [women in southern Mexico] refer to sexual relations with their partners as '*cuando hace uso de mí*'—'when he makes use of me,'" and local emergency rooms regularly treat women unconscious due to domestic violence.[8] Influential transnational postures of sexism and violence, as well as more culturally specific norms like *marianismo*, shape women's and men's expectations and behaviors in ways that heighten vulnerability. As a result, Marrujo notes, "an undocumented Central American woman for whom sexual relations has rarely, if ever, been consensual, may consider a *coyote* or supervisor's demand for sex expected male behavior."[9] These threats to women's well-being—physical, psychological, economic—frequently also threaten families on multiple sides of national borders.

Divided Families

From 1970 to 2010, the overall US immigrant population increased four-fold, whereas the Mexican and Central American population increased by a factor of twenty.[10] Due to a variety of factors—including country quotas and drastically mismatched labor needs with visa avenues—a substantial proportion of the immigrant population from these countries remains unauthorized. The Immigration Reform and Control Act of 1986 failed to provide status to family members of its beneficiaries, and the surge in petitions has contributed to backlogs so lengthy that immigrants sometime switch categories while they wait as they age or get married. US backlash against family preference categories is evident in fearful rhetoric, proposed *point systems*, and partisan deadlock surrounding legislative reform.

Beyond material need and family reunification, escalating violence increasingly fuels migration from some Central American communities. Given that homicides have only increased as Central American governments have implemented *iron fist* policing since 2003—in Honduras, for example, about seventy youth have been murdered *per month* over the past three years—many minors feel they have no other option than to flee home. Thirty percent of Central American youth are neither employed nor in school.[11] A 2014 UN High Commissioner for Refugees study of more than four hundred unaccompanied minors found widespread experience of violence or threats by organized crime groups, including gangs, drug cartels, or by state actors in countries of origin (48 percent), recruitment or exploitation by human smuggling organizations (39 percent), and abuse at home (22 percent).[12] As a result, the number of unaccompanied children crossing the US border has doubled annually from 2011 to 2014. Smuggling networks profit from these lower-risk passengers who frequently turn themselves in upon crossing.

Today 16.5 million people in the United States live in *mixed status families*. Of the roughly 4.5 million US-citizen children who have at least one parent residing in the United States without a regular status, tens of thousands undergo the deportation of a parent annually. In 2013, Immigration and Customs Enforcement removed 72,410 immigrants who reported they had US-born children. The detrimental impact of family separation has been poignantly evident in US federal, state, and local enforcement mechanisms that have escalated in recent years. In the aftermath of detention or deportation, families face major economic instability, and affected children suffer poor health and behavioral outcomes. Such foreseeable consequences violate fundamental norms regarding human dignity and care for the vulnerable.

Interrogated Values

In spite of immigrants' resilience, many of the patterns outlined obscure their full humanity as spouses, parents, and children. An operative value hierarchy prioritizing capital to people diametrically opposes Christian values and is as subtly formative as it is harmful to families. From Pope Paul VI's concern for the survival of children and well-being of families in light of international development,[13] through Pope Benedict XVI's critique of global economic threats to integral human development in *Caritas in veritate*,[14] to Pope Francis's lament at Lampedusa that we have forgotten how to weep for young men and women migrating to support family members who meet death en route,[15] Catholic social teaching decries systems that deny basic goods to families in the name of economic instrumentalism.

Beyond a critique of economic idolatry, the sanctity and social mission of the family developed in Christian ethics reorient immigration stakes away from deportation quotas or political calculations. Families comprise our most intimate relationships such that protracted separation threatens our very human subjectivity. Policies that undermine family unity frustrate this core relationally. Ada Maria Isasi-Díaz characterizes the family as the central institution in Latina/o culture, noting it functions as a duty, a support system, and a primary identity marker.[16] Hence, for those migrant women whose agency is caught up in motherhood, the inability to provide for or reunite with children can fracture integrity in profound ways.

Hebrew and Christian Scriptures are replete with examples of displaced families revealing a pattern not unlike what we encounter today: "Families are forced to uproot themselves, leaving behind their homes, their relatives and friends, the security of their lands and their provisions, the familiarity of their language and support of their communities."[17] A Christian family ethic offers significant resources for reorienting the immigration paradigm in several constructive ways: its profoundly relational anthropology, the family as *domestic church* and mediator of covenantal love, and the family's social mission.

Rooted in a Trinitarian anthropology, Catholic social thought integrates a family's intimate communion with its charge to mutually engage the broader social good. If families serve as basic cells of civil society—*schools of deeper humanity*—social conditions must protect their participation in the demands and benefits of the common good. Deprivation of dignified labor opportunities and traumatic enforcement mechanisms signify hostile social forces impeding immigrant families' access to social goods. In *Familiaris consortio* and *Centesimus annus* Pope John Paul II connects families' call to reveal love and bring children into and up through the world to their vocation to practice hospitality and give witness through a preferential option for the poor.[18] Particularly in light of this social mission, conditions that perpetuate family separation undermine human subjectivity and harm the common good. Even a cursory retrieval of the sanctity and social mission of the family squarely challenges harmful immigration policies. Yet the social contexts explored also suggest several caveats about idealized notions of family that hinder familial flourishing—particularly for migrant women and otherwise vulnerable family members.

Proposed Developments

According to this integral family humanism, families are public goods and "our ability to build just societies resides therefore primarily in our ability to build just families."[19] Given this responsibility, it is important to examine how migrants' experiences also serve as a source for Christian ethics in ways that might develop dominant Christian family ethics. The social contexts explored suggest several caveats in this regard: (1) inadequate approaches to the work of social reproduction, (2) the multiva-lence of *familismo*, and (3) the function of idealized familial norms.

Assumptions about the complementarity of the sexes that often lurk below Christian family ethics bolster uneven burdens for the work of social reproduction with ontological status. Pope Francis continues recent papal emphases on women's *feminine genius*, which he notes finds a particular, even if not exclusive, expression in motherhood. The language he uses suggests a *deeper theology of women* need not meaningfully contest the *equal but different* status (*valued not clericalized* status) that hinders women's flourishing in *public* and *private* venues alike. This separate spheres' ideology has helped sustain not only inequities in the workplace but also a lack of mutual accountability in shared household and parenting responsibilities.[20] Feminist ethicists have long emphasized tensions that persist between Christian teachings on equal human dignity or women's social contributions and emphases on women's maternal function and gender complementarity. Assumptions about the nature of women and caregiving work function to legitimize a *second shift*—felt most poignantly by women at the bottom economic rungs—and pit women against one another in shouldering the work of social production.[21]

These assumptions also obscure the relationship of the work of production to that of reproduction.[22] The maternal *genius* often burdens women with pluri-form caregiving duties rather than calling forth intergenerational solidarity marked by shared responsibility and adequate compensation. How societies organize the necessary work of social reproduction (such as dependent care, nurturance, and socialization) vis à vis the work of material production constitutes a social justice issue.[23] In contrast to the de facto liabilities caregivers face in the reigning economy and culture that assume an anthropology of isolated individualism, the "equality of women requires a political economy in which . . . being in need of care, and being responsible for the care of others, *are* the human norm."[24]

The lack of sustained attention to the impact of the political economy on family well-being masks "the actual connections between the deprivation of low-wage workers and the lifestyle of others."[25] In many cases upper- and middle-class women are liberated from domestic tasks by relying on low-wage workers, rein-forcing traditional, gendered divisions of labor. Anthropologist Jennifer Hirsch describes "outsourcing of caring" in vivid terms: "now the changing of diapers of both the very young and the very old—as well as the cleaning of the toilets of those who are, however temporarily, between Huggies and Depends—is done largely by darker-skinned hands."[26] This problematic shift in the organization of social reproduction too often remains peripheral to ethical discourse on family life, labor justice, and migration.[27] As Mary Romero's landmark analyses reveal, domestic labor arrangements are not only embedded in systems of domination but serve to sustain North American illusions of meritocracy and equality.[28]

The complex ways in which economic globalization has alternately under-mined and reinforced gender inequalities[29] are also evident in the ways cultural values like *familismo* impact and are altered by migrant experiences. A consideration of how a Latin American understanding of family might tutor an individualistic ethic, on one hand, and is altered by migration and diaspora experiences, on the other, illuminates how traditional Christian family ethics can both support and constrain women. It challenges Christian ethics to expand its notion of kinship networks, make more visible the oppression of women within the home, and expose inadequate construals of *family values*.

Familismo typically refers to a strong value placed on family relationships, community, and intergenerational kinship networks. Family serves as the primary organizing structure in most Latin American migrants' lives, for their social identity is relational.[30] The traditional cultural value of *familismo* intensifies the connection of familial relationships to women's identity: women serve as the backbone that binds this unique cultural, economic, social (and often religious) network of familial relationships. Migrant women are frequently accompanied by children or family members, whether at church, socializing, or on the job. Kinship networks extend laterally and vertically, and boundaries among members transcend genetics. A focus on the nuclear family evidenced in dominant Western Christian family ethics often overlooks these extended family solidarities.

The value *familismo* places on collective goals over individual well-being both challenges and is challenged by the autonomous ethos more predominant in the United States. Its kin networks "facilitate familistic reciprocity behavior," which studies indicate provides "powerful protective effects on health and emotional well-being."[31] On the other hand, women often face discrimination within *familismo*. The experience of migration to the United States has, in some cases, liberated women from social contexts that had constrained or harmed them. In her study of Mexican immigrant women who have been victims of sexual violence, sociologist Gloria González-López found that two sets of gendered dynamics emerged: "family honor anchored in notions of female purity and motherhood; and fear of the repercussions associated with contesting male violence."[32] Participants who migrated from Jalisco and Mexico City alike reported becoming passionate opponents of coercive marriage and legal systems that fail to protect rape survivors.[33] In many Latin American nations, sexual assault and violence against women are legally framed as crimes against family honor rather than as crimes against the victim's human rights.[34] One woman raped after migrating noted that, "although she experienced emotional trauma . . . geographical distance from her family and a sense of anonymity in a foreign country protected her from potential family confrontations and feelings of guilt." She noted she told no one so as not to shame her family, reflecting both the constraints of *familismo* and the different social consequences of sexual violence in her new setting.[35]

Hirsch's research on changing relational norms among Latin American migrant women and men indicate intergenerational shifts among Mexican transnational communities. She identifies generational shifts from compliance with gendered behavioral ideals of obedience to emphases on mutuality in companionate marriage and a relative softening of gendered division of labor in the home.[36] Beyond evolving relationship dynamics, Hirsch notes several key areas of difference in sending and receiving immigrant communities with respect to women and family matters: the privacy and social organization of public space (noting that a sense of invisibility in receiving countries can be empowering for women); legal protections against domestic violence (willingness of government to intervene in receiving but not in sending countries); and economic opportunities for women (the power to give orders is no longer an "economically earned right" for men alone).[37] The portrait is more complex than one wherein (limited) US notions of gender parity deserve praise or blame, but they do point to the multivalent nature of cultural and religious values related to family life and their malleability in light of migration experiences and economic necessity.

In her study of Latina immigrant laborers in Durham, North Carolina (USA), sociologist Chenoa Flippen's analyses reflect the intersecting dynamics that shape migrant women's labor experiences. She finds that women who have minor children abroad are more likely to work than other women, whereas married women and those with coresident children are less likely to work and experience significant family-related inactivity when they do work. She notes this indicates the need to recognize the complex ways "gender roles and family arrangements [and their relation to work] are profoundly altered through migration." Flippen's findings that married women's labor force participation remains more sensitive to legal status than marital status mitigate assumptions about Latino patriarchal constraints on women's paid employment and shift focus to structural conditions.[38] Participants' childcare and laundry employment often accommodated young children at work; this alleviated family responsibilities' impact on market work, at once enabling women to perform both roles and reinforcing gendered notions of caring work.[39] Hirsch's and Flippen's intersectional approaches offer Christian family ethics a helpful model for more adequately considering how family members' gender, class, race, ethnicity, and citizenship status intersect with expectations of relationship roles, household reproduction, and other labor.

Whereas the policies outlined at the outset have harmful concrete effects on family units, the discourse of *broken* families fails to capture the flexible strategies transnational families accomplish. Just as we must analyze which social frameworks effectively value families given intersecting constraints, considering which practices best permit mutuality and flourishing may be complicated. *Familismo* can perhaps broaden a dominant US Christian notion of kinship restricted by idealized nuclear family assumptions and underscore the ways in which solidarities can both connect and conceal, suggesting the importance of autonomy and interdependence alike. *Mujerista* perspectives rooted in the significance of *la familia* while rejecting patriarchal and authoritarian structures give witness to Jesus's inclusive and just kin-dom.[40]

As the profiled cases indicate, families negotiate a diversity of opportunities and challenges across borders, which the exclusive glorification of *familismo* or of nuclear family as refuge serve to obscure. Ahistorical portrayals of marriage and family in Christian ethics can issue inadequate ideals. An emphasis on the spousal meaning of body in terms of utter self-gift yields a marital sexual ethic that risks overlooking social forces that can abet sexual exploitation and violence. Conditions fostering *loneliness sex* among migrants and protracted family separation damage marital and family relationships. The iconic Christian symbol of motherhood of the *Virgin Mary peacefully cradling a newborn baby* does not fully speak to the experiences of many mothers who work tirelessly to feed their children.[41] Likewise, disproportionate emphasis on Our Lady of Guadalupe's innocent purity and compliant motherhood can fail to connect with women's felt concerns in harmful ways.

Idealized family norms not only miss significant realities and voices, they serve to reinforce oppression. Lisa Sowle Cahill rightly cautions, whereas a gospel identity should convert families to the hospitality and neighbor regard outlined above, "historically, the so-called Christian family has often been coopted by existing social structures, especially those that reproduce economic and gender inequities."[42] The task for Christian families to embody countercultural identities remains ever urgent, yet migrants' experiences suggest that this may look different for families without the luxury of responding in hospitality per standard prescriptions. In Philomena Cullen's words,

> It is when the Church relates to actual diverse families rather than to the non-existent idealized version that it becomes in the inclusive universal family of God that Jesus directed it to be . . . from the messiness of our family lives today [we] dare to find the action of a liberatory God [who] calls on us to . . . build an inclusive theology of the family that is based on justice, mutuality and reciprocal love.[43]

Conclusions

A Christian family ethic inattentive to the transnational family dynamics neglects significant factors that complicate strict ideals. The experiences traced herein signal intersecting structural and cultural forces—beyond relativism or hedonism—that impact actual families' lives. The analysis indicates supporting families demands cultural norms that equitably share and value caregiving work, economic and political policies that unite families, and enforcement strategies that do not hinder family and community well-being.

It also demands familial and sociopolitical supports that enable women to be economically productive members of a family. Rather than uncritically denigrating or glorifying migrants' survival strategies or family networks, it is important to bear in mind ways in which they are shaped by the challenges of economic insecurity; this dynamic suggests that ethics and social policies alike must not focus on changing family behaviors alone but also improving economic conditions and supporting a range of existing family arrangements.

Attending to women and children on the move and families in limbo across the Americas exposes patterns at odds with Christian commitments to human rights and the sanctity of family life. In turn, idealized family and gender norms risk reifying particular virtues or cultural models in isolation and can overlook significant barriers to familial flourishing. These caveats prompt contemporary Christian family ethics' important emphases on families' inherently sacred and social dimensions toward more inclusive and reality-based norms for families and communities. Even as dominant lenses in immigration debates conceal via partial or false narratives (e.g., distortions of security, rule of law, or economic concerns), it is urgent to also interrogate ways in which dominant ethical frameworks similarly mask complex realities and genuine values when they overlook the experiences of vulnerable agents. Familial patterns of distributive injustice across the double (or triple) *shift*, the trials of separated family members, and migrant women's courage in the face of formidable barriers highlight shortcomings of ethical methods that assume agency without constraint. Cross-border encounters challenge Christian ethics to reconsider assumptions about the scope and nature of threats to families' well-being and shape responses that more adequately foster loving and just communities.

Notes

1. Portions of the moral arguments developed here I first published in *Kinship across Borders: A Christian Ethic of Immigration* (Washington, DC: Georgetown University Press, 2012).

2. Chenoa A. Flippen, "Intersectionality at Work: Determinants of Labor Supply Among Immigrant Latinas," *Gender & Society* 28, no. 3 (June 2014): 404–34, at 404–5.

3. Amnesty International, "Invisible Victims: Migrants on the Move in Mexico," (London: Amnesty International Publications, 2010), (part 1 introduction).

4. Randy Capps et al., "A Profile of the Low-Wage Immigrant Workforce," Urban Institute, Brief No. 4 (November 2003).

5. Irma Morales Waugh, "Examining the Sexual Harassment Experiences of Mexican Immigrant Farmworking Women," *Violence Against Women* 16, no. 3 (March 2010): 237–61.

6. Ibid., 242.

7. Andres Cediel, "Rape in the Fields," *PBS Frontline* (June 25, 2013).

8. Olivia Ruiz Marrujo, "The Gender of Risk: Sexual Violence against Undocumented Women," in *A Promised Land, A Perilous Journey: Theological Perspectives on Migration*, ed. Daniel Groody and Gioacchino Campese (Notre Dame, IN: University of Notre Dame Press, 2008), 232.

9. Ibid., 228.

10. See Kate Brick, A. E. Challinor, and Marc R. Rosenblum, *Mexican and Central American Immigrants in the United States* (Washington, DC: Migration Policy Institute, 2011), 1–2.

11. National Jesuit Conference and the Washington Office on Latin America, "Myths and Facts on the Central American Migration Surge," http://www.jesuits.org/.

12. UN High Commissioner for Refugees, "Children on the Run: Unaccompanied Children Leaving Mexico and the Need for International Protection" (Washington, DC: UNCHR, March 12, 2014).

13. Pope Paul VI, *Populorum progressio* (March 26, 1967), no. 80.

14. Pope Benedict XVI, *Caritas in veritate* (June 29, 2009).

15. Tom Kington, "Pope criticizes indifference toward immigrants' plight," *Los Angeles Times*, July 8, 2013.

16. Ada María Isasi-Díaz, "Kin-dom of God: A Mujerista Proposal," in *In Our Own Voices: Latino/a Renditions of Theology*, ed. Benjamín Valentín (Maryknoll, NY: Orbis Books, 2010),181.

17. Robert Fortune Sanchez, "Migration and the Family," *Catholic Mind* 79 (February 1981): 19–20.

18. Pope John Paul II, *Familiaris consortio* (November 22, 1981), nos. 44, 45, 47; *Centesimus annus* (May 1, 1981), no. 48.

19. Philomena Cullen, "Social Justice and the Open Family," in *Catholic Social Justice: Theological and Practical Explorations*, ed. Bernard Hoose Cullen, and Gerard Mannion (London: T&T Clark/Continuum, 2007), 218.

20. See Christine Firer Hinze, "U.S. Catholic Social Thought, Gender, and Economic Livelihood," *Theological Studies* 66 (2005): 568–91 for a lucid assessment of these intersecting challenges.

21. See Arlie Russell Hochschild, *The Second Shift* (New York: Penguin Books, 1989); and Arlie Russell Hochschild, *The Time Bind: When Work Becomes Home and Home Becomes Work* (New York: Henry Holt, 1997).

22. Barbara Hogan, "Feminism and Catholic Social Thought," in *The New Dictionary of Catholic Social Thought*, ed. Judith A. Dwyer (Collegeville, MN: Liturgical Press, 1994), 397–98.

23. Gloria H. Albrecht, *Hitting Home: Feminist Ethics, Women's Work and the Betrayal of "Family Values"* (New York: Continuum, 2002), 139.

24. Ibid., 148.

25. Ibid., 141.

26. Jennifer S. Hirsch, "'Love Makes a Family': Globalization, Companionate Marriage, and the Modernization of Gender Inequality," in *Love and Globalization: Transformations of Intimacy in the Contemporary World*, ed. Mark B. Padilla et al. (Nashville, TN: Vanderbilt University Press, 2007), 103.

27. Linda Bosniak, "Citizenship, Noncitizenship and the Transnationalism of Domestic Work," in *Migration and Mobilities: Citizenship, Borders and Gender,* ed. Seyla Benhabib and Judith Resnik (New York: New York University Press, 2009), 131.

28. Mary Romero, *The Maid's Daughter: Living Inside and Outside the American Dream* (New York: New York University Press, 2011), 47. See also Mary Romero, *Maid in the USA* (New York: Routledge, 1992).

29. Hirsch, "Love Makes a Family," 102.

30. Victoria Malkin, "Reproduction of Gender Relations in the Mexican Migrant Community of New Rochelle, New York," in *Women and Migration in the U.S.-Mexico Borderlands: A Reader*, ed. Denise A. Segura and Patricia Zavella (Durham, NC: Duke University Press, 2007), 426.

31. William A. Vega, "The Study of Latino Families: A Point of Departure," in *Understanding Latino Families: Scholarship, Policy, and Practice*, ed. Ruth E. Zambrana (Thousand Oaks, CA: SAGE Publications, 1995), 7, 14.

32. Gloria González-López, "'Nunca he dejado de tener terror,': Sexual Violence in the Lives of Mexican Women," in *Women and Migration in the U.S.-Mexico Borderlands:*

A Reader, ed. Denise A. Segura and Patricia Zavella (Durham, NC: Duke University Press, 2007), 228.

33. Ibid., 236.

34. Rosa Kinda Fregoso, "Toward a Planetary Civil Society," in *Women and Migration in the U.S.-Mexico Borderlands,* ed. Segura and Zavella, 51.

35. González-López, "'Nunca he dejado de tener terror,'" 236.

36. Hirsch, "Love Makes a Family," 95.

37. Ibid., 446–50.

38. Ibid., 430.

39. Ibid.

40. Isasi-Díaz, "Kin-dom of God," 185–86.

41. Cathleen Kaveny, "Defining Feminism: Can the Church and World Agree on the Role of Women?" *America* 204, no. 6 (February 28, 2011): 17.

42. Lisa Sowle Cahill, *Family: A Christian Social Perspective* (Minneapolis, MN: Fortress Press, 2000), 83.

43. Cullen, "Social Justice and the Open Family," 212.

LIFTING THE VEIL

Theological Reflections on Marriage Migration

Gemma Tulud Cruz

A Demographic Gaze

When current patterns of global integration were established in the 1980s, marriage migrations became noticeable in terms of numbers. These migrations intensified in the 1990s when processes associated with globalization accelerated. Today, the dramatic rise in, and the global nature of, cross-border marriages[1] is such that *The Economist* refers to it as one of the world's biggest social trends.[2] In the Philippines alone, the US Embassy reports that there are more than 11,000 fiancé/fiancée and spouse visa applications each year.[3]

Data shows that cross-border marriage is on a slow but steady rise worldwide. This could be seen in a study by the Centre for Demographic Studies (Barcelona) and the Minnesota Population Center of the censuses of more than fifty countries on every continent for people aged twenty-five to thirty-nine. The most significant fact found in the study is the large difference between levels in rich and developing ones. In most developing countries, the share of men married to foreign women was less than 2 percent in 2000. In contrast, three rich countries—the United States, Britain, and France—account for half the total in the sample.[4] Such disparity between developed and developing countries is stark in Asia, the part of the world where cross-border marriages have been rising most consistently.

Every year, a large number of women from developing countries in Asia, particularly from Vietnam and the Philippines, migrate as brides to developed countries in East Asia. Foreign brides currently comprise 4 to 35 percent of newlyweds in Japan, South Korea (hereinafter Korea), Taiwan, and Singapore.[5] Cross-border marriages also involve other Asian countries such as the ethnic Chinese (mainly Hakka) from the Pontianak area of Indonesia who predominate in the flow of Indonesian brides to Taiwan. Women from India, Bangladesh, Pakistan, and Sri Lanka, meanwhile, dominate marriage-related migration to the United Kingdom, where spouses constitute the largest single category of migrant settlement.[6]

Issues and Challenges

Like every social phenomenon, which brings about external and internal transformations, there are issues and challenges that are attendant to cross-border marriages. To be sure, such issues and challenges go beyond victimization, which is often the perspective in which this phenomenon is analyzed and critiqued.

Decline of Marriage

The decline of marriage and, consequently, the family inevitably figures in discussions on cross-border marriages. In Asia, in the past two decades, educated and/or employed women may no longer be willing to accept the traditional role of a married woman, which involves taking care of all household chores and the parents-in-law while men work and become the breadwinners, because these women can work and support themselves without getting married. Consequently, these women, particularly in East Asia, may opt not to marry, resulting in the so-called marriage strike. In many cases, they delay marriage or, as is considered normal in Asia, choose to marry men of higher economic status who may not necessarily be a compatriot. The attraction of a cosmopolitan lifestyle and the availability of better job opportunities, which lure these women to the urban areas, also mean that local men in the rural areas have to contend with a further reduced pool for potential wives. This is true not just in Asia but in many agricultural communities worldwide. Unsuccessful efforts of these rural-based men to try to find spouses in their country then force them to turn to another country to find their brides. In Japan, the practice became a trend following the involvement of rural local governments in arranging cross-border marriages for their male residents in response to the problem of attracting Japanese brides to farm households.[7]

Cross-border marriages could, therefore, be analyzed in relation to a decline of marriage and the family that is primarily plaguing developed countries worldwide. This decline is rooted in the flight from marriage not just by women[8] but also by men who are either choosing not to marry or marry much later, and, in many cases, choosing to have less children. In 2013, for example, 53 percent of women and 47 percent of men who are eighteen and older in the United States were unmarried.[9] *The Economist* puts this decline in concrete terms as far as Asia is concerned:

> Marriage ages have risen all over the world, but the increase is particularly marked in Asia. . . . The mean age of marriage in the richest places—Japan, Taiwan, South Korea and Hong Kong—has risen sharply in the past few decades, to reach 29–30 for women and 31–33 for men. A lot of Asians are not marrying later. They are not marrying at all. Almost a third of Japanese women in their early 30s are unmarried; probably half of those will always be. Over one-fifth of Taiwanese women in their late 30s are single; most will never marry. In some places, rates of non-marriage are especially striking: in Bangkok, 20% of 40–44-year old women are not married; in Tokyo, 21%; among university graduates of that age in Singapore, 27%.[10]

The decline is also reflected in a growing number of married people, including women, who are choosing not to have children at all,[11] contributing to the collapse in the birth rate. Fertility in East Asia has fallen from 5.3 children per woman in the late 1960s to 1.6 at present. In countries with the lowest marriage rates, the fertility rate is nearer 1.0.

Last but not the least, the decline could also be seen in the proliferation of "commercially-arranged marriage migration" or "commodified marriage"[12] as these lack, at least at the beginning, one of the foundations and/or prerequisites of marriage, that is, love. The involvement of money as a service fee to marriage brokers or introduction agencies could be perceived as a stain on the marriage. Marriages in Korea, for example, are often arranged by a broker in a process that takes two or three days and costs the Korean groom US$20,000–30,000. The fact that the most significant problem of Filipino women married to Japanese men is the failure of the latter to fulfill the promise of regular financial support for the former's families also gives a window into this seemingly problematic motivation for marriage.[13] The financial strings attached to this type of marriage arguably taints it. "Sham marriages," whereby marriage is considered only as a ticket to visa or settlement, and the divorces that occur in, or as a result of, these cross-border marriages, is also symptomatic of what could be perceived as the devaluation of marriage.[14]

(Dis)empowerment

Despite its problematic reputation, cross-border marriage has intensified and is predicted to continue its upward crawl worldwide primarily because of the hope and promise it offers to the various actors and players. Marriage brokers are obviously clear winners. Countries of origin, on the other hand, suffer as they lose so many of their women, sometimes in just one area or region. In 2004 alone, a total of 19,594 women in nineteen northeastern provinces in Thailand chose to marry Western men. In some villages, as many as one-third of families have female members who have opted for Western husbands.[15] At the same time, sending countries and the brides' families benefit from the flow of money and goods and other forms of sociocultural capital that foreign wives provide. Destination countries, meanwhile, often feel they are on the losing end so they usually have an array of marriage-related immigration policies that get updated and become more restrictive over the years. The United Kingdom increased not only the minimum age for spouses to twenty-one but also the probationary period for spousal visa holders to apply for settlement from two to five years. Malaysia, meanwhile, maintains an array of secular and religious permits that foreigners must get not only for marriage but also for residence and work.[16] Still, it cannot be denied that foreign brides fill a gap in these countries' marriage market and prop up their fertility rate, not to mention serve as cash cows for national budgets. Australia, for instance, has increased the visa application charge for partner visas by 50 percent such that the partner visa fee, priced at AUS$4,575 until December 2014, was increased to AUS$6,865 starting

January 2015.[17] And while countries like Japan and Korea worry about the negative effects on the ethnic homogeneity that historically characterizes their societies, the diversity that cross-border marriages, and migration in general, bring could also be seen as beneficial to the health and vitality of destination countries.

The men or the grooms, particularly those from East Asia who look for brides in poor(er) Asian countries, are actually already marginalized by the marriage market in their own countries. They are in a sense the *leftover* men who cannot find a wife in their country due to various reasons such as their location (rural), occupation (farmer), age (older), lower educational background, and subscription to traditional views on marriage and gender roles. Having a young, poor wife from a developing Asian country also further subjects them to unsavory treatment from their compatriots. Last but not the least, they fall victim to women who want them only for their money and/or citizenship as some brides disappear, leave, or divorce them after residency or citizenship status has been granted.

Nevertheless, it cannot be denied that men get the better side of the bargain as they not only hold the power to choose the spouse; they also hold advantageous positions on account of their socioeconomic status, race, or ethnicity, the circumstances surrounding the arrangement of the marriage, and the fact that their country becomes the country of settlement. More importantly, they not only get a wife or someone who will bear them (more) children but also a domestic worker and a caregiver for their parents, which then enables them to go out to work.

The worst of the lot undoubtedly falls on the women. The majority of foreign wives have different ethnicities from their husbands and have no history of visiting or working in their destination country prior to marriage. For these reasons, they generally have a limited understanding of the destination country as well as a low ability to use the destination country's language. This, of course, has serious implications on their quality of life both in the public and private sphere, that is, the family, especially when the children are fluent in the fathers' language but not the language of the mothers. Loneliness and isolation is also common among foreign wives, especially for those who marry men who live and/or work in rural or remote areas such as mining or agricultural towns (e.g. the Australian outback).

In addition to the normal problems associated with geographic and cultural adjustment, cross-border marriages are further burdened by negative public attitudes in the destination country regarding the identity as well as the character and motivations of the brides. The label *mail-order bride*, for example, is an Australian colloquialism that emerged in the 1970s for Filipino women who married Anglo-Australians, with the pejorative implication that such women were either prostitutes or prepared to marry for financial gain. It is a caricature that penetrated the Australian collective imagination in the film *The Adventures of Priscilla: Queen of the Desert* in the character of Cynthia who was portrayed as a gold-digging Filipina whore beyond redemption. As a result the Philippine-born community, in general, and Filipinas married to Anglo-Australians, in particular, have been subject to a *sexualized citizenship* on top of racialized otherness.[18]

Such sexualized citizenship, understood as the conferment of nationality and the expropriation of belonging based on the sexual division of labor and the goods and services rendered by those who received the citizenship, is often the lot of poor foreign women married to rich men in developed countries. This means that the migration of these women is portrayed and understood in terms of what they can do with their sex, which includes performing sex, giving birth as the reproductive role of their sex, unpaid domestic labor premised on sexual differences, and the specialized affective labor that the foreign wives' racialized and sexualized class provides. These women, in other words, buy their citizenship through the exercise of their sex; the lowest *trick* in jumping the immigration queue,[19] rendering their citizenship questionable and illegitimate.

While the cause and effects of sexualization outlined above may hold true for all foreign brides from developing countries in Asia, the racialization that is layered by local politics into the sexualization is worse for certain ethnic groups. On paper, for example, Malaysia has a five-year continuous residency requirement for foreign wives to receive a residence permit. Mimicking ethnic politics in Malaysia, however, there are cases of foreign wives married to Malay men who have received their permanent residence permit in five years, whereas for wives of Chinese Malaysians, it takes seven years, and for wives of those of Indian descent, nine years.[20] In Taiwan's case ethnic nationalism plays a key role such that those from (mainland) China are most opposed.[21] Even in Europe only very few countries grant the foreign spouse full residence and employment rights immediately upon entry.[22] Such rights are clearly vital to ensure that foreign wives do not remain dependent on their husbands for their immigration status and ability to work since work provides some form of economic and psycho-social security.

Last but not least, foreign wives experience disempowerment through various forms of violence. Some young women are victims of cruelty, neglect, physical abuse, and trafficking.[23] Cowed victims of domestic violence suffer in silence rather than compromise their visa status, the material help they provide for their family back in the country of origin, or the future immigration of other family members. Husbands who fail in the husband-provider role may vent their frustration on their wives and children. The bodily harm experienced by *mail-ordered brides* in Australia, for example, has been well documented: victims were drowned, shot, knifed, slashed, hit on the head with a hammer, pushed into water, strangled, cut up, stabbed thirty times, strangled with a lamp cord and then set on fire, bashed in the head, among others. Sometimes the body of the *mail-order bride* was simply made to *disappear* as if she never existed.[24]

At the same time, it is clear that foreign brides experience various forms of empowerment. The women, who are often poor, see marriage with a man from a richer country as a means of advancement and a way of helping their families back home. In fact, marriage migration may often be the most efficient and socially acceptable means available to disadvantaged women to achieve a measure of social and economic mobility.[25] Various scholars point to migration as a means used by women to escape from patriarchal gender roles and relations, including a problematic or abusive marriage. Numerous literature also points to the empowering role of migration for women. Citing some of this literature, Oliva Espin enumerates the benefits:

> Newly-encountered sex-role patterns in the "host culture," combined with greater access to paid employment, create for women the possibility to live a new way of life. Some women become employed outside the home for the first time after the migration. Many of them encounter new opportunities for education. All of them are confronted with the alternative meanings of womanhood provided by observing the lives of women in the host country.[26]

Foreign wives also experience some form of empowerment in their contributions to the cultural; economic; and, to a certain extent, political life of their destination countries. For instance, Filipino wives in Mount Isa, a remote mining town in Australia, provide considerable contributions to the town's labor force and civic life such that they enjoy some form of political clout. They are also invaluable sources of help for one another in times of distress.[27]

Theological Reflections

The previous section unpacked the two key issues and challenges arising from cross-border marriages. The current section critically unveils and explores the theological themes that relate to these issues and challenges. Due to space constraints only two key themes will be engaged.

Marriage

Cross-border marriages obviously offer both promise and peril for Catholic theology on marriage if these marriages are scrutinized from the perspective of key marriage-related texts. In the Scriptures there is the classic text on Jesus's teaching on divorce with the oft-repeated passages "For this reason a man will leave his father and mother and be united to his wife, and the two will become one flesh. So they are no longer two, but one flesh. What therefore God has joined together, let no man separate" (Matt. 19:5–6). These passages certainly provide wisdom for cross-border marriage couples. As mentioned previously, East Asian grooms look for a bride in Vietnam or the Philippines precisely because they are looking for women who would have no problem living with and taking care of their aging parents. The serious difficulties the marriages and, in particular, foreign wives face when authority dynamics and cultural differences with the in-laws kick in, make the exhortation on leaving the father and the mother, interpreted here literally and figuratively, a much-needed practical moral boost for cross-border marriages. The above-mentioned passages from Matthew strip the in-laws of authority to meddle over their son's or daughter's personal, particularly marital and family, affairs, which could sometimes extend to decisions on the education of grandchildren. Supporting the empowerment of vulnerable poor(er) foreign wives/mothers who are forced to live with their in-laws, *Gaudium et spes* (GS) insists that "the parents themselves and no one else" should ultimately make the judgment in the education and formation of the children (GS, no. 50).

The church's antidivorce stance, however, would be another matter. While the durability of many cross-border marriages has been evident, it is no secret that there are grooms who have been previously married and/or divorced before engaging in cross-border marriages and that there are cross-border marriages that end in divorce due to serious reasons such as domestic violence. This antidivorce stance, which has been staunchly defended in key texts on marriage in the traditions such as Augustine's famous threefold *good* of marriage (in this case fidelity and sacrament),[28] *Castii connubii* (CC), nos. 32 and 34, and *Gaudium et spes*' exhortation that conjugal love is not to be "profaned by adultery or divorce" (GS, no. 49), pose problems for foreign wives trapped in an abusive or violent marriage, even while there have been shifts in the Catholic theology on marriage.[29]

The commercial and financial aspects surrounding many cross-border marriages are also questionable from the point of view of the tradition. John Chrysostom, for example, is of the view that marriages are not to be arranged for political or mercenary motives for "marriage is not a business venture but a fellowship for life."[30] The materialistic and instrumentalist character of such marriages could be of concern, as well, in view of the church's reference to an authentic married love informed and guided by divine love (GS, no. 48) and on what constitutes "true love between husband and wife" as described in GS, no. 49. A more nuanced understanding of the imbrication of marriage in a variety of socioeconomic and political circumstances could help. Women's marriage migration is often seen as a social institution determined merely by kinship and custom and, to this extent, outside the realm of political economy and the operation of modern market forces. Therefore, regarding marriage in purely religious terms, for example, as a sacrament that's "ordained toward the begetting and educating of [more] children" (GS, nos. 48, 50) without taking into serious account its roots and relationships with economics, politics, contexts, etc., also marginalizes cross-border marriages.

Since the majority of Asian cross-border marriages are interfaith marriages, the emphasis on the intergenerational sharing of the faith and on marriage in the faith in the most recent *Instrumentum laboris* of the 2014 Synod of Bishops on the family presents a challenge for understanding the religious dimensions of cross-border marriages.[31] How about cross-border marriages where the ceremony is held in the other religion? Is their marriage less of (or not) a sacrament?

To be sure, marriage between people of the same culture is already complex in itself considering differences in family upbringing, beliefs, and value systems. Those in cross-border marriages require double efforts toward mutual understanding because the greater the distance between the cultures of people, the more diverse are the cultural expectations and assumptions regarding marriage and family life.[32] It would perhaps be more fruitful to view such unions not so much with a romantic or universal view of marriage but one that stresses more the idea of companionship and growth. From this perspective it could be argued that a deep and lasting genuine relationship is the true test of the morality of marriage not so much sex and the sexual act or the formal institution of marriage.

Gender Roles and Relations

Traditional gender roles and relations clearly play a key role in cross-border marriages right from their inception and, arguably, throughout the couples' lifetimes. As discussed in the preceding section it is the reason and the lifeblood of many cross-border marriages and, at the same time, the root of the suffering of the men and, in particular, women who resort to it. Official Catholic teachings do not completely reject the patriarchal ideas that reinforce traditional roles that account for women's experience of suffering, violence, even death in some instances of cross-border marriages. Examples of this include teachings such as "the primacy of the husband with regard to the wife and children" (CC, no. 52), the focus on motherhood as the distinguishing function of women (CC, no. 11), and the reinforcement of women's domestic role as mothers in GS, no. 52.

While significant developments on the part of the church can be seen, such as John Paul II's recognition of the work and contribution of women to society, and the affirmation of the equal dignity and responsibility of women with men,[33] the use of the model of *complementary* male and female natures does not go far enough to address the manifold problems women encounter on account of their gender. "It is at least debatable whether the full equality of women with men in marriage, family, and society is compatible with seeing women primarily as compassionate nurturers and men as representing God to other family members."[34]

Meng Yanling offers an interesting compromise on the complementarity issue by using the term *mutual complementarity* in her analysis of the idea of the helper (*ezer*) in Genesis 2:20–22. By insisting that helper has no sense of *higher* or *lower*, Meng points out that it is not a conferral of status but must be understood as a mutual partner. Meng notes that a fuller expression of the mutual complementarity of the union between a man and a woman is when the man, on seeing the woman, calls her "bone of my bone, flesh of my flesh" (Gen. 2:23) for "only when male and female are united, mutually helping, can perfection be achieved . . . Between male and female there is not opposition but mutual help."[35] The *Instrumentum laboris* does make reference to the killing of women in intimate relationships and the damaging effect on women and children of psychological, physical, and sexual violence and abuse in families. However, it does not go far enough as it only calls for action for the church "in her ministry to the family." There was no mention of church teachings, policies, or pastoral practices that may be reinforcing the violence.

In fact, for the document to say that the violence is, "arising from a false culture based on possessions"[36] is somewhat puzzling and disappointing.

The weight of familial and social expectations, with a special reference to Asia, was also mentioned in the document, but the concern was mainly for children and educational expectations.[37] No mention was made on the weight of such expectations on girls and women, which is an equally strong and persistent problem all over the world, especially in Asia, as shown in the experience of foreign brides/wives.

Conclusion

A situation where women and men are not forced to leave their home country to marry someone else under problematic circumstances is clearly the goal that needs to be set. At the same time, the church cannot remain indifferent to the millions of cross-border marriages and bi/multiracial families all over the world, which have to contend with serious challenges that are peculiar to their situation. If it takes seriously Pope Francis's stance of mercy and compassion, both in its theology and practice, the church can certainly go a long way in helping and accompanying cross-border spouses and their families negotiate life with(out)borders. At the same time, stop-gap pastoral solutions are not enough, especially given the fact that cross-border marriages are here to stay in view of systemic inequality and the irreversible processes of globalization. Mercy must be accompanied by social justice. A helpful step, from a theological perspective, is the articulation of a theological ethics that recognizes the difficulties and, at the same time, complexities of cross-border marriages. Even more helpful, I posit, is a theology of marriage that celebrates what is/may be made possible in these unions such as a view of marriage as a unique form of friendship or human connection.

Notes

1. This essay uses the term *cross-border marriage*, also known as international marriage, intercultural marriage, cross-cultural marriage, or mixed marriage, with a focus on Asian women and on *commercially arranged marriage migration*. *Cross-border marriage* refers to marriages that join individuals with different citizenship statuses but do not link family or community groups, as compared to *transnational marriage*. It is also used to emphasize cultural, ethnic, religious, or social differences between the marriage partners regardless of other commonalities that may exist. For a listing and definition of terms for various marriage-related migrations, see Lucy Williams, *Global Marriage: Cross-Border Marriage Migration in Global Context* (London: Palgrave Macmillan, 2010), 8–9.

2. In rich countries alone, such unions number around ten to fifteen million. See "Herr and Madame, Señor and Mrs: International Marriage," *The Economist*, November 12, 2011, http://www.economist.com/.

3. See "Over 60,000 Yearly Apply for Non-Immigrant, Fiancé, Fiancée, Spouse Visas—US Embassy," November 2, 2014, http://globalnation.inquirer.net /.

4. Ibid..

5. Ibid.

6. See Katharine Charsley, "Marriage-Related Migration to the UK," *International Migration Review* 46, no. 4 (Winter 2012): 861–68.

7. Tomoko Nakamatsu, "International Marriage through Introduction Agencies: Social and Legal Realities of 'Asian' Wives of Japanese Men," in *Wife or Worker: Asian Women and Migration*, ed. Nicola Piper and Mina Roces (Lanham, MD: Rowman and Littlefield, 2003), 181.

8. For example, the large influx of foreign brides coincides with an unprecedented drop in marriage rate among women, particularly educated women in East Asian countries. See Daiji Kawaguchi and Soohyung Lee, "Brides for Sale: Cross-Border Marriages and Female Immigration" (working paper, Harvard Business School, Cambridge, MA, 2012), http://www.hbs.edu.

9. See United States Census Bureau "America's Families and Living Arrangements Table A1," http://www.census.gov.

10. "Asia's Lonely Hearts: The Decline of Asian Marriage," *The Economist*, August 20, 2011, http://www.economist.com. Melody Chia-Wen Lu and Yang Wen-shan, eds. *Asian Cross-border Marriage Migration: Demographic Patterns and Social Issues* (Amsterdam: Amsterdam University Press, 2010) is also a valuable resource.

11. Melanie Notkin, *Otherhood: Modern Women Finding a New Kind of Happiness* (Berkeley, CA: Seal Press, 2014) discusses women who do not have children either by choice or based on life's circumstances.

12. There are 3,100 matchmaking agencies in Japan and around 1,000 in Korea. Some of the dating agencies in Singapore even specialize in foreign brides, particularly from Vietnam. Gavin W. Jones, "International Marriage in Asia: What Do We Know and What Do We Need to Know," *Asia Research Institute Working Paper Series No. 174* (January 2012): 13.

13. Restitute Ogsimer and Agnes Gatpatan, "Filipino Women in Cross-cultural Marriage: Their Emerging Roles in the Catholic Church in Japan," *Journal of Sophia Asian Studies* 26 (2008): 44.

14. See, for example, Doo-Sub Kim, "The Rise of Cross-Border Marriage and Divorce in Contemporary Korea," in Lu and Wen-Shan, *Asian Cross-border Marriage Migration*, 127–54.

15. See Ratana Tosakul, "Cross-border Marriages: Experiences of Village Women from Northeastern Thailand with Western Men," in Lu and Wen-shan, *Asian Cross-border Marriage Migration*, 179–200.

16. See Michelle Lee and Nicola Piper, "Reflections on Transnational Life-Course and Migratory Patterns of Middle-Class Women—Preliminary Observations from Malaysia," in Piper and Roces, *Wife or Worker*, 121–36.

17. See Australian Government Department of Immigration and Border Protection, "Fees and Charges for Visas," http://www.immi.gov.au.

18. Shirlita Africa Espinosa, "Reading the Gendered Body in Filipino-Australian Diaspora Philanthropy," *Journal of Multidisciplinary International Studies* 9, no. 2 (July 2012): 11.

19. Ibid.,10.

20. Lee and Piper, "Reflections on Transnational Life-Course and Migratory Patterns of Middle-Class Women," 132.

21. See Ming-Chang Tsai, "'Foreign Brides' Meet Ethnic Politics in Taiwan," *International Migration Review* 45, no. 2 (Summer 2011): 243–68.

22. Eleonore Kofman et al. *Gender and International Migration in Europe* (London: Routledge, 2005) sheds light on this.

23. See Thérèse Blanchet, "Bangladeshi Girls Sold as Wives in North India," in *Marriage, Migration, and Gender*, ed. Rajni Palriwala and Patricia Uberoi (New Delhi: Sage Publications, 2008): 152–79.

24. See Chris Cunneen and Julie Stubbs, *Gender, Race and International Relations: Violence against Filipino Women in Australia* (Sydney: University of Sydney, 1997), 55–79; and Centre for Philippine Concerns-Australia—Brisbane, "Violent Deaths and Disappearances of Filipino Women and Children since 1980 (August 6, 2011), http://cpcabrisbane.org.

25. Rajni Palriwala and Patrcia Uberoi, "Exploring the Links: Gender Issues in Marriage and Migration," in Palriwala and Uberoi, *Marriage, Migration, and Gender*, 23–24.

26. Oliva Espin, *Women Crossing Boundaries: A Psychology of Immigration and Transformations of Sexuality* (New York: Routledge, 1999), 4.

27. See Mina Roces, "Sisterhood is Local: Filipino Women in Mount Isa," in Piper and Roces, *Wife or Worker*, 73–100.

28. The third *good* is offspring.

29. For a substantive discussion on this, see Bernard Cooke, "*Casti Connubii* to *Gaudium et Spes*: The Shifting Views of Christian Message," in *Marriage in the Catholic Tradition: Scripture, Tradition, and Experience*, ed. Todd Salzman et al. (New York: Crossroad, 2004), 113.

30. John Chrysostom, "Vainglory," in Max Ludwig Wolfram Laistner, *Christianity and Pagan Culture in the Later Roman Empire; Together with an English Translation of John Chrysostom's Address on Vainglory and the Right Way for Parents to Bring Up Their Children* (Ithaca, NY: Cornell University Press, 1951), cited by Lisa Cahill, *Family: A Christian Social Perspective* (Minneapolis: MN: Fortress Press, 2000), 56.

31. Synod of Bishops, *Instrumentum laboris*, no. 41.

32. Ogsimer and Gatpatan, "Filipino Women in Cross-cultural Marriage," 42.

33. See John Paul II, *Letter of Pope John Paul II to Women* (June 29, 1995), http://www.vatican.va; and *Mulieris dignitatem* (August 15, 1988), http://www.vatican.va.

34. Lisa Cahill, "Equality in Marriage: the Biblical Challenge," in Todd Salzman et al., *Marriage in the Catholic Tradition: Scripture, Tradition, and Experience*, 67.

35. Meng Yanling, "Women, Faith, Marriage: A Feminist Look at the Challenges for Women," *Chinese Theological Review* 18 (2004): 92.

36. Synod of Bishops, *Instrumentum Laboris: The Pastoral Challenges of the Family in the Context of Evangelization* (2014), 66, http://www.vatican.va.

37. Ibid., 76.

Part V

Virtues in the

Migration Context

Fortitude in the Midst of Weakness

The Case of Haitian Migrant Associations in Ecuador

Mauricio Alarcón Burbano, SJ

Though Ecuador has long been known as a sending country (mainly to Spain and the United States), it also evidences the process of return and international *im*migration. The presence, in particular, of a Haitian population in Ecuador is recent, although this population has a complex and painful migration throughout history.[1] According to the data of the National Directorate of Migration, during the decade between 2005 and 2014, 40,565 entries and 10,391 departures of Haitians were registered, for a total positive net migration of 30,174.[2] Ninety-five percent of these entries occurred in the period between 2010 and 2014. While these are approximations,[3] the fact remains that since the earthquake of January 12, 2010, the Haitian population in Ecuador has increased significantly.

Ecuador is also a route for both short- and long-term transit for the Haitian population. Gabriela Bernal,[4] an anthropologist who developed a study of Haitians in Quito, confirms that those who come for the short term are most likely linked to the trafficking of migrant peoples, making their stop in Ecuador as they journey further south (crossing from Peru into Brazil). Haitians who come for the long term are hoping to find educational and labor opportunities. With respect to the reasons for leaving Haiti, it is important to keep in mind that the earthquake in 2010 was a trigger within the wider context of social and political instability. Bernal considers that there are diverse factors influencing their exit and subsequent arrival in Ecuador. Following the 2010 earthquake, many moved to the rural zones trying to rebuild their lives, but Hurricane Sandy in 2012 caused the destruction of crops (70 percent, according to the International Labor Organization), leading to further displacement of populations toward the urban zones. However, life in the urban context did not solve their problems since they were met by cities destroyed and a generalized environment of violence. Under these circumstances, Haitians leaving their country making their way to Ecuador will claim that "there is no longer anything in Haiti."

The latest Constitution of the Republic of Ecuador (2008) defines the country as a "plurinational" and "intercultural" state, where human mobility falls under the aegis of "rights of priority persons and groups" (chap. 3). The same establishes that "no human being shall be identified or considered as illegal because of his/her migratory status" (art. 40), along with advocating for the "principle of universal citizenship" (art. 416). Because of the Haitian earthquake, the government of Ecuador issued Executive Decree Number 248 (signed by president Rafael Correa), which opened the possibility of regularizing Haitian citizens who were in Ecuador as irregular residents on the condition that they arrived in the country on or before January 30, 2010. However, the majority of Haitians arrived after that date, leaving them outside the opportunity to regularize their migrant status. Two years after the earthquake, Haitian migrants in Ecuador asked the government for channels to legalize their status because lack of proper documentation makes them vulnerable to abuse and labor exploitation. Although the situation of illegal immigrants was not resolved, thanks to requests from the Haitian associations, the Haitian embassy and consulate were established in Ecuador in mid-2013, which facilitates the acquisition of a police record, one of the documents needed to settle and work in Ecuador.

In addition to the advances of the 2008 Constitution, there is a Law of Foreigners from the 1970s, which sustains a hierarchy of access to rights, leveled according to migrant status, and where refugees and irregular immigrants populate the lowest rung. In addition, public opinion among Ecuadorians regarding foreigners is differentiated.[5] US citizens and Europeans are generally accepted by the public while those coming from a south–south migratory context, such as Colombians, Peruvians, Cubans, and Haitians, are rejected or suffer from poor public opinion.

In addition to their exclusion due to their Afro-Caribbean heritage, irregular Haitian migrants are condemned to economic exclusion (when finding precarious employment). Still, despite experiences of rejection, Haitians have a will to integrate, since they show favorable levels of relating to nationals and participating in shared social spaces. Fortunately, they find spaces where they can face the challenges of linguistic integration.[6]

Haitian Associations[7]

Civil and voluntary groups provide benefits not only to those associated with them but also to the corporate social body, bearing contributions such as the intrinsic benefit of organizations, political education, civic socialization, representation of interests, and public deliberation.[8] Collective norms and social trust increase when people participate in various voluntary associations, therefore generating social capital with positive effects on the common good and the nourishment of democratic character.[9]

Haitians in Ecuador have two civic association initiatives in the city of Quito. These initiatives constitute a shining light in the darkness, since they provide a timely word and accurate information to its Haitian compatriots, in the midst of the frustrations and uncertainties of the migratory project. The first association of Haitians, the Association of Resident and Refugee Haitians in Ecuador (AHRRE) was created in 2009. The second association, Haitian Community of Ecuador, surfaced in 2011. Both initiatives added up to one hundred members in 2013. They are weak associations since they lack a specific location (meeting in ecclesial and neighborhood spaces), are young (they have little experience), and do not have a fixed budget or subsidies from Ecuadorian public or state administration. Both groups are informal, meaning that they establish relationships of cooperation without need of formal rules or statutes. This does not mean the absence of norms, but rather it indicates a margin of flexibility in their procedures according to their activities toward their ends and depending on the context in which these efforts develop. An informal approach becomes a strategy allowing the opening of flexible channels of communication. The only limit imposed on this openness is a legal one. That is, they are open to counseling all Haitians, but they cannot make concessions in the case of people who might be involved in human trafficking.

Leading in Difficult Circumstances[10]

The Association of Resident and Refugee Haitians in Ecuador is led by a woman—who I shall call María—even though the majority of people in the association are men. María arrived in Ecuador over ten years ago due to the political upheaval in her country, events that led to the overthrow of Haitian president Jean-Bertrand Aristide. At that time, her family decided to go to Ecuador because they considered its people friendly and good hearted. María traveled first with her small daughter, in the hopes of reuniting with her husband. Unfortunately, the long wished-for reunion never took place as her husband was murdered. This was followed by dark times marked by tears and confusion in a strange land, but María had to overcome these and find the strength to move forward with her young daughter. What she did not imagine was that years later she would have to find renewed strength to encourage and bring an intimate word in Creole to fellow Haitians who were arriving in Quito.

María did not start out with the goal of becoming the coordinator of an association of Haitians. The invitation to lead came from a local parish priest. María had previous experience with a participatory association in Haiti and was able to incorporate a group for the defense of the rights of women (*Fem la Kaya*), which aimed to move forward a law that would guarantee respect for Haitian women. In this way, María's leadership skills were forged, grounded in her own experiences as a woman in a difficult context in which men have the public role while women are confined to the private sphere of the home and its domestic chores. Because of the sexual violence already present in Haiti, women within the familial context are cared for and perhaps overprotected. For this reason, it might seem normal that men control and support women in the private sphere. This makes men more visible in the public spaces in Quito, while women remain hidden. This fact partly explains the scant presence of women in initiatives of Haitian associations. From these experiences of pain and hope, María developed the strength to move ahead in Ecuador, bearing on her shoulders the weight of other migrant compatriots.

The Haitian Community of Ecuador has various coordinators, among them a fellow named Manuel. He arrived in Quito in 2011 along with his wife and his two small children in a flight from the Dominican Republic. From an early age, Manuel was interested in the process of participation, and sustained a practice of community service while in Ecuador. In his words, "if there is no one to serve and help Haitians, who are my compatriots, I feel that I'm missing something [. . .] It pains me to see my brothers suffering, and all foreigners who live here in Ecuador." Along with other Haitians who have more experience living in the country, the Haitian Community of Ecuador saw the need to organize as they noticed the lack of knowledge about laws and procedures in Ecuador, which would lead their compatriots to be easily misled or taken advantage of. They committed themselves to bring true information through social media, a radio program, and availability by phone when Haitians require some advice. This visibility has allowed them to establish spaces for civil participation.

María and Manuel have to lead in a context made difficult because of the lack of resources. Their initiatives are marked by *resistance*[11] because their mere existence is carried out in a hostile context inside and outside of their associations. Inside, there is a natural weakness because they don't have a specific site, they are young associations (with little experience), and cannot count on a fixed income stream. Outside, these two Haitian associations have only a small network of institutional support.[12] This is because most public and nongovernmental institutions taking care of "forced migrants" concentrate on those who fulfill the classical parameters of refugee. Regardless of this weakness, they exhibit a strength that was sustained thanks to the support of the *word*.

The Support of the Word

The word *support* has many meanings; here it refers specifically to maintaining, sustaining, comforting, heartening, and strengthening. Haitian associations find their support on the basis of the word in two ways: in a general sense, the human word becomes a source of strength for Haitians; on a more personal level, leaders find support in the Word, that is, in the Christian message that cannot be reduced to the *letter*, but that is indeed life, and in which ecclesial communities are mediated.

An Intimate Word That Engenders Trust

The two Haitian associations share the task of bringing an intimate human word that constitutes support to the Haitian community in the midst of weakness. Haitians have to give up their native tongue (Creole) in order to carry out their lives in the mainly Spanish-speaking context of Quito. Therefore, finding a compatriot that can assess and encourage them in Creole is an effective way of building closeness and trust.

The communication of the word is made easier through virtual media; the Haitian Community of Ecuador has a Facebook page in which posts are written in Spanish, French, and Creole. This social network turns into an information space for topics of interest to the Haitian community. Along with the virtual and written word, there is also space for the voice transmitted over the airwaves through the show "Chita Tande,"[13] an expression in Creole meaning sit and listen inspired by the immigrant experience that must be heard from the Ecuadorian immigrant context in order to be understood.

Manuel is conscious that only with the *truth* can one build *trust*: "we never speak a word that we cannot comply with for them [. . .] if I can give advice, I will give it. If I cannot, then I don't. Once I saw that the question was a psychological problem, and I sent that person to Jesuit Refugee Services, where there is no charge for this service." In María's case, her lengthy experience in Ecuador and in past associations have formed in her a unique perspective that makes her capable of inspiring other Haitian and Afro-Ecuadorian women in Quito.

The Word as Support

The two Haitian associations are groups with a civil character, with no goal to proselytize. Within migration processes, however, one not only take suitcases along but also the whole sociocultural baggage that will be reestablished in dialogue with the host country. Haitian immigrants bring with them their religious expressions, whether from their Christian Catholic, Protestant, or Evangelical traditions, in addition to their African religious expressions.[14]

María and Manuel participated in Catholic community spaces in their places of origin. These spaces have allowed them to strengthen their faith and hope, as well as develop their abilities for communication and leadership that can be put to use today in Ecuador.

María was raised in Seventh-Day Adventist Evangelical environment, but she moved toward Catholicism thanks to her partner, and subsequently husband, whom she met at the university. Her partner was a committed Catholic who had been a seminarian in the past. She was moved by the fact that he was not only interested in preaching heavenly promises but that he actually was concerned about earthly realities. Her husband used to say, "Jesus Christ did not remain quiet. Jesus Christ was not frightened. If Jesus Christ was afraid we would not be here!" This is how María, along with her husband, got to know a Christian perspective in which faith and justice walk together.

Manuel's case is different since he was part of ecclesial spaces ever since he was a child. Manuel formed a committee in which over twenty altar servers distributed Eucharistic duties for the week. He developed leadership qualities as leader of the altar servers. Upon completing high school, he went to the city of Port Au Prince where he continued actively participating in ecclesial initiatives: youth ministries and as a delegate for the district at age eighteen. Two years later, he became the secretary general of the Catholic youth ministries.

The ecclesial experiences of María and Manuel in Haiti brought them the support of the Word in difficult moments. Currently, the support of the Word continues to be important in their lives. However, they have not been able to participate fully in a Catholic parish in Quito since they do not have a context that celebrates the liturgy in their language and culture.[15] In contrast, Christian Evangelical Haitians have been able to organize religious celebrations in the Creole language in Quito, which have been facilitated because the Christian Evangelical institutional structures are more flexible than the institutional structures of the Catholic Church.

Fortitude as a Virtue of these Associations

Frequently we find approaches that describe the "forced migrant" as a universal victim, dehistoricized and apolitical.[16] Frequently this perception influences how humanitarian aid is doled out by public and civil organizations (nongovernmental organizations), and ecclesial initiatives of solidarity. This runs the risk of masking the potential of migrants who, regardless of difficulties, are able to be agents of their own civic associative processes.

In both associations described above, Haitians exhibit a paradox. Migrants participate in each, even though they are excluded from full social participation with respect to citizenship and the fullness of rights. However, their capacity to organize evidences a will to social integration and civic participation that goes beyond the classic model of nation-state (where citizenship is restricted to nationality). Civic participation is also expressed from the diverse spaces in which the migrant acts in promotion of the common good: neighborhood spaces, educational spaces, associative, etc.

Social integration is a two-way process where both migrant and host society participate and interact. Therefore, it is important to put into effect policies for social integration in the spheres of education, health, housing, and labor. Before the impossibility of full social and civic integration, Haitian migrant associations become spaces of resistance. This is not a passive resistance, but rather active support, which in this case is exhibited by the *word* in its human and ecclesial meaning. This resistance is more evident in Ecuador where organizations with a civil character are going through difficult times.[17] Strength or fortitude in the midst of weakness emerges in this context and is grounded in concrete experiences.

Fortitude refers to courage amid adversity. In the classical context of Homer, courage has heroic connotations, and it is not merely an individual quality. Rather, it is also a quality needed to sustain the community.[18] It is evident that in the cases of the leaders presented here, their commitment is support for those Haitians who participate in the associations. This support is mainly ethical, not economic, since these are associations with few resources.

According to Aristotle, the virtues "find their place not just in the life of the individual, but in the life of the city and that the individual is indeed intelligible only as a *politikon zoon*."[19] Courage or fortitude is a middle point between rashness and timidity. Therefore, it also requires prudence: "the person of fortitude must rely on true prudence in order to figure out the proper course of brave action."[20] Haitian associative initiatives are worked out in the fluid context of undocumented migrants who arrive to Ecuador ill informed, without knowledge of the language, and sometimes deceived by trafficking networks that falsely promised them education and work. Under these conditions, leaders must exercise prudence since any misstep in their services can end up in expectations or promises that cannot be met and could even get them in trouble with the state. As affirmed by Abdelmalek Sayad, a "social hypercorrection" is required from the immigrants since socially and morally, they are considered suspect.[21] This suspicion is made more evident when it coincides with ethnocentric patterns such as a black skin color, Spanish language with an accent, etc. In other words, migrants run the risk of being discriminated against because they are not Ecuadorian, do not speak Spanish, and are black. Haitian associations in the midst of this hostile context show their strength by developing spaces of communication that have political impact, not with regard to political parties, but with respect to civic participation.

Throughout the tradition, particularly in Augustine and Thomas Aquinas, Christian fortitude has been associated with the fourth Beatitude in Matthew 5:6 ("Blessed are they who hunger and thirst for righteousness, for they will be satisfied"). According to Romanus Cessario, "In making this connection, we are reminded that the gift of fortitude especially points to the realization of evangelical justice in the world."[22] In this case study, both association leaders experienced the support of the Word in Catholic communities within the context of their home country: Haiti. If Haitians as a group have not been able to actively join a parish ecclesial community in the host country, this does devalue the commitment of leaders who, inspired by their Christian identity, hunger and thirst for justice.

Strength or fortitude in the face of the weakness of the associative processes for Haitians can be related to the theo-anthropology of the death and resurrection of Christ applied to the migratory phenomenon. *Erga migrantes caritas Christi* affirms, "The experience of migration can be the announcement of the paschal mystery, in which death and resurrection make for the creation of a new humanity" (no. 18). This passage, written in the context of Christian hope can be applied also to fortitude since without hope, there can be no fortitude, as Josef Pieper affirms.[23]

In the Paschal mystery Jesus Christ is elevated as the risen one who triumphed over death. For those of us still journeying in this world, death and resurrection are not separate from the context of human finitude where structural and personal sin promotes injustice.[24] Haitian migrants are a people forced to leave their country (devastated by the 2010 earthquake) and who, up to now, have not received feasible solutions from the international community. World powers prefer to focus their attention on those places that bring a strategic advantage in the political or economic sphere, while ignoring those realities where the human drama is evidenced in its rawness. In contrast to this "globalization of indifference"—as Pope Francis affirmed[25]—we are met with local initiatives led by the migrants themselves, that, rather than being informal and weak, witness to a fortitude full of hope. It is here that we glimpse a true sign of the resurrection!

(Translated from Spanish by Mariá Teresa Dávila)

Notes

1. "One of the most notorious migrations in the Caribbean sub-region is the employment of Haitian braceros (strong armed ones) in the Dominican Republic's sugar cane harvest." Stephen Castles and Mark Miller, *The Age of Migration: International Population Movements in the Modern World,* 3rd ed. (London: Palgrave MacMillan, 2003), 150.

2. Calculation based on annual databases of international entries and exits. http://www.ecuadorencifras.gob.ec/.

3. These data must be considered as estimates. The actual number of Haitians leaving Ecuador must be greater than the number presented in the official statistics because there are Haitians in transit crossing the Ecuadorian border into Peru as irregular migrants, whose departure is not recorded in the official statistics.

4. Interview conducted June 27, 2013.

5. Luis Verdesoto and Beatriz Zepeda, "Ecuador, Las Américas y el Mundo 2010," *Opinión pública y política exterior* (Quito, Ecuador: FLACSO, 2011).

6. Linguistic integration takes place through friends, churches, and the Spanish School advanced by the work of Jesuit Refugee Services. This service was transferred to the Gobierno Autónomo Descentralizado de la Provincia de Pichincha in July 2014.

7. This investigation used a qualitative methodology with data obtained in the summer 2013.

8. Archon Fung, "Associations and Democracy: Between Theories, Hopes, and Realities," *Annual Review of Sociology* 29 (2003): 515–39.

9. Robert D. Putnam, *Bowling Alone: The Collapse and Revival of American Community* (New York: Simon & Schuster, 2000).

10. Names have been changed to protect the identity of the subjects interviewed.

11. Fung, "Associations and Democracy: Between Theories, Hopes, and Realities."

12. "The only civil society organization that has worked with Haitians in Ecuador in a continuous manner is the Jesuit Refugee Service." Gabriela Bernal, "Haitian Migration to Brazil: Ecuador, a Transit Country," in *IOM: Haitian Migration to Brazil: Characteristics, Opportunities and Challenges* (Buenos Aires, Argentina: IOM, 2014), 67.

13. This program is broadcast weekly through the station of "Casa de la Cultura Ecuatoriana," though it ceased in 2015 due to its coordinator's new job.

14. Roman Catholic 80 percent; Protestant 16 percent (Baptist 10 percent, Pentecostal 4 percent, Adventist 1 percent, other 1 percent); none 1 percent; other 3 percent. Roughly half of the population practices voodoo. "Index Mundi: Haiti Demographics Profile 2014," http://www.indexmundi.com.

15. While there are reliable pastoral initiatives promoted by Catholic organizations, such as Pastoral de la Movilidad Humana, Cáritas, Misión Escalabriniana, and Jesuit Refugee Services, these are not able to offer the pastoral care of a parish.

16. Ted C. Lewellen, "The Anthropology of Forced Migration," in *The Anthropology of Globalization* (Westport, CT: Bergin & Garvey, 2002), 178.

17. Some civil society organizations consider that Executive Decree 16 (in effect since June 4, 2013) has restricted the right to freedom of association in Ecuador.

18. Alasdair MacIntyre, *After Virtue*, 2nd ed. (London: Gerald Duckworth, 1985), 122.

19. Ibid., 150.

20. Romanus Cessario, *The Virtues, or, The Examined Life* (New York: Bloomsbury Academic, 2002), 168.

21. Abdelmalek Sayad, *La double absence: Des Illusions de l'emigré aux souffrances de l'immigré* (Paris: Le Seuil, 1999), 404.

22. Cessario, *The Virtues, or the Examined Life*, 175.

23. Josef Pieper, *Justicia y fortaleza*, trans. M. Garrido (Madrid: Rialp, 1972), 258.

24. "A structural sin is recognizable as sin by the destruction of the social bonds, through violence, lies, alienation, and submission." Mathias Nebel, *La categoría moral de pecado estructural* (Madrid: Trotta, 2011), 310.

25. Vatican Radio, *Pope on Lampedusa: "The Globalization of Indifference"* (July 8, 2013), http://www.news.va.

Hospitality and Solidarity

Virtues Integral to a Humane Refugee Policy

Deogratias M. Rwezaura, SJ

Because hospitality and solidarity remain key virtues in many African settings, on crossing borders, African refugees are often received by residents close to the border before any organization responds to their pressing needs. The late Julius K. Nyerere, the first president and founding father of the United Republic of Tanzania and the 1983 Nansen Award winner, referred to refugees as *resident guests* whose needs must first be attended to before they are asked why they fled. These virtues are increasingly being eroded in Eastern Africa as elsewhere by stringent refugee and migration policies that treat migrants as a threat to national security, a hazard to the environment, grabbers of citizens' job opportunities, and competitors for meager resources.

Inspired by the wisdom of Nyerere, I contend that hospitality and solidarity remain integral to the process of local integration, resettlement, or voluntary return to one's home country in dignity and safety. This essay draws on African virtues of hospitality and solidarity, examines them in light of the experience of the forcibly displaced, and recommends that they function as a yardstick for a critical review of refugee policy in Eastern Africa. In the essay, I will privilege the voices of the forcibly displaced and how they experience these virtues while allowing their voices to dialogue with existing regional policies on the subject matter.

When a Guest Decides to Stay Longer

Africans have for many years practiced the virtues of hospitality and solidarity. Hospitality might be understood in varied ways. I take it here to mean "a deeply human and Christian value that recognizes the claim that someone has, not because he or she is a member of my family or my community or my race or my faith, but simply because he or she is a human being who deserves welcome and respect."[1] Solidarity, too, has been used by many scholars and practitioners in various contexts. I understand it in the words of Jon Sobrino and Juan Hernández Pico "as another name for the kind of love that moves feet, hands, hearts, material goods, assistance, and sacrifice toward pain, danger, misfortune, disaster, repression, or death of other persons or a whole people [in order to] share with them and help them rise up, become free, claim justice, rebuild."[2]

In practice, these virtues of hospitality and solidarity form part of a child's upbringing in most African settings. A child will often be reprimanded for failure to welcome guests in the absence of parents. In the absence of his or her immediate host, any person can receive a guest, for a guest belongs to the community. In most cases, when a guest arrives, the host takes it as duty to inform the neighbors who, in solidarity, participate in making the guest feel at home. Rarely, if at all, is a guest in an African context asked when he or she intends to go back home. A guest might even decide to stay so long as he or she makes a transition from being guest to resident by participating fully in the affairs of the host community. As young children, we used to sing hospitality songs, one of which encouraged the community to welcome guests on the first and second day, and hand them a hoe for cultivation on the third day. Communal hospitality renders a guest welcomed and incorporated within the wider context. When extended to the forcibly displaced, such hospitality becomes an integrating virtue that helps alleviate their suffering and attend to their needs.

Hospitality demands that a guest be treated with dignity due the person. It also clearly instructs that once a guest decides to stay for whatever reason, he or she must join the rest and go to farm or do work in any other productive activity his or her host is engaged in. This wisdom blends hospitality with proactive solidarity that leads to productivity and dignified living. A guest becomes a resident and participates actively in the day-to-day undertakings of his or her host community or family. As such, hospitality can be seen to create necessary avenues for people to actualize their potential. Wage labor and other forms of gainful employment, which accord every person the dignity of participating productively in community, cease to be a privilege of the minority but a shared source of life. Refugees and asylum seekers have the right to work.[3] Work in this way becomes an integrating value where people forced to flee their homes cease to be seen as strangers,[4] but rather as *resident guests*.[5]

In his *ujamaa* (extended familyhood[6]) policy, Nyerere practiced hospitality as solidarity with the refugees. The borders remained porous, and he considered them as artificial creations separating families, clans, and community ties. Land, precious as it remains, was shared with refugees, and citizenship was granted to those who desired to be naturalized. In 1978, Tanzania naturalized Rwandese refugees,[7] and 162,000 Burundian refugees were offered citizenship by Tanzania in 2010.[8] As resident guests, refugees were also seen as part of the extended African family who needed to be sheltered and enabled to be self-reliant so long as they remained in Tanzania. The headman of Katumba settlement in Tanzania captures well the value of treating refugees as resident guests with dignity. He says "we are now a branch on the tree called Tanzania."[9] The open door policy rooted in Nyerere's respect for the dignity of all stemmed from his high practical esteem for African and Christian values and his Pan-African movement philosophy.[10]

Resident Guests or Unwanted Refugees?

Treating the forcibly displaced with dignity calls for local integration within a host community, in countries of resettlement, and upon return to their countries of origin in safety and dignity. Yet one cannot become fully integrated without fully participating in the productive activities of the host community. Lack of participation in social and economic activities renders refugees dependent on handouts rather than being allowed to actualize their potential through education, both formal and informal, depending on their capacity and talents. Value for work and participation in gainful employment allow refugees to become residents who should never lose their ability for productivity due to stringent laws. Again the case of the 1972 Burundian refugees in Tanzania stands out as a clear example of hospitable refugee policies that empower rather than degrade refugees.[11]

Sadly, full integration in host communities and countries has become increasingly diminished by stringent laws that pay less attention to the dignity of the forcibly displaced and more to the security, the integrity of national boundaries, and the concern for limited resources. Consequently, refugees flee insecurity in search of safer places to rebuild their lives and those of their families only to be treated as sources of insecurity. These attitudes and laws doubly jeopardize the forcibly displaced and retraumatize them. In fact, rather than formulating policies of hospitality toward the stranger in need of protection, some countries have put in place policies of hostility.[12] A keen look at the existing refugee acts and policies across East Africa reveals the extent to which solidarity and hospitality no longer inform the treatment of forced migrants.

Kenya's Refugee Act of 2006

For many years, Kenya has been hospitable to refugees from across its immediate neighbors in South Sudan, Ethiopia, Somalia, and Uganda, as well as its distant neighbors from Burundi, the Democratic Republic of Congo (DRC), and Rwanda, to mention the most prominent. Refugees reside in Kakuma camp located in northwestern Kenya and Dadaab camps located in northeastern Kenya as well as in urban areas. Official records by the UN High Commissioner for Refugees (UNHCR) put the number of refugees and asylum seekers hosted by Kenya as of July 2014 at 569,772, excluding 20,000 stateless people.[13]

While Kenya continues to extend hospitality to refugees, as the above statistics clearly indicate, unconstitutional and illegal directives and policies that go against international, regional, and national instruments meant to protect and promote the rights of refugees have often tainted Kenya's human rights record with regard to the treatment of refugees. The directive issued in December 2012 ordering all refugees residing in urban centers to relocate to the refugee camps and closing all urban refugee registration centers serves as an example.

The directive was quashed by the High Court of Kenya in July 2013 for violating the rights of refugees to freedom of movement and threatening their fundamental freedoms: their right to dignity and their right to fair administrative action. The High Court also ruled against the directive for violating the state's responsibility toward people in vulnerable situations and for threatening the principle of *nonrefoulement* contained in section 18 of the Refugee Act, 2006.[14] Despite the ruling in defense of refugees' rights as enumerated above, the then cabinet secretary for interior and coordination of national government, Mr. Joseph Ole Lenku, issued a press statement on March 25, 2014, directing that all refugees residing in Kenya's urban settings relocate to designated camps. He further intimated that failure to adhere to this would lead to prosecution of refugees and anybody hosting them in undesignated places. He again declared all registration centers in the urban settings of Nairobi, Nakuru, Isiolo, Mombasa, and Malindi closed, instructing Kenyans to report any refugee residing outside designated camps. As in the case of the December 2012 directive, the cabinet secretary cited security challenges in urban centers and the need to streamline the management of refugees as the reasons behind the press statement.

These directives have not only violated refugees' freedom of movement but have also blatantly disregarded gains achieved by refugees residing in urban areas, in terms of livelihood, education, access to health, local integration, and contribution to local economies. A forced relocation of refugees to the camps denies them the chance to actualize their potential, diminishes their efforts toward overcoming dependence, and locks what Loren B. Landau and Marguerite Duponchel have termed a "a gateway to a durable solution."[15] While national security and that of every Kenyan resident needs to be guaranteed by the state, this should not be done at the expense of refugees' rights. Some refugees have lived in urban areas for more than fifteen years and for security reasons cannot live in designated camps. These directives clearly indicate how policy makers are no longer making decisions anchored in African virtues of solidarity and hospitality that privilege the centrality of human people in any society.

Uganda's Refugee Act of 2006

Uganda remains by far the most generous country with the most hospitable policy for refugees in the region. Currently opening its doors to refugees fleeing the conflict in South Sudan, Uganda has been host to refugees from Rwanda, Burundi, and the DRC, as well as Kenyans who fled the 2007–2008 postelection violence and Somalis who fled the 2010 famine. The 2006 refugee act enshrines international instruments, the country's Bill of Rights, as well as the 1951 UN Convention and the 1967 protocol for the protection and assistance of refugees. Prior to 2006, the government had been guided by the repressive Control of Alien Refugees Act, from which the UNHCR had distanced itself. Enacted in the name of national security, it restricted refugees' right to move freely within its territory by according refugee status only to those who reside in refugee settlements. These settlements, as clearly argued by Lucy Hovil and Moses Chrispus Okello, did not only physically restrict refugees but also hampered their ability to develop fully as people with civil and political rights, as well as social, economic, and cultural rights.[16]

Tanzania's Refugee Act No. 9 of 1998 and the National Refugee Policy of 2003

Under Nyerere's leadership, Tanzania's approach to the hosting of refugees was guided by an *open door policy*. The policy "reflected the government's behavior and attitude toward refugees emanating from the spirit of Pan-Africanism and respect for humanity."[17] In a spirit of *ujamaa*, refugees were regarded as *resident guests* in hope that with their countries attaining independence, they would easily move back and live in safety and dignity. While guided by an open door policy in its treatment of refugees, Tanzania also had in place legislation–the Refugee Control Act No. 2 of 1965, which was quite restrictive but was repealed by the Refugee Act No. 9 of 1998. The 1998 act, while adhering to international instruments—such as the 1951 UN Convention Relating to the Status of Refugees and its 1967 protocol, as well as the 1969 Organization of African Unity Convention Governing Specific aspects of Refugee Problems in Africa—had its limitations as summarized by Khoti Kamanga.

The enactment of a new refugee statute would appear to have been used to accomplish four . . . interrelated objectives. Firstly, to signal disengagement from the Open Door policy of Nyerere's administration, with a view to making Tanzania a less attractive destination for asylum seekers, and sending a deterrent message to authorities in refugee-generating countries. Secondly, to convey to the international community disenchantment with the humanitarian assistance system for being insufficiently responsive to the impact of refugees on economically impoverished, fragile Tanzania. Thirdly, to assure the populace that the government is determined to address the problem of seemingly endless refugee influxes which are a direct cause of insecurity, environmental degradation, unemployment, moral decadence and electoral tensions. Fourthly, to enact an instrument that equips the relevant authorities with the legal means to deal with the problem[18]

The 2003 National Refugee Policy was formulated to combat economic, security, environmental, and social challenges in keeping with the safeguards for refugee protection and in "the spirit of international co-operation and burden sharing."[19] With this policy, however, the shift is made from seeing refugees as resident guests under the open door policy to regarding them as a burden to the national economy, environment, social services, and security. In recognition of the fact that some criminal elements take advantage of group status determination for refugee status (prima facie), the policy stipulates that "any asylum-seeker or refugee who engages in military activities . . . be separated and interned in a separation facility."[20] National interests started to trample the fundamental rights of refugees to freedom of movement, gainful employment, local integration, and naturalization.[21]

The reality is not different when people are forced to cross seas and oceans in search of safe and dignified lives in Europe and the Gulf States of Yemen, Saudi Arabia, Bahrain, and Oman. The October 2013 incident near the coast of Lampedusa, where hundreds of African refugees were honored in death rather than in life, serves as the most recent example.[22] Xenophobia in South Africa[23] is a clear indication of the erosion of African virtues of hospitality and solidarity espoused by *ujamaa*. These incidents reduce solidarity and hospitality to a circle of friends, and homogeneous communities, and lack the wider application of these virtues to the entire humanity. Yet, as Fr. Adolfo Nicolas, the current superior general of the Society of Jesus has reminded us, hospitality is boundless.

The Healing Dimension of Hospitality as Solidarity

The broken relationships that *ujamaa* seeks to mend require an ongoing reconciliation model that remains integral to all forms of hospitable and bonded communities. Jesuit Refugee Service (JRS) brings to the table concrete forms of reconciliation that enable the forcibly displaced to be at home with themselves, with their host communities, and with God.[24] Voluntary return in dignity and safety hinges on favorable conditions in countries of origin, which include reconciled and healed communities ready to welcome (be hospitable to) their compatriots. This does not easily come about when one's ancestral land has been taken away while in exile, and one has to be allocated another piece of land to start life afresh. Emotional and religious sentiments remain strongly attached to the land and while another piece of land may be found, delinking oneself with one's ancestral land especially for the forcibly displaced from rural areas does not come with ease. This is where hospitality, solidarity, and reconciliation come together to address root causes of conflicts or possible causes of future conflicts in order to proactively prevent the cycle of violence. Understood in the context of armed conflict, "reconciliation seeks to stop present violence, heal the wounds of past violence and prevent outshoots of violence returning in the future."[25]

In his message to JRS during the organization's thirtieth anniversary, Nicolas referred to hospitality as the building of reconciled communities and a bridge to people whom society separates on the basis of race, nationality, religion, gender, or tribe. Creating a space where people—who have every right to mistrust each other because of atrocities committed to them and to their loved ones—can come together to rebuild their lives is indeed "hospitality in action." It allows wounded people to be healed, feel at home not only in host communities but, more importantly, among themselves.[26]

Conclusion

Forced migration policies that make people feel so connected to host communities, indeed as *branches of the one tree* called humanity, require more than just legislation. They are rooted in inspirational leadership grounded in human values that recognize the dignity in all who, for no fault of their own, are forced to flee their homes. The increasing stringent policies toward people who flee their countries and homes in search of safety and dignity deny the fundamental realization that as branches of one family tree, we are in solidarity. The degradation of any of us is a diminishment of humanity. Hospitality to the forcibly displaced affirms our common humanity, and solidarity with them recognizes this affirmation.

In this essay I have contended that hospitality and solidarity are critical virtues to forced migration policies that seek to treat people as people. Rooted in African traditions and practices, these virtues need to always be taken into account in formulating refugee policy in Eastern Africa, as elsewhere on the continent. Failure to see refugees as primarily people with dignity can lead to seeing and treating them as disposable and hence as undeserving of hospitality in solidarity with them.

Notes

1. Adolfo Nicolás, "Hospitality Fosters Reconciliation" (November 20, 2010), http://www.jrsusa.org.

2. Jon Sobrino and Juan Hernández Pico, *Theology of Christian Solidarity*, trans. Phillip Berryman (Maryknoll, NY: Orbis Books, 1985), vii.

3. See articles 17, 18 and 19 of the UN Convention and Protocol Relating to the Status of Refugees, http://www.unhcr.org.

4. United States Conference of Catholic Bishops, "Strangers No Longer: Together on the Journey of Hope," USCCB and Conferencia del Episcopado Mexicano (2003), http://www.usccb.org/.

5. Sreeram Sundar Chaulia, "The Politics of Refugee Hosting in Tanzania: From Open Door to Unsustainability, Insecurity and Receding Receptivity," *Journal of Refugee Studies* 16, no. 2 (2003): 154, 156.

6. Shirley Graham, *Julius K. Nyerere: Teacher of Africa* (New York: Julian Messner, 1975), 148.

7. Charles P. Gasarasi, "The Mass Naturalization and Further Integration of Rwandese Refugees in Tanzania: Process, Problems and Prospects," *Journal of Refugee Studies* 3, no. 2 (1990): 97–100.

8. See UNHCR News Stories, "UNHCR Welcomes Tanzania's Decision to Naturalize Tens of Thousands of Burundian Refugees" (April 16, 2010), http://www.unhcr.org.

9. Anne-Lise Klausen et al., "Joint Evaluation: Evaluation of the Protracted Refugee Situation (PRS) for Burundians in Tanzania" (October 2010), http://www.unhcr.org.

10. Beatus B. A. Kitururu, *The Spirituality of Hospitality: African and New Testament Perspectives,* (Nairobi, Kenya: CUEA Press, 2009), 59.

11. Klausen et al., "Joint Evaluation," 17–21.

12. Irene Duffard Evangelista, "On Policies of Hospitality and Hostility in Argentina," *Forced Migration Review* 45 (February 2014): 75.

13. UNHCR, "2015 UNHCR Country Operations Profile—Kenya," http://www.unhcr.org.

14. Republic of Kenya in the High Court of Kenya at the Nairobi Milimani Law Courts Constitutional and Human Rights Division, Petition no. 19 of 2013 consolidated with Petition no. 115 of 2013, paras. 100(a) and (b), http://www.urpn.org/. *Nonrefoulement* obliges states to refrain from forcibly repatriating refugees to countries where they would be persecuted.

15. Loren B. Landau and Marguerite Duponchel, "Laws, Policies, or Social Position? Capabilities and the Determinants of Effective Protection in Four African Cities," *Journal of Refugee Studies* 24, no. 1 (March 2011): 15.

16. Lucy Hovil and Moses Chrispus Okello, "The Right to Freedom of Movement for Refugees in Uganda," in *Refugee Right: Ethics, Advocacy and Africa*, ed. David Hollenbach (Washington, D.C.: Georgetown University Press, 2008), 80–82.

17. The United Republic of Tanzania, Ministry of Home Affairs, *The National Refugee Policy* (Dar es Salaam, September 15, 2003), no. 3.

18. Khoti Kamanga, "The (Tanzania) Refugees Act of 1998: Some Legal and Policy Implications," *Journal of Refugee Studies* 18, No.1, (2005): 104–5.

19. The United Republic of Tanzania, *The National Refugee Policy*, nos. 4, 5.

20. Ibid., no. 10.

21. Ibid., nos. 15, 17.

22. Barbara Molinario, "UNHCR Urges Italy to Improve Facilities on Lampedusa as Boat Tragedy Death Toll Rises" (October 9, 2013), http://www.unhcr.org/52556a469. html. Many more migrants continue to die in the Mediterranean Sea en route to Europe with the numbers estimated at 1,500 for the first quarter of 2015. For details, see "Mediterranean Migrant Deaths: EU Faces Renewed Pressure," (April 20, 2015), http://www.bbc.com/news/world-europe-32376082.

23. "South Africa's Zuma Vows to End Attacks on Migrants," (April 18, 2015), http://www.bbc.com/news/world-africa-32365157.

24. The United Republic of Tanzania, *The National Refugee Policy*, nos. 15, 17.

25. Elias Lopez Perez, SJ, "The Spirituality of Reconciliation in JRS," in *Recreating Right Relationships: Deepening the Mission of reconciliation in the Work of JRS*, ed. Danielle Vella (Rome: Jesuit Refugee Service, 2013), 90.

26. Read the story of Victoria who had succumbed to the violence and alcohol abuse of camp life but who trained under JRS and became a great counselor to victims of abuse "Peace and Reconciliation in Kitgum," *JRS Eastern Africa Newsletter* 49 (July 2012): 13.

Fair Trade Tourism

Practicing Hospitality and Keeping the Sabbath in a Foreign Land

Patrick T. McCormick

International tourism brought nearly 500 million travelers to developing nations in 2012, and generated nearly $350 billion in exports for these nations, making the industry the second largest source of foreign exchange for the world's poorest forty-nine nations. But local residents and communities often see little of the income or good jobs generated by a flood of first-world tourists that can degrade and exhaust these vacation paradises, and a booming sex tourism industry that enslaves millions of women and children. Fashioning a theological ethics for the tourism trade might begin by turning to the biblical notions of hospitality and Sabbath, both of which call the modern tourist to provide adequate care and protection to the host communities in emerging economies that provide half a billion tourists with their vacation rest.

Growth of International Tourism

According to the World Tourism Organization (UNWTO), tourism is the world's largest industry and employer, earning 9 percent of the world's gross domestic product (GDP) and employing over 250 million people, or one out of every eleven workers.[1] As Martha Honey notes, "If it were a country, [tourism] would have the second-largest economy, shadowed only by the United States."[2] UNWTO reports indicate that international tourism accounts for 30 percent of the world's exports of services and 6 percent of overall exports of goods and services. It is currently the leading source of foreign exchange earnings for nearly 40 percent of the world's nations. In 2012, tourists around the world took over one billion international trips, generating over $1.3 trillion in exports, or about $3.5 billion a day, with an additional five to six billion trips taken that year by domestic tourists, pushing tourism's contribution to the world economy to approximately $7 trillion.[3]

International tourism has increased fortyfold (6 percent annually) since 1950, when 25 million international trips generated $13 billion in revenues, and this sector is predicted to grow to 1.8 billion trips by 2030. A growing percentage of that international travel is taking tourists to the developing world. Since 1980, emerging economies have increased their share of the international tourist trade from 30 to 47 percent and are expected to attract 57 percent of the market by 2030. In 2012, just under 500 million of the slightly more than 1 billion international tourist trips were taken to developing nations, earning $386 billion in exports, and by 2030 the UNWTO predicts that 1 billion of the 1.8 billion international trips taken that year will be to destinations in emerging economies.[4]

Emerging economies have been particularly keen on securing a larger slice of the tourist pie, borrowing and investing billions on marketing and infrastructure. Poor and indebted countries have been encouraged to grow their tourist trade so they might diversify their economies, generate investment, increase foreign exchange earnings, generate employment, and boost domestic spending on education and health care, all without the sort of resources required for mining, manufacturing, or oil development.[5]

And the strategy has been somewhat effective. Between 1992 and 2010, annual income from tourism in the world's forty-nine poorest nations leapt from $1 to $10 billion, and today tourism is the first or second largest source of export earnings in twenty of these countries.[6] Meanwhile, one hundred of the world's poorest nations now earn up to 5 percent of their GDP from foreign tourists, with tourism accounting for 6 percent of exports and 60 percent of service exports. Only oil remains a larger source of foreign exchange for these countries, and the World Trade Organization reports that the tourist industry represents the only sector where developing nations regularly run a trade surplus.[7]

International tourism has also generated significant employment in developing nations. About 65 percent of the jobs tourism creates each year are in the developing world. Each new hotel room can generate one or two positions, and in places like the Bahamas, the Maldives, and Saint Lucia, nearly half of the jobs are tied to tourism. Many of these positions go to women, who make up about 46 percent of the workers in the hotel, catering, and restaurant industries, and who can often find part-time and entry-level positions or self-employment opportunities selling food and crafts.[8]

Costs of International Tourism

Still, international tourism has not been an unmixed blessing for developing countries.

Much of the wealth generated by this industry stays in or leaks back to wealthy multinational corporations, advanced economies, or corrupt local officials, while the burdens/costs imposed by tourism are outsourced to the local communities.

Leakage

Overall, about half of the income from international tourism leaks out of developing countries, due in no small part to the fact that foreign-based companies and chains dominate the tourist sector in many of these nations. When international travelers arrive on foreign-owned air carriers and stay in foreign-owned hotel chains, about four-fifths of tourist dollars stay with these companies. If tourists purchase cruise or other all-inclusive vacation packages, the hosts in the developing country will see even less of their money. And the situation is likely to worsen as international economic agreements force developing countries to give foreign and multinational chains and operators more access to their tourist markets, allowing these behemoths to further marginalize local businesses.[9]

Unjust Labor Practices

Most of the jobs in the tourism sector open to local workers in developing nations are in low-paying, entry-level, menial, dead-end positions in the service sector. Local employees in the tourist trade are regularly exploited by being overworked and underpaid, and remain vulnerable because they lack adequate protection from unions or government regulations.[10] In addition, there is evidence the women in tourism are largely relegated to low-status jobs and often suffer from gender stereotyping and exploitation.[11] Indeed, working conditions in the tourist sector in emerging economies often replicate colonial patterns of exploitation and marginalization. This is particularly true in the exploding cruise industry, where open ship registry allows employers to circumvent national labor and environmental regulations, resulting in many employees working twelve to sixteen hours a day, seven days a week for as little as $50 (plus tips) a month.[12]

So while tourism has created millions of jobs in developing nations, most of the better-paying management positions go to foreigners or workers from the cities. Local residents can usually only find work cleaning, cooking, caddying, carrying bags, or driving a cab, and may often find themselves trapped in a culture of servitude, treating their foreign guests as colonial or neocolonial masters and mistresses.[13] As Lisa Mastny notes, "The International Labor Organization (ILO) reports that tourism workers earn 20 percent less on average than workers in other economic sectors . . . (and) some 13–19 million children now work in tourism."[14]

Environmental Pollution/Degradation

The arrival of hundreds of millions of tourists from industrial nations has had a decidedly negative impact on the environment and resources of tourist communities in developing countries. Tourists from industrial nations come to these once-remote sites to savor their natural beauty and charm, but they also bring first-world expectations for comfort and amenities, and the infrastructure required to satisfy their industrial appetites can overwhelm the local resources. Tourism and travel is responsible for 5.3 percent of the world's carbon emissions.[15]

The environmental impact of international tourism begins at home, or at least at the airport. Commercial airliners are dirtier polluters than any other form of passenger transport, and about 43 percent of international travelers fly to their destination.[16] In some developing nations, 90 percent of tourists arrive on a plane. Rising carbon dioxide emissions from the planes in our increasingly busy skies contribute to global warming trends threatening the very rainforests and coastlines in developing nations that so many tourists want to visit.[17]

On their arrival, millions of these travelers settle into one of the many high-rise hotels or resorts spreading across the once empty beach and displacing colonies of smaller, locally owned facilities. Global tourism added about four million new hotel rooms to its registry in the 1990s, mostly in large complexes.[18] Constructing these bedroom behemoths and their accompanying golf courses often harms the dunes, wetlands, and coral reefs tourists have come to visit and deprives the local community of important farmland; and once in operation, these modern resorts place tremendous stress on local resources.[19] At an average resort, a single tourist can use over one hundred pounds of fossil fuel a week, and filling pools, cleaning laundry, and watering golf courses means that international tourists often use four to seven times as much water as locals, not infrequently contributing to shortages and escalating rates. Watering a single eighteen-hole golf course can take over half a million gallons a day.[20]

And these resorts and hotels generate a great deal of waste, often without adequate sewage treatment facilities, leading to the pollution and degradation of beaches, coral reefs, and other local habitats.[21] Cruise ships pose an even greater environmental threat. Each week, a typical cruise ship generates 1 million gallons of graywater, 200,000 gallons of sewage, and 8 tons of garbage. Each day the cruise ships dump 90,000 tons of untreated sewage and trash into the world's oceans, and this problem could worsen as more and larger ships are constructed to meet an expanding appetite for cruises.[22]

Travelers themselves can also exhaust a local environment. Busloads and caravans of tourists often overwhelm the fragile ecosystems and habitats they have come to visit. Automobile and foot traffic wear down the lush green of rainforests and national parks and reserves, and wear out the paths and steps to ancient sites. Visitors and hikers litter and trample. Scuba divers and snorkelers scrape and chip. And local animals lose their fear of humans and are distracted from hunting and feeding.[23]

Sex Tourism and Trafficking

Finally, millions of women and at least two million children are enslaved in a sex tourism industry earning criminal trafficking syndicates hundreds of billions of dollars a year.[24] Jump started by the arrival of US military rest and recreation centers during the Viet Nam War, Thailand's booming sex tourism industry has trafficked millions of women and children from the surrounding region, attracted tens of millions of male tourists from industrial nations, and inspired the expansion of this illegal trade into other developing countries, where sex tourism can provide nearly a sixth of the nation's GDP.[25] About a third of the females entrapped in this trade are under eighteen, and fourteen- to nineteen-year-olds make up the largest group of sex workers in developing countries. Traffickers kidnap children or buy them from desperately impoverished parents, often with promises of good jobs.[26] Once entrapped in this trade, women and children are victimized, abused, exposed to violence and deadly infections, and stigmatized as social outcasts.[27]

Theological Grounds for a *Fair Trade* Tourism

Two biblical notions could help us develop a theological ethic to address the challenges and difficulties of modern tourism: hospitality and the Sabbath command. In differing ways, each of these scriptural principles summons us to protect the rights and dignity of host communities providing international tourists with their vacation rest.

Hospitality

While modern society sees hospitality as the practice of good manners or an industry providing for the needs of paying guests, "the ancient peoples of the Near East considered hospitality as an essential value," and "most of the ancient world regarded hospitality as a fundamental moral practice . . . necessary to human well-being and essential to the protection of vulnerable strangers."[28] In a similar spirit the Bible describes hospitality to strangers as an essential virtue, and offers two reasons for the practice of this virtue: first, the stranger one entertains might be a divine messenger, and second, believers should imitate and extend the hospitality God showed to their ancestors when they were oppressed aliens in Egypt and needy sojourners in the wilderness.

"Do not neglect to show hospitality," Hebrews 13:2 advises, for "by doing this some have entertained angels unawares," referring to the hospitality offered by Abraham and Sarah and Lot and his wife in Genesis 18 and 19. But even more importantly, the Bible directs us to remember and imitate God's own hospitality to the Hebrews when they were aliens in Egypt and sojourners in the desert. "When an alien resides with you in your land, you must not oppress him," God tells the Israelites in Leviticus 19:33–34. "He is to be treated as a native born among you. Love him as yourself, because you were aliens in Egypt." Anyone failing to show this hospitality betrays the God who "shows love towards the alien who lives among you, giving him food and clothing" (Deut. 10:18).

The biblical command to show hospitality to the needy stranger continues in the New Testament, where Jesus, who repeatedly takes on the role of the vulnerable alien, commands his disciples to provide for the needs of the vulnerable stranger, make room for them at their tables, and wait on them as servants. In Matthew's parable of the Last Judgment and the Lucan parables of the Good Samaritan and the Rich Man and Lazarus, Jesus instructs his followers to provide for the needs of vulnerable strangers. In the accounts of his radical table fellowship Jesus teaches his followers to breach the walls of class, race, and gender by welcoming and befriending the alien and outsider. And in the six accounts of the multiplication of loaves and fishes and John's account of the Last Supper Jesus directs his disciples to take up the role of servants, treating the needy alien as their honored guests and masters.

Biblical hospitality, then, commands believers to provide needy aliens with adequate food, shelter, and protection; demands that the stranger be welcomed as a companion and friend and offered a place at the table; and requires that hosts breach and dismantle the walls of privilege or exclusion by becoming servants of those in need.

Applied to the modern setting of international tourism, this biblical hospitality generates parallel obligations on modern travelers who must take steps to protect and provide for the basic needs of host communities serving them in emerging economies, welcome these hosts as friends and companions, and take steps to dismantle colonial and exploitive structures imposed on these communities.

For while the biblical practice of hospitality usually had hosts extending care to travelers and aliens, the true basis of the duty to be hospitable was generated by the need and vulnerability of the other, not by their status as sojourner. In a modern context where well-to-do travelers from advanced economies interact with exploited and vulnerable hosts in emerging economies, the duty to practice biblical hospitality lies with the wealthy traveler. And, indeed, many of those extending hospitality in biblical accounts were themselves aliens or sojourners, as was surely the case with Sarah and Abraham, Lot and his wife, and Luke's Good Samaritan. So the duty of hospitality also obliges sojourners. And at least part of the duty to prac- tice hospitality toward the exploited, endangered, and vulnerable host communities serving hundreds of millions of international tourists comes from the fact that these very travelers impose burdens on their hosts, commodify their culture, and exhaust and degrade their environment.

The biblical virtue of hospitality demands that international tourists find a way to adequately protect and provide for their vulnerable hosts, recognize the dignity and culture of their alien hosts and welcome them as companions, and to breach or dismantle exploitative and neocolonial structures that oppress and marginalize those providing their vacation rest.

Sabbath

The context of modern international mass tourism is one in which hundreds of millions of middle- and upper-class workers from the industrial and postindus- trial world seek *rest* from their labors in advanced capitalist economies by escaping to vacation spots in emerging markets where they will be hosted and served by domestic low-cost labor that is generally vulnerable (lacking adequate legal protec- tions or negotiating positions) and often exploited (underpaid and overworked).

In the interface of traveler and host in international tourism in emerging economies, some of the worst elements of the developed world's labor practices intrude on the developing world and, instead of exporting the accumulated rights, protections, and benefits of postindustrial labor, international tourism in emerging markets often replicates colonial patterns of exploitation and discrimination, with vacationing tourists renting cheap domestic servant labor that does not enjoy the benefits, rights, or protections of laborers in the developed world.

This is true of tens of millions of workers from emerging economies in the tourism sector, and even more horribly true of the millions of women and children sold or entrapped in the sex tourism and sex trafficking industries that make up a part of the practice of international tourism. So, hundreds of millions of tourists vacationing from their industrial and postindustrial labors in advanced economies cooperate in the exploitation of overworked, underpaid, unprotected and not infrequently abused and violated laborers.

In addition, international tourism exports patterns of environmental exploitation of the industrial age to developing countries, outsourcing much of the environmental costs of international tourism to vulnerable communities in emerging economies, without offering the accumulated environmental protections currently demanded and provided for in advanced economies.

It is this exploitation of labor and land in the context of seeking rest from work that makes the Sabbath command a critical tool for theological analysis.

Patrick D. Miller argues that the Sabbath command is the central command of the Decalogue found in Deuteronomy 5 and the springboard for the liberating "Sabbatical Principle" that moves from Moses's request for "rest" for Hebrew slaves to the liberation of all peoples called for in the Sabbatical and Jubilee commands.[29]

Ellen Davis argues that the Sabbath command issued in Deuteronomy 5 is a divine gift liberating former slaves from bondage and transforming their servitude into free and human labor. This same command, Leo XIII argued in *Rerum novarum* (no. 32) provides the basis for the right to rest enjoyed today by the hundreds of millions of laborers from advanced economies who vacation in emerging markets. Yet this Sabbath command is also a summons, demanding that resting workers extend a similar respite to all other laborers, including, in particular, both those who toil as their own servants and those vulnerable and unprotected strangers who labor in their midst. According to Deuteronomy 5:12–15, ancient and modern workers freed from bondage must remember their own previous enslavement and liberation by sharing their current freedom and rest with servants and strangers who labor for them.

For the Sabbath command in Deuteronomy 5:12–15 not only directs the reader to rest from labor on the seventh day but also demands this rest be extended to our male and female slaves and the resident alien within our gates, "so that your male and female slave may rest as you do." And we should extend this liberating rest to servants and foreigners because we, too, "were once slaves in the land of Egypt, and the LORD, your God, brought you out from there with a strong hand and outstretched arm."

This Sabbath command to share God's liberating rest with servants and strangers must surely apply to the servants and workers waiting on and hosting the nearly 400 million international tourists taking their vacations in emerging markets.

Miller and Davis argue that Sabbath is a liberating rest, a rest that renders our work good or human and transforms the bad or oppressive toil of Genesis 3 (curse) and Pharaoh's Egypt (which resists and reacts to Moses's call for a liberating rest for Hebrew slaves in Exodus 5:1–9). The Sabbath command in Deuteronomy 5 recalls the liberating rest offered to the Hebrews in Exodus and calls for an extension of this liberation to all peoples. But this same liberating rest is also a springboard for a progressive liberation of all workers and peoples, and even of creation itself. The Sabbath functions as a mustard seed or leaven that encroaches on the bad toil of Pharaoh's and Caesar's empires and constantly presses for a transformation into a more human practice of labor.

According to Miller, the request Moses and Aaron make repeatedly for a short rest for the Hebrews leads to their ultimate liberation and to the weekly rest of the Sabbath that transforms a community of toiling slaves into a society of free people laboring together in dignity. This Sabbath command further unfolds in what Miller calls the "Sabbatical Principle," which produces the Sabbatical and Jubilee commands in Leviticus. In these extensions of the Sabbatical Principle workers trapped in poverty, debt, and slavery are liberated from their condition and given a fresh start by a year of rest that breaks the cycle of bad work, debt, and bondage that was the lot of far too many in the ancient world. At the same time the seven-year rest offered to the land provided gleanings for the landless poor and a rest for soil exhausted by relentless toil of advanced agricultural societies. And the Jubilee year caps off the liberating arc of the Sabbath and the Sabbatical Principle by adding the return of the land to those indebted families who had been forced to sell their birthright in a labor economy that drove them into poverty, debt, slavery, and landlessness.[30]

Each of these three stages of the Sabbatical Principle (Sabbath, Sabbatical, and Jubilee) offers workers trapped in a cycle of exploitation and oppression a liberating break from and a re-creation (new start) of history that interrupts the escalating pace of history in which toil consumes more and more of our lives and drives people into poverty, debt, slavery, and death.

At the same time, the Sabbath and Sabbatical Principle challenge the idolatry of work and the belief in salvation through works, and interrupt the escalating practice of oppressive labor that consumes all our days and all peoples. And the Sabbath and Sabbatical Principle also address the preservation of the land and the natural world, providing a rest for the beasts of the field and a rest every seven years for the land itself. Both of these indicate that good work, or work transformed by the Sabbath and the Sabbatical Principle would also resist the exploitation and degradation of the environment.[31]

The implications of the Sabbath and Sabbatical Principle for those involved in the industry of modern international tourism, particularly as it is played out in emerging or developing economies, are many.

To start, the Sabbath and Sabbatical Principle make it clear that good work must include an adequate and genuine rest for all workers—particularly unprotected and vulnerable servants and aliens—and indeed for all creation. The same good work, shaped by the Sabbath and the Sabbatical Principle, must preserve the rights, benefits, and protections of all workers, and of the land itself. Thus, good work is by its nature sustainable and does not exploit or exhaust the laborer or the land. And any rest taken from work must not impose unjust labor on others or on their environment. Practicing the Sabbath in a foreign land requires extending that Sabbath protection to host communities and their environment.

This means that the Sabbath command and Sabbatical Principle demand that tourists from advanced economies should only rest in ways that extend the liberating gift of the Sabbath to all in the human household, and certainly to those unprotected and foreign laborers supporting the tourist industry. So, the work of local tourism employees must be safeguarded by limits on overtime, provision of just wages and safe working conditions, and establishment of adequate protections of the rights of workers. And the abuses of sex tourism and sex trafficking must be eradicated. Deuteronomy 5:12–15 makes it clear that none can rest while the rights of other workers are not protected, and no authentic Sabbath is celebrated while the foreign slave is oppressed.

Hence, the interaction between international travelers from advanced economies and laborers and communities in emerging or developing economies should not be an occasion to replicate the exploitive and oppressive economics of colonialism but must be a path for extending the accumulated rights, benefits, and protections of workers in advanced economies. The Sabbatical Principle is a mustard seed or leaven that is meant to liberate all peoples and lands from oppression, and it is only the Pharaoh's unjust rest that is based on the oppressed labor of others.

Nor can the practice of international tourism be used as a means to export or outsource the externalities and environmental burdens generated by the vacations of hundreds of millions of workers. Instead, the Sabbath command and Sabbatical Principle require that genuine rest be extended to other creatures and to the land itself, both as a way of allowing the land to serve all peoples (especially the landless poor) and as a means to restoring lands degraded and exhausted by an idolatrous worship of toil that consumes the land and its peoples.

Conclusion

In spite of the problems and burdens associated with international tourism, developing nations and many indigenous peoples remain eager for the income and employment generated by this trade.[32] Still, the hospitality international tourists owe the people and communities they visit is not satisfied by paying the hotel or tour bill, or by leaving a tip. The industrial nations and multinational corporations and chains that send millions of middle- and upper-class tourists to vacation in developing nations have a duty to ensure that the people and communities recruited to serve the clientele of these playgrounds are adequately protected and provided for, that the beaches, rainforests, and savannahs tourists come to visit and trek through are not polluted or destroyed, and that the animals and plants tourists come to see and photograph are not endangered or decimated by their visit.

For the good sojourner, hospitality means recognizing the people and communities that host us as companions and neighbors. It means treating them and their culture with regard and respect, protecting them from abuse and exploitation, and making a commitment to ensure that they receive a just wage and benefit fairly from the industry in their midst. Hospitality requires a commitment to a just and sustainable tourism industry, ensuring that sojourners tread lightly, "minimizing impact through environmentally and culturally sensitive architecture and regulating the number and modes of behavior of tourists."[33] Such an industry must also provide "financial benefits and economic empowerment to the local (and indigenous) people . . . respecting the local culture and supporting human rights and democratic movements."[34]

Being a good sojourner was a costly practice for the Samaritan on the road to Jericho, and a lifesaving one for the man he aided. For many of us vacationing in developing countries, practicing hospitality will make our sojourn more expensive, but it may also prove to be life giving, both for the communities we visit and for the children and grandchildren of host and guest alike.

At the same time, the Sabbath command and Miller's Sabbatical Principle direct millions of international tourists seeking their vacation rest in developing economies to extend the accumulated rights and benefits of industrial and postindustrial labor to the vulnerable and exploited tourist workers toiling on their behalf. No one should take their rest on the backs of those stripped of a liberating Sabbath and cursed like Adam to toil all the days of their lives.

And the same Sabbath command instructs international tourists to rest in a way that does not overburden or exhaust other creatures or the land itself. For the Sabbath command and the Sabbatical Principle direct us to rest in ways that sustain creation and that extend the liberating gift of the Sabbath to all of nature.

Notes

1. World Tourism Organization, *UNTWO Tourism Highlights: 2013 Edition* (Madrid: UNWTO, 2013), 2–4.

2. Martha S. Honey, "Treading Lightly? Ecotourism's Impact on the Environment," *Environment* 41, no. 5 (1999): 9.

3. World Tourism Organization, *UNTWO Tourism Highlights,* 2–6.

4. Ibid., 2–7.

5. Elizabeth Becker, *Overbooked: The Exploding Business of Travel and Tourism* (New York: Simon & Schuster, 2013), 19.

6. World Tourism Organization, *Tourism and Poverty Reduction* (Madrid: UNWTO, 2011), 1.

7. Lisa Mastny, *Traveling Light: New Paths for International Tourism* (Washington DC: Worldwatch Institute, 2001), 19–20.

8. Ibid., 24–25.

9. Ibid., 21–24.

10. Deoni Duncan, "The Ethics of Tourism," *Review and Expositor* 108, no. 4 (2011): 528–30.

11. World Tourism Organization, *Global Report on Women in Tourism 2010* (Madrid: UNWTO, 2011), 7–11.

12. Christine B. N. Chin, "Mini United Nations Crew on Cruise Ships," *International Feminist Journal of Politics* 10, no. 1 (2003): 2–9.

13. Paul Jeffrey, "Gathering Stones in Paradise," *Christian Century* 110, no. 17 (May 19, 1993): 542; Chin, "Mini United Nations," 7–12.

14. Mastny, *Traveling Light*, 24.

15. Becker, *Overbooked*, 20.

16. Andrew Holden, "Achieving a Sustainable Relationship between Common Pool Resources and Tourism: The Role of Environmental Ethics," *Journal of Sustainable Tourism*, 13, no. 4 (2005): 341–42.

17. Mastny, *Traveling Light*, 29.

18. Ibid., 30.

19. Jeffrey, "Gathering Stones in Paradise," 542–43.

20. Mastny, *Traveling Light*, 32.

21. Jeffrey, "Gathering Stones in Paradise," 544.

22. Mastny, *Traveling Light*, 33.

23. Ibid.

24. Becker, *Overbooked*, 115–16.

25. Aaron Sachs, "The Last Commodity: Child Prostitution in the Developing World," *World Watch* 7, no. 4 (1994): 24–30; Becker, *Overbooked*, 115.

26. Dennis Coday, "Trial Draws Attention to Child Sex Tourism," *National Catholic Reporter* (November 3, 2000):10; Nina Rao, "Sex Tourism in South Asia," *International Journal of Contemporary Hospitality Management* 11, no. 2 (1999): 97.

27. Chris Beyrer and Julie Stachowiak, "Health Consequences of Trafficking of Women and Girls in Southeast Asia," *Brown Journal of World Affairs* 10, no. 1 (2003): 107–12.

28. Hampton Morgan, "Remember to Show Hospitality: A Sign of Grace in Grace-less Times," *International Review of Mission* 87, no. 347 (1998): 535; Christine D. Pohl, *Making Room: Recovering Hospitality as a Christian Tradition* (Grand Rapids, MI: Eerdmans, 1999), 17.

29. Patrick D. Miller, "The Human Sabbath: A Study in Deuteronomic Theology," *Princeton Seminary Bulletin* 6, no. 2 (1985): 81–97.

30. Ibid., 92–94.

31. Ibid., 95.

32. Mastny, *Traveling Light*, 28.

33. Honey, "Treading Lightly?" 7.

34. Ibid.

"Always Remember Where You Came From"

An Ethics of Migrant Memory

Peter C. Phan

The voice, rich and resonant, tinged with part nostalgia, part pride, rumbled from an old black man, deep furrows in his brow but radiant with hope and strength. It being Black History Month in the United States, he was asked what advice he would like to give to his fellow black Americans. Eyes strained at the camera, the right index finger raised for emphasis, he intoned, "Always remember where you came from." The message was solemn and persuasive. Television trades only in sound bites, however, and so the old man was not afforded the time to elaborate on his pithy counsel. But it was not difficult to conjure up, behind those words "where you came from," years of unspeakable suffering and humiliation and violence when black slaves, like cattle, were bought and sold, forced to serve their white masters as their gods, and lynched when they rebelled.

"Always Remember Where You Came From"

With a black man in the White House (though himself not a descendant of slaves), it can be easy to forget this long and painful chapter of their history. The old black man's timely admonition to his fellow black nationals to remember where they came from was all the more poignant in light of recent shootings and killings of unarmed black men by white police officers who were not even indicted, stories that went viral on global social media.[1]

The old man's admonition to remember one's roots was compelling not only for black Americans but also for millions of migrants and refugees who have come to the United States, especially after the passage in 1965 of the Hart–Celler Act, a byproduct of the civil rights movement and part of President Lyndon Johnson's Great Society program. The primary aim of this act was to abolish the racially based quota system imposed by the 1921 National Origins Formula that favored the immigration of people from Central, Northern, and Western Europe. The law replaced the racial quotas with preference categories based on family relationships and job skills that were in demand to boost the American economy. However, after 1970, following an initial influx of migrants from those European countries, immigrants started pouring in from unexpected countries such as Korea, China,

India, the Philippines, Vietnam, and Pakistan, as well as the countries of Africa and Central America, and then most recently, from the Middle East. Compared with their predecessors, the great majority of these new migrants, whose racial and ethnic origins had been judged by nativists to be unassimilable into the American melting pot, did not come voluntarily in search of a better economic future but to flee from war and violence.

For the descendants of predominantly white migrants from Europe in the nineteenth and early twentieth centuries, their ancestors' experiences of leaving their countries and their loved ones in search of a better life in the United States, painful as they were, are now but distant and dim memories. They are ensconced in long-forgotten family lore or buried in dusty national archives. By contrast, for recent migrants from Asia, Africa, Latin America, and the Middle East, the victims of war and torture, memories of their pain and suffering are agonizingly fresh: blood-oozing wounds and mutilations branded on their bodies, rape and piracy on the high seas, hunger and thirst in the jungle and the desert, despair and anguish carved into the deep folds of their psyche, haunting them on sleepless nights or jerking them awake with screams of terror.

To these migrants and refugees, what does the eloquent injunction "Always remember where you come from" mean? Perhaps, for black Americans who are urged to forget the horrors of slavery to bring about a color-blind society, and for descendants of white immigrants who are not aware of their roots due to the passage of time or because they are now part of the dominant social group, remembering one's past is an urgent ethical imperative lest forgetfulness of where they came from blunts their sense of solidarity with the new immigrants. But for arrivals after the 1970s, most of whom are refugees escaping from war and violence, does the old man's advice to remember where they came from not wiggle the knife deeper into their physical and psychological wounds? While it is debatable whether such remembering produces a beneficial or harmful effect on the migrants' psychological well-being, it may be asked whether it constitutes a *moral* duty for them and, if so, why.

Most treaties on the ethics of immigration have emphasized the duty of the host country and the local church to welcome the strangers and the migrants into their communities. The virtue of hospitality has received the lion's share of scholarly attention, which is unsurprising, given the sacred duty of hospitality in ancient societies and in biblical history. Kristin E. Heyer writes eloquently on "inhospitality to immigrants" as a social sin and "civic kinship and subversive hospitality" as the hallmark of Christian immigration ethics."[2] Jesuit ethicist William O'Neill draws on biblical texts to offer rich reflections on Christian hospitality and solidarity with the stranger.[3] For O'Neill, hospitality toward migrants is often paired with solidarity with them. These twin attitudes are examined in one of the most comprehensive texts on the theology of migration.[4] In one of the earliest texts on the theology of migration in Asia, hospitality is also twinned with solidarity.[5] A recently published book that deals with migration and mission also has a chapter on hospitality to migrants.[6]

Politically, the practice of hospitality, especially in the United States, France, and the United Kingdom, has taken the form of a sanctuary movement, which works to provide asylum to refugees who have reasonable proof of being likely to be subjected to persecutions in their own countries on account of one of five protected grounds: race, religion, nationality, political opinion, and social group. Susanna Snyder has written one of the most insightful studies of migration, asylum seeking, and the role of the church.[7]

Presupposing all these reflections on hospitality and related virtues toward the stranger, my essay takes a somewhat different tack by focusing not on the ethical responsibilities of the citizens and the churches of the host countries but on those of the migrants themselves. Of course, migrants, and refugees in particular, live in extremely precarious circumstances and need a welcoming home to recover their human dignity as well as ample assistance to secure their well-being. But they are not, and must not be treated as, objects of charity. They are primarily agents charged with moral responsibilities. Among the latter, I would argue, is the duty of *remembering*. In what follows, I first explain *why* migrants should remember "where they came from," to cite the old man's solemn injunction. Next, I discuss *what* they as migrants should remember of their pasts. Lastly, I examine *how* migrants should remember their past for the sake of the host country, the receiving church, and the migrants themselves.

Why Should Migrants Remember?

At first glance, it seems counterintuitive that migrants ought to remember "where they came from." For most migrants, especially those who voluntarily leave their own countries in search of better economic opportunities for themselves and their families or those who have done well in their adopted countries, *home* is at worst a place plagued by poverty and backwardness, at best a destination for occasional, nostalgic visits, but not a place to remember with pleasure, much less their final resting place. The primary concern of these voluntary migrants is to blend into the so-called melting pot as quickly and as effectively as possible so as to guarantee acceptance into the new society and allow professional success. To urge them to remember where they came from sounds like a tasteless joke. This is true particularly of their children, the one-and-half and second generations, who most often know next to nothing of their parents' country of origin, its history, language, and culture, and for whom a journey of discovery of their family roots would often take the form of academic research. If they happen to travel to their ancestors' homeland, the trip is more an imaginative reconstruction of what their migrant parents would have gone through than an actual journey down memory lane.

By contrast, people who are forced to flee their native countries for physical safety, most of whom do not possess the necessary skills to succeed economically and socially in the new countries, tend to remember their homelands and their former lives there with fondness and longing. Unfortunately, however, they are forced to emigrate under painful circumstances, often with as much of their material possessions as they literally can carry. Because their flights to safety and freedom are invariably filled with anguish and tragedies, refugees are psychologically conditioned to suppress memories of their escape. If they remember their former lives at all, their memory is tinged with sadness and nostalgia, and when doing so, their memory is distorted by exaggerating the quality of their standard of living in the old country in contrast to the lowly one they now have.

Because of real or perceived heavy losses, often including the deaths of their family members and friends, refugees often succumb to feelings of bitterness and hatred toward the people whom they deem responsible for their losses and current condition. They do not adapt easily to the culture of the host country, remaining permanent foreigners living in a foreign land. They often endlessly plot—mostly in grandiose rhetoric—a revolution against or an overthrow of the—illegitimate in their eyes—government that has caused their exile and robbed them of their freedom, and dream of an eventual return to the old country and of being buried there. This has happened to many of my fellow Vietnamese refugees—including my parents—who fled to the United States after the Communist takeover of South Vietnam in 1975. To these refugees, the injunction to remember where they came from—especially if by this expression is meant the inhuman circumstances forcing their migration—is tantamount to asking them to descend to hell once again. Thus, to voluntary migrants, this mandate sounds like a tasteless joke; to forced migrants and refugees, a cruel one.

Why then ought migrants remember where they came from, and indeed, what are the things they must keep in their memory? For the first question, the most direct and peremptory answer is that this is a *divine command*. Again and again, Yahweh enjoins the Israelites to remember where they came from: "You shall not wrong or oppress a resident alien, for you were aliens in the land of Egypt" (Exod. 22:21). Again, "You shall not oppress a resident alien; you know the heart of an alien, for you were aliens in the land of Egypt" (Exod. 23:9). Again, "When an alien resides with you in your land, you shall not oppress the alien. The alien who resides with you shall be to you as the citizen among you; you shall love the alien as yourself, for you were alien in the land of Egypt" (Lev. 19:33–34).[8] These words repeated throughout the Hebrew Scripture serve as the ethical foundation for Israel's various duties to the strangers and aliens among them.

It is true that these words are addressed not to migrants as such but to *former* migrants who have settled in the new land and are now citizens. But arguably the command, "remember where you came from," applies to both since most often migrants, both voluntary and forced, eventually become citizens. If anything, the obligation is even more stringent for erstwhile migrants, as they are more tempted to forget their past now that they enjoy all the privileges accruing to them as successful citizens. Furthermore, the Israelites-now-citizens may be psychologically inclined to erase their experiences as aliens and slaves in Egypt because they were painful experiences that Yahweh does not fail to recall to their memory: "I have observed the misery of my people in Egypt. I have heard their cry on account of their taskmasters. Indeed, I know their sufferings" (Exod. 3:7).

Indeed, it is this memory of past suffering associated with migration that grounds ethical behaviors to migrants. Yahweh reminds the Israelites that they have a connatural empathy with migrants because "you know the heart of an alien" (Exod. 23:9) But how can one know the depths of "the heart of an alien" if one does not nurture in one's own heart the memory of oneself as a migrant? Without this memory of oneself as migrant, how can one identify oneself with other migrants and fulfill the Lord's command: "You shall love the alien as yourself" (Lev. 19:34? "Yourself" here is a migrant/alien, not a citizen, or a generic human being. It is oneself as *migrant* that is the measure of one's love toward other migrants, even if legally one is now no longer a migrant. Perhaps the divine command may be paraphrased as "You shall love the migrant in the measure in which you love yourself *as* a migrant." In other words, being migrant is a *permanent* identity and not a phase of life that can eventually be shed as one acquires a better social status. And it can become permanent—an "indelible character"—to use an expression of Catholic sacramental theology—imprinted in the "heart" only if one always and constantly remembers where one came from.

There are thus at least two fundamental reasons why migrants ought to remember where they came from. First, theological: to proclaim the great works of God (the *magnalia Dei*) and to rejoice and give thanks to God for the deeds God has done for all migrants—to quote Mary's words in her Magnificat: "My soul magnifies the Lord and my spirit rejoices in God my Savior . . . for the Mighty One has done great things for me" (Luke 1:4–47, 49). Of these mighty deeds Yahweh himself reminds the Israelites before making a covenant with them: "You have seen what I did to the Egyptians, and how I bore you on eagles' wings and brought you to myself" (Exod. 19:4). The God of the Hebrews, the God of Abraham, Isaac, and Jacob, is a God who loves and accompanies the migrants with mighty deeds: God is a migrant God (*Deus migrator*). To remember having been a migrant then is an act of *imitatio Dei*, and to act justly and lovingly toward migrants is nothing less than an act of liturgical worship, glorifying, praising, and thanking God for God's mighty deeds, carrying on God's wings the ancient "aliens in Egypt" and migrants of all times and in all places.

Second, *ethical*: to do for migrants what God has done for them. There is an intrinsic and indissoluble connection between the theological and the ethical reasons. Note the conjunction "for" in the words that follow the command to love the migrants: "*for* you were aliens in the land of Egypt." The reason why we must not wrong and oppress the migrants is *because* we were, or more precisely, *are* migrants. The underlying ethical reasoning seems to be as follows: First, being a migrant enables one to know "the heart of a migrant"; second, knowledge of the migrant's heart is cultivated by remembering one's own personal experience of being a migrant; and third, remembering one's past as a migrant provides the ethical grounding for one's just and loving treatment of migrants. Remembering "where one came from" is therefore a moral imperative in the ethics of migration.

What Must Migrants Remember?

Granted the moral imperative for migrants to remember where they came from, what exactly does "where they came from" stand for? How much of it should be remembered, or forgotten? Is migration memory always selective? If so, what is the principle of selection? It is common knowledge that we remember clearly things that bring us joy and pleasure; today, thanks to ubiquitous digital cameras, we can record them and e-mail photos to friends so that they too can share in these happy moments simultaneously, in real time. It is also a well-known fact that we easily remember life-changing events, be they happy, such as marriage and the births of our children, or painful and tragic, such as divorce and the deaths of our loved ones, even though in the latter case we may try (albeit rarely with success) to erase them from our memory because they bring renewed pain and suffering when remembered. Be that as it may, memories, remembered as well as suppressed, are the stuff that makes us who we are—our ever-shifting identity—just as imagination, which lives on hope, is the construction site of our final destiny.

Migrants, like everyone else, remember and forget things that are pleasurable, as well as things that are painful, and, like everyone else, they tend to suppress the latter, especially those surrounding their flights from their countries. Thus, "where they came from" is not an objective collection of fixed facts and events of their past but a highly selective medley of memories, some embellished, others diminished, some real, others imagined, that make up the psychological and spiritual blocks with which migrants rebuild their lives in the new country. Notwithstanding this amalgamative and partial character of their memories, there are certain realities of where they came from that migrants ought to, and indeed should, be encouraged and empowered to preserve and promote, in order to maintain their self-identity and bring their own contributions to the common good of their host country.

The first part of "where they came from" that migrants must remember is of course their culture and all the things that go under this broad umbrella term. While it is important for migrants to learn the local language and to familiarize themselves with the history and cultural traditions of the host society in order to be able to fulfill the duties of citizenship responsibly, it is their right, as well as their duty, to preserve and promote their own language, cultural traditions, and values, and to transmit them to their children. Happily, today, at least in the United States, this cultural right is by and large respected, in the educational system as well as in the society at large, as the melting-pot paradigm of cultural assimilation has been abandoned in favor of multiculturalism. In general, there is a deep and genuine appreciation for and promotion of cultural diversity, especially in countries with a large presence of migrants. There are, of course, pockets of political resistance and cultural chauvinism, but efforts at imposing a national language and a homogeneous culture are doomed to failure. The reason for this is that migrants' constant connection with their countries of origin is greatly facilitated by the omnipresent reality of globalization, the widespread use of social media, the rampant accessibility of the Internet, and the ease of international travel. Geographically, "where they came from" can be brought close to migrants with a click of the mouse; culturally, ethnic foods, music, entertainment media, fashion, and newspapers and magazines are available around the corner.

Sadly, however, migrants, and especially their children, are sometimes embarrassed by their cultural customs and practices. In the new country, these may appear as quaint, old-fashioned, and even superstitious, subject to misunderstanding and ridicule by their new, modern neighbors, and in a misguided effort at shedding their ethnic background, migrants are tempted to jettison their age-old and rich cultural heritage. Furthermore, migrants may be prevented from celebrating their native customs and feasts by their work schedule and calendar differences (for example, the lunar New Year's Day celebrations). In view of this very real danger of forgetting where they came from, it is all the more imperative for migrants to find ways to remember and celebrate their cultural traditions in the new country.

Another part of "where they came from" is the migrants' religious heritage. Unlike earlier immigrants from Europe, migrants to the United States since the 1960s bring with them their own, non-Christian religious traditions—typically, Hinduism, Buddhism, Sikhism, and Confucianism from Asia and Islam from Africa and the Middle East—and are not willing to renounce their faith and convert to Christianity, and in the process are turning America into the "most religiously diverse country on earth," to quote the title of Diana Eck's popular book.[9] Many migrants to European countries, such as Britain, France, and Germany, bring Islam with them, and their religious practice is consistently more vibrant than that of Christians of mainline churches. Of course, for migrants, remaining faithful to their non-Christian religions in the new country is challenging. They are under heavy pressure to convert to Christianity, not only from proselytizing Christians but also from life in the pervasive albeit nominal Christian society with its Christian calendar and festivals (for example, Christmas and Easter) and interfaith marriages.

Fortunately, with the proliferation of non-Christian places of worship and religious organizations, non-Christian migrants in the West (though, unfortunately, less so for Christian migrants in non-Christian countries) can continue to practice and propagate their religions. This growing and increasingly vocal presence of non-Christian migrants in the heartlands of Western Christianity constitutes a formidable challenge to hitherto dominant Christianity. It is here that migrants can make an important contribution to the religious life of their adopted countries but only on condition that they do not forget their own non-Christian religious faiths. The coexistence of many diverse, at times conflictive, religious traditions makes interreligious dialogue both a real possibility and an urgent need, with enormous benefits to not only the migrants and their new fellow religious believers in the host countries but also to the religious communities in their home countries, where religiously inspired wars and violence have often caused their migration in the first place.

A third element of the migrants' past that must be remembered is their own brand of Christianity. Again, as they participate in the life of Western Christian churches, migrants are unavoidably shaped by their worship styles, spiritual practices, and organizational structures, which are often governed by result-oriented efficiency, streamlined bureaucracy, financial solvency, and legal protection. These concerns are, of course, legitimate and even necessary to assure a smooth functioning of church activities in a complex society. However, the dark side of all this is that Christian "communities" tend to operate like corporations and not like the "family of God."[10] It is here that Christian migrants from the so-called third world can bring to the Western churches their experiences of local churches as neighborhood communities or *comunidades de base* where lay leadership, popular devotions, shared prayer, group solidarity, and personal friendship play a large role in church life. It is a fact, albeit not yet widely acknowledged, that the presence of Catholic migrants has "rescued" many dioceses in the West, especially the United States, with their numerous priestly and religious vocations, and revitalized parishes with their regular church attendance and generous financial contributions. It is also a fact, similarly not yet widely recognized, that migrants have transformed the membership, organization, and spiritual life of Christian churches in Asia such as those of Japan, Taiwan, Hong Kong, and South Korea.

Finally, for migrants, part of "where they came from" that must be remembered and even publicly honored includes their individual and unique experiences of migration. Of course, these experiences are extremely diverse: migration experiences of voluntary migrants are very different from those of refugees. Voluntary migrants do not normally incur economic losses and physical pain; still they may suffer cultural shock, discrimination, separation from their families, and loneliness. Forced migrants and refugees, by contrast, in addition to the above-mentioned pain, are always subjected to traumatic and life-shattering suffering. More than other migrants, they are psychologically conditioned to erase from their memory their migration experiences. Though this erasure may sometimes be necessary for their psychological well-being, total forgetfulness will not only be detrimental to their spiritual development but also will deprive them of making one of the most precious contributions to the ethics of migration. Without this memory, it is impossible to form "the heart of an alien," which is the deepest source and motivation for ethical behavior toward migrants, as Yahweh's command makes it clear: "You shall not oppress a resident alien; *you know the heart of an alien,* for you were aliens in the land of Egypt" (Exod. 23:9; emphasis added). Consequently, these memories of migration should be recorded; preserved in museums and archives; and celebrated in literature, art, and liturgical celebrations.

If an effective ethics of migration is to be developed, it must not only be based on the abstract principles of human rights and justice but also bathed in the blood and tears; the hunger and thirst; the grief and pain; the torture; and, yes, the deaths of so many migrants on their way to freedom. Perhaps this is "the where they came from" that runs the greatest risk of being erased and forgotten not only by the migrants but also by the now-citizens whose migrant roots have dried up and withered and whose memories of their ancestors' migration have been lost forever in the mists of the past. If we want an ethics of migration that will propel both citizens and migrants to act justly and lovingly toward strangers and aliens in our midst, we must practice the old black man's injunction: "always remember where you came from."

How Must Migrants Remember?

How must migrants remember where they came from, especially the pain and suffering inflicted on them by their political enemies who caused their exile? In the recent literature on the spirituality for peacemaking and reconciliation, there is an emphasis on not to *forgive and forget* past acts of injustice and violence but on opening up the space for the victim's journey toward God, his or her enemies, and the self. This spirituality goes beyond the strategies and methodologies of conflict resolution and applies to reconciliation between both individuals and among groups and nations. In this spirituality of reconciliation and peace-building an important role is given to memory and remembering. Miroslav Volf explores the challenges of reconciliation in contexts of persisting enmity in which the dividing line between victims and perpetrators is thin, and in which today's victims can become tomorrow's perpetrators.[11] For Volf, "embrace," as a spiritual attitude toward the oppressor, is marked by acting with generosity toward the perpetrator of injustice and maintaining flexible identities with porous boundaries. Embrace, which is made possible by God's grace, does not negate the necessity of justice.

As a model of embrace, Volf cites the father's attitude toward his son in the so-called parable of the Prodigal Son in which the father forgives his son and accepts his new identity as the father of the prodigal son. For Volf, however, the supreme exemplar of embrace is Christ's action in his death as an *inclusive substitute* for the ungodly. On the cross, Christ forgives and opens his arms to embrace sinners, thus creating a space for them in God. For Volf, embrace is ultimately rooted in God's unconditional love and in God's Trinitarian nature in which there is the mutual indwelling of the three divine people whose identity boundaries are therefore reciprocally porous. Volf points out that total embrace will be achieved only eschatologically, at the *Last Judgment*, which he interprets as the final reconciliation between God and humanity in which judgment is not eliminated but is an indispensable element of reconciliation. Of relevance to our question of how migrants should remember where they came from, is truth-telling in the context of enmity and conflict, especially truth-telling about the past, a theme that Volf explores in much greater depth in later work.[12] Volf suggests the practice of remembering *rightly*. The question is not whether to remember but how. One does of course forget things but not things that leave an indelible mark on one's body or psyche or soul. These cannot be forgotten, but how must they be remembered?

The book was sparked by an event in the author's life in 1984, when as a conscript in the army of the then-Communist Yugoslavia, he was considered a security threat simply because he was a son of a pastor, had studied theology abroad, and had an American wife. He was spied on by his comrades and was subjected to interrogations, though not physical torture, especially by a captain, a certain G. The question that kept haunting Volf after he was freed was how he should remember this abuse, especially Captain G. himself, not with hatred and a desire for vengeance, but out of fidelity to Jesus and his God who command us to forgive and love our enemies. The required task, then, is not simply to forgive the victimizer, but to love him or her. For Volf, remembering the wrongdoing rightly involves remembering it and its implications with regard to three realities: the injured, the community out of which the injury arose and to which it may be applied, and the perpetrator himself or herself.

For Volf memory of wrongs suffered is a Janus-faced organ: as a *shield*, it can help form our identity, bring about healing, produce justice by acknowledging the reality of wrongs, link us with other victims, and protect victims from further violence. Sadly, as a *sword*, it can also wound, breed indifference, reinforce false self-perceptions, and reinjure.

This leads to the question of how we as Christians should remember. Volf suggests a triple remembering: "remember truthfully," "remember so as to be healed," and "remember so as to learn."[13] In this way, Volf argues, we remember not simply as individuals but also as members of a community that can teach us to remember rightly, that is, "remembering that is truthful and just, that heals individuals without injuring others, that allows the past to motivate a just struggle for justice and the grace-filled work of reconciliation."[14]

But *how long* should we remember? Volf argues for the possibility of a healthy forgetting or nonremembering. He goes further in asserting that "memories of suffered wrongs will not come to the minds of the citizens of the world to come, for in it they will perfectly enjoy God and one another in God."[15] Important in Volf is that in heaven, "we will not forget so as to be able to rejoice; we will rejoice and therefore let those memories slip out of our minds."[16] Thus, the "end" of memory is both its *termination* (since we should not remember forever) and its goal or *telos*, that is, "the formation of the communion of love between all people, including victims and perpetrators."[17]

Remembering Truthfully

As alluded to above, migrants tend to remember their past tendentiously, either exaggerating their pain and suffering, or erasing the most traumatic ones of them, or embellishing their former lives in the old country. However, in order for them to regain their human dignity, migrants must remember where they came from truthfully. This truthful remembering, which corresponds to Volf's *"Remember truthfully,"* has three aspects: first, establishing the facts of abuses against oneself; second, disclosing the structures of lying and the patterns of violence of the oppressive regime; and third, making public the history of abuses through reports and honoring the memories of the victims.[18] Knowing the truth is absolutely essential for achieving real reconciliation since systematic violence is built on "a narrative of the lie" intended to destroy and replace the truths that provide the victims with a sense of self-identity and security.[19] This truth seeking is not only necessary for the possibility of closure for the survivors and the relatives of the victims but also establishes a pattern of truthfulness on which a new moral order can be built.

Remembering Justly

Knowing the truth, however, does not necessarily lead to the migrants' reconciliation with those who inflict pain and suffering on them. Indeed, it may lead to revenge, hatred, and retribution. To achieve reconciliation, knowing the truth must be followed by doing justice. Without justice, reconciliation is immoral. But what kind of justice? Certainly, not simply punitive justice whereby the wrongdoers are apprehended, tried, convicted, and punished. Punitive justice must also be corrective, providing the wrongdoers with an opportunity for moral conversion; otherwise, punitive justice is not very different from revenge.

Instead, a fuller vision of justice must be considered that includes restorative justice, which seeks to make amends by providing reparation or restitution for the victims. In this three-part understanding of justice, migrants, and specially refugees, have the right to recover what they have lost. Even though reparation can only ease and not erase the damages and the pain inflicted on the victims (the dead cannot be brought back to life, health cannot be restored, and the lost years cannot be recovered!), nevertheless it is a necessary and important symbol for the recovery of the dignity of the victims. Second, there is structural justice by which inequalities in the society are removed. Third, there is legal justice by which a just and equitable legal system is established and the rule of law maintained. In these two levels of justice, migrants can play an important role by making use of all the means at their disposal in their new countries, including political organizations and economic pressure.

Remembering Forgivingly

The third (and, by common agreement, the hardest) part of reconciliation is forgiveness. This "remembering forgivingly" corresponds to Volf's "Remember so as to be healed." One reason why forgiveness is hard is that at first sight it appears to require forgetting the violent deeds suffered. But, of course, most victims of physical torture and political repression find it impossible to forget their wounds as these are indelibly burned into their flesh and their psyche, and consequently feel that forgiveness is beyond their power. To forgive seems to imply betraying the past, especially the dead. Here it is useful to note that rather than "forgive and forget," we should "remember and forgive."[20] Or, as Schreiter puts it, "*in forgiving, we do not forget; we remember in a different way.*"[21] It is possible to remember in a different way because in forgiving, the balance of power has shifted from the oppressor to the victim: it is the victim, and the victim alone, who has the power to forgive. In forgiving, the victim breaks loose of the oppressor's hold, becomes free of the power of the past, and is able to live by a story other than that of fear and suffering.

There is another reason why forgiveness is hard. Normally, a condition for forgiveness is the offender's acknowledgment of guilt, repentance, and asking forgiveness from the victims. But it is a rare oppressor who sincerely does these things, not even when confronted with his or her evil deeds. More often than not, wrongdoers shamelessly deny any responsibility or flee to another country and there enjoy a comfortable life off their ill-gotten wealth, while their victims are left with a greater sense of injustice. It is here that human forgiveness takes on the characteristics of divine forgiveness. According to the Christian faith, God forgives humans not because of but *prior* to their repentance, out of God's gratuitous love and mercy. It is God's forgiveness that leads the sinner to repentance and not vice versa. Repentance is not the condition but the *fruit* of God's forgiveness. In imitation of God's gratuitous mercy and love, and by God's grace and power, the victims forgive their torturers and oppressors, *prior* to and not as a consequence of their repentance and asking for forgiveness, with the hope that this forgiveness will lead them to repentance and change. God's forgiveness, the victim's forgiveness has a gift-like and miraculous quality. Ultimately, it is this gratuitous forgiveness—beyond truth and justice—that makes real reconciliation between abusers and victims possible. Only then can the legal and social processes of amnesty and pardon be put into action.[22]

Remembering Constructively

The ultimate goal of truth finding, restoring justice, and forgiveness is to build a society in which all can live in freedom, equality, and harmony, and in which, at the minimum, abuses of human rights will not occur again. This task of social reconstruction corresponds to Volf's "Remember so as to learn." Such praxis for change requires, establishing structural justice through various social reforms and legal justice through the reform of law and the judiciary. Moreover, there is the need of a democratic system of government in which all citizens can exercise their civil rights and duties. There is a need, as well, of an economic system in which all have an equal opportunity at earning a living wage and in which the basic needs of the poor and the weak are provided for. Last but not least, the cultural and religious dimensions of human life must also be nurtured and developed through education, the mass media, and other means, so that the whole person, and not only certain dimensions of it, can achieve full flourishing. Perhaps the contribution of migrants to this fourth aspect of remembering is often indirect but no less effective, by means of individual and collective activities to promote justice, peace, education, social services, and economic development during their diaspora. Their role is, of course, vastly expanded if they, or their descendants, can one day return to their old countries to take part in the reconstruction of their homelands.

"Always remember where you came from!" The old black man's words continue to reverberate down the corridors of the history of migrations—old and new. Unless migrants understand *why* they must remember their past, *what* of this past they must remember, and *how* they should remember it, they will fail to meet the challenges and forfeit the unique opportunities the *Deus migrator* has given them.

Notes

1. Jonathan Capehart, "From Trayvon Martin to 'Black Lives Matter,'" *Washington Post*, February 27, 2015, http://www.washingtonpost.com.

2. See Kristin E. Heyer, *Kinship across Borders: A Christian Ethic of Immigration* (Washington, DC: Georgetown University Press, 2002), especially chaps. 2 and 5.

3. See William O'Neill, "Christian Hospitality and Solidarity with the Stranger," in *And You Welcomed Me: Migration and Catholic Social Teaching*, ed. Donald Kerwin and Jill Marie Gerschutz (Lanham, MD: Rowman & Littlefield, 2009), 149–55.

4. See Daniel G. Groody and Giacchino Campese, eds., *A Promise Land, A Perilous Journey: Theological Perspectives on Migration* (Notre Dame, IN: University of Notre Dame, 2008). The essays that discuss hospitality and solidarity at some length include Donald Senior, "'Beloved Aliens and Exiles': New Testament Perspectives on Migration," 20–34, and Peter C. Phan, "Migration in the Patristic Era: History and Theology," 35–61.

5. See Anthony Rogers, "Globalizing Solidarity through Faith Encounters in Asia," in *Faith on the Move: Toward a Theology of Migration in Asia*, ed. Fabio Baggio and Agnes M. Brazal (Quezon City, Philippines: Ateneo de Manila University Press, 2008), 203–18.

6. See Timothy A. Lenchak, "Israel's Ancestors as *Gerim*: A Lesson of Biblical Hospitality," in *God's People on the Move: Biblical and Global Perspectives on Migration and Mission*, ed. vanThanh Nguyen and John M. Prior (Eugene, OR: Pickwick, 2014), 18–28.

7. See Susanna Snyder, *Asylum-Seeking, Migration and Church* (Burlington, VT: Ashgate, 2012).

8. English translation of the Bible is taken from *The New Revised Standard Version*.

9. See Diana Eck, *A New Religious America: How a "Christian Country" Has Now Become the Most Religiously Diverse Nation on Earth* (San Francisco: Harper San Francisco, 2001). See also Robert Wuthnow, *America and the Challenges of Religious Diversity* (Princeton, NJ: Princeton University Press, 2005).

10. The image of "family/household of God" is used in the New Testament to refer to the church (see, for instance, 1 Tim. 3:15). Though this image can be misused to justify patriarchalism and androcentrism, as has often been done in the Christian tradition, it can also convey intimacy and mutuality.

11. Miroslav Volf, *Exclusion & Embrace: A Theological Exploration of Identity, Otherness, and Reconciliation* (Nashville, TN: Abingdon Press, 1996).

12. Miroslav Volf, *The End of Memory: Remembering Rightly in a Violent World* (Grand Rapids, MI: Eerdmans, 2006).

13. See Miroslav Volf, "Memory of Reconciliation—Reconciliation of Memory," *Proceedings of the Fifty-ninth Annual Convention, Catholic Theological Society of America*, 59 (2004): 1.

14. Ibid., 128.

15. Ibid., 177.

16. Ibid., 214.

17. Ibid., 232.

18. This truth finding about human rights violations was one of the three tasks assigned to the Truth and Reconciliation Commission in South Africa, the other two being determining reparations for the victims of gross human rights violations and granting amnesty to perpetrators of human rights abuses who have made a full and frank disclosure of their misdeeds.

19. See Robert Schreiter, *Reconciliation: Mission and Ministry in a Changing Social Order* (Maryknoll, NY: Orbis Books, 1992), 34–36.

20. See Donald W. Shriver, *An Ethic for Enemies: Forgiveness in Politics* (New York: Oxford University Press, 1995) 6–9.

21. Robert J. Schreiter, *The Ministry of Reconciliation: Spirituality & Strategies* (Maryknoll, NY, 1998), 66.

22. On amnesty and pardon in the process of reconciliation, see ibid., 124–26; R. Scott Appleby, *The Ambivalence of the Sacred: Religion, Violence, and Reconciliation* (Lanham, MD: Rowman & Littlefield (2000), 167–204; and William Bole, Drew Christiansen, and Robert Hennemeyer, *Forgiveness in International Politics: An Alternative Road to Peace* (Washington, DC: United States Conference of Catholic Bishops, 2004).

Part VI

Theo-anthropological Reflections

MIGRATION FOR LIVELIHOOD

Hope amid Untold Miseries of Tribal Girls

Prem Xalxo, SJ

"This is a people despoiled and plundered, all of them trapped in holes, hidden away in prisons. They are taken as booty, with no one to rescue them, as spoil, with no one to demand their return" (Isa. 42:22).

The words of Prophet Isaiah reflect, to a certain extent, the plight of the tribal domestic working women in various metropolitan cities of India. My social apostolate with them during my formation as a Jesuit scholastic inspired me to study their situation and future prospects. As a theology student in 1998, I used to go to Greater Kailash, a posh locality of New Delhi, for a social apostolate amid them. Since I could avail myself for my social apostolate mostly on Sundays, my focus was based primarily on Christian domestic working women. I had heard and read about them, but that was my first personal encounter with them. They had migrated to New Delhi to earn a living by working mostly in nontribal families as *Aayas* or maidservants. Despite their precarious working conditions and frequent physical, verbal, mental, sexual, emotional, and psychological harassment, violence and exploitation, they seemed to be happy and lively on Sundays. That was the only day when they had the chance to meet and share their *sukham-dukham* (experiences of joys and sorrows), as it is known popularly. The church premises offered a perfect venue for their gathering.

In the same year, we organized a common festival for all the *tribals* living in New Delhi. The occasion was the *Karam* festival, a feast celebrated at the conclusion of the planting season by almost all tribal communities of north India. Seeing the huge crowd, I realized for the first time the magnitude of migration of the tribal women to the metropolitan cities. As the master of ceremony of the cultural activities, I could see the euphoria in their faces and in their way of singing and dancing; but I wondered how long such joy and excitement would last!

On December 29, 2013, I participated in one of the weekly meetings of a group of the tribal domestic working women held on the premises of the Indian Social Institute, New Delhi. Under the umbrella of *Adivasi Jeevan Vikas Sanstha* (Tribal Life Development Society), run by JESA (Jesuits in Social Action), around two hundred women gather every week in the Institute for the Holy Mass. Although not all of them are Christians, they feel at home in sharing their works and living conditions. All of them receive possible legal and other logistic assistance. To keep in touch with their tribal roots, some cultural activities are also organized occasionally for them. I interviewed thirteen women from different socioreligious backgrounds. Their stories and experiences represented the general feeling among those attending the regular Sunday meetings.

Major challenges in working with these women include instilling in them a sense of human dignity, equality and justice, and strengthening their tribal roots and identity, and their communitarian spirit. Over the years, many initiatives have been taken to improve their situation. An anthropological, theological, and ethical study of their joys and hopes, grief and anxieties (cf. *Gaudium et spes*, no. 1) amid untold miseries might be a stepping stone to tap further possibilities for their integral well-being.

Profiles of the Tribal Domestic Workers

The majority of domestic working girls hail from the tribal areas of Assam, Bihar, Chhattisgarh, Jharkhand, Madhya Pradesh, Orissa, West Bengal, and the other seven northeastern states of India. They belong to five major tribes of India—Oraon, Munda, Kharia, Ho, and Santhal—and are "known as *adivasis*, a Hindi term, which literally means original inhabitants. It is one of the common names given to agrarian or primitive peoples of India."[1] It is important to note that the term *primitive* is not used anymore, and these tribes do not have any caste system. Their population is concentrated in Jharkhand, one of the smallest states of India, but rich in minerals and natural resources. Right from the independence of India in 1947, all the successive federal and state governments have been interested only in exploiting the natural resources. Development-induced displacements have constantly forced the tribals away from their traditional land without any proper compensation or resettlement. Government and multinational companies set experience and skill as the terms and conditions for employment in factories or mining establishments, which most of the tribals do not have. Unfortunately, corruption and nepotism play a major role in bringing even unskilled laborers from outside leaving the tribals "excluded and marginalized: without work, without possibilities, without any means of escape" (*Evangelii gaudium*, no. 53) to fend for themselves.

These tribals depend primarily on the produce of the field and the forest for their subsistence. Because of a lack of proper irrigation facilities, their agriculture depends on the monsoon rains. In recent years, the erratic monsoon, gradual deterioration and degradation of cultivable land, shrinking water resources, and insufficient agricultural produce have caused havoc in their lives. Along with the produce of the field, they also depend on the forests for their livelihood. In the name of saving the forests, the forest officials have outlined various restrictions to prevent them from using the forest. With two major sources of livelihood gradually being dried up, they are forced to migrate to other states as unskilled laborers to work in agricultural fields, factories, or construction sites. In summary, "ecological degradation, landlessness and land alienation, unemployment and poverty"[2] are the primary reasons for their migration.

John Lakra, a tribal Jesuit who has done extensive research on tribal sociocultural and religious traditions and customs, maintains that the tribals are "basically simple, sincere and honest people, hardworking and having a wonderful sense of cooperation and community."[3] True to the observation, the tribal women, are simple, honest, sociable, soft-spoken, enduring, extremely hardworking, and possess an inherent capacity to adjust to any situation or place. A large number of them, despite working in the fields, running after the household animals, and doing the daily chores, study hard and complete their graduate and postgraduate studies. The Christian missionaries have done extraordinary work in the field of education in the entire tribal area. However, a good number of the tribal women discontinue their studies after a certain stage because of the lack of resources. Rampant poverty and unemployment in the rural areas force them to migrate to the cities either willingly or unwillingly. One can imagine the life of a lone migrant young girl in a strange nontribal family in a totally unknown place. For her, the mere fact of being uprooted from a closely knit tribal community and being placed alone in a "strange land" (Ps. 137:4) forces her to face a massive challenge in the search for an identity and human dignity amid innumerous untold miseries in the form of physical, sexual, and psychological exploitations. Her struggle to sustain sociocultural, moral, and religious values offers the immense possibility of some deep anthropological, theological, and ethical reflections on the situations of the worldwide domestic workers. Can their miseries be brought to light or their cries of despair be heard (Exod. 3:7)?

Pull–Push Factors and Human Trafficking

The age-old formula of supply and demand in the market economy can explain the pull–push factors of migration. Despite India being projected as one of the growing economic giants, an extremely uneven development is evident in semi-urban and rural areas. The rich have become richer; some have climbed the ladder of development to reach a totally new economic status; but a vast majority of the Indian population has remained untouched by economic growth. The process of industrialization, urbanization, and modernization has opened up new possibilities and opportunities for employment, creating a new group of rich middle class. The growth of "the urban middle class, especially the increase in the number of women working outside their homes and the availability of cheap domestic labor,"[4] function as a major pull factor to attract the less privileged tribal communities for such labor.

The rural set-up offers almost negligible possibilities of any creative work or job opportunities to the tribal women. Some of them observe the pathetic situation of their family members and peers who journey everyday to the nearby cities in search of a daily wage job. The construction companies or some rich families come to hire them for a day and pay according to their work. The scene represents the parable told by Jesus, "For the kingdom of heaven is like a landowner who went out early in the morning to hire workers for his vineyard. He agreed to pay them a denarius for the day and sent them into his vineyard" (Matt. 20:1–2). Not all are hired for work; some remain there till the end of the day and return home empty handed. Living amid such desperate situations, if someone offers the possibility of a better life in the cities, they do not hesitate to jump into the abyss of uncertainties and challenges. The prospect of earning money on their own and helping their families pulls them to the cities, and the misery, poverty, and hopelessness work as push factors.

Amid the pull–push factors of migration, human trafficking raises some serious ethical questions. Over several decades, human trafficking has become a burning issue confronting the northern states of India. Realizing the seriousness of the problem, the central government has already drafted the Domestic Workers (Registration, Social Security and Welfare) Act 2008, which states, "with no rights and rules to fall back on, most of the domestic helps have become contemporary slaves. It is also a known fact that many women and children are trafficked and exploited by the placement agencies, which operate openly without any form of restrictions and regulations." However, there has not been any further progress in ratifying the act or in taking some concrete steps to stop the human trafficking.

There are multiple groups at work behind human trafficking. The first group is the mafia-type placement agencies that charge a huge sum of money as a registration fee from those looking for a maidservant. Their agents guarantee a regular supply by recruiting young women from the impoverished semiurban and rural areas. The agents receive thousands of rupees as commission and pay substantial kickbacks to the police to ensure the continuity of human trafficking. They roam around discreetly in the remote villages, take time to identify the possible victims, and befriend them through their peers and relatives. Once they gain their confidence, they lay a trap and deceitfully convince them of good jobs and better lives in the cities. If a group of young women is ready and willing, a meticulous plan is drafted to traffic them out of the village via bus and railroad.

The second group of human traffickers might be composed of the relatives and friends of the victims. Their method is the same as the first group. The major difference is that the people in this case are known to the victims and their families, and so laying the trap becomes easy and the result is fast. While living with the possible victims, they almost brainwash them by selling the dream of a better life in the cities. On the pretext of taking the victims to the house of another relative or friend or to a public function, they traffic them to the cities.

The third group of human traffickers is the domestic working women who return to the native villages for their holidays. Quite often, they have made a commitment before leaving for home to bring one or two young women along with them at the conclusion of their holidays. Some young women choose willingly to go to the cities and are even encouraged by their parents to go because the options are limited at home.

Once trafficked into the cities, the young women are handed over either to the placement agencies for a hefty commission or directly employed in some families. Some are even sold to the brothels. The newly trafficked women are kept with others in a small room just large enough to cook and sleep, with little space for privacy, until they are employed by someone. Once employed, their daily routine includes "cleaning (sweeping, swabbing and dusting), washing (clothes and dishes), cooking or preparation for cooking such as chopping vegetables and making dough, ironing, housekeeping and extensions of these outside the home such as shopping."[5] Despite all this, their living and working conditions are pathetic, with no limits on working hours; no respect for their work; and no protection or social security from physical, mental, and sexual exploitations. Their employer forces them to bring a substitute when they are sick or want a leave in case of emergency. Without any formal contract, they live under constant fear that "their services can be terminated at any point of time."[6] Sometimes they are thrown out of the house on the pretext of theft or no work. In most cases, FIR (First Information Report), a written complaint against any cognizable offense, is never registered, which is mandatory to initiate the criminal justice process. Their lack of knowledge of the legal procedures or "little confidence in complaint mechanisms or stigma due to breach in confidentiality can also be responsible for the silence."[7] Unfortunately, there is no community or structural support system to pursue such cases, which, in turn, encourages human trafficking.

Case Studies

In October 2013, a story appeared in almost every local newspaper about the rescue of a young domestic working woman in Delhi. She was so badly tortured and beaten by her employers that at the time of her rescue, she had severe head injuries and wounds on almost every part of her body. She confessed that she was ill treated, abused verbally, and physically beaten almost every day; so much so that she was forced to drink urine and made to sleep in the bathroom.[8] After the public uproar, her employers were arrested by the police. In another case of brutality, Delhi police arrested a couple who had locked up their thirteen-year-old domestic servant in their apartment and had gone for holidays in Thailand.[9] Such stories rarely become a public issue.

My interviews with the thirteen young domestic working women on December 29, 2013, in the Indian Social Institute, New Delhi yielded some startling revelations. Although some seem to enjoy good treatment, respect, and freedom in their workplaces, they are reminded time and again by different people and circumstances that ultimately they are the maidservants. Not having any other option, they face all challenges with tremendous courage and patience. Not all the case studies present a gloomy state, of course. My younger brother had four maidservants from Jharkhand over a period of fifteen years. One remained for almost ten years and went back to her village only to get married. My brother and sister-in-law desperately needed someone to take care of their two children and the house while they were away at work for the whole day. My sister-in-law did scold these servants sometimes, but nonetheless, they were treated well. They participated in almost all family activities such as meals, prayers, and social festivities. There are many such cases where the domestic working women are adopted as one of the family members in an atmosphere of respect, confidence, and mutual trust.

Some Fundamental Ethical–Theological Questions

Most of the tribal women whom I interviewed and interacted with during my formation period seemed to be happy and content with their work and their working conditions. However, their feeling of being alone, abandoned, and away from home often tortured and traumatized them. Even if they received good treatment from their employers, the maidservant mentality invariably sprang forth time and again to segregate them from the rest of the family. During my recent interaction with them, it surfaced again that the biggest sorrow for them was not being treated as equal human beings. Unfortunately, the derogatory terms used and the negative attitudes shown toward them by their own tribal community members seemed to be even more painful and agonizing. This raises some serious ethical and theological questions regarding what it means to be human and the role of the church in instilling respect and dignity toward the other in this context.

Migration: The Only Answer?

Most of the domestic working women in New Delhi belong to the Oraon tribe, whose forefathers migrated to Chotanagpur Plateau around the fifth century B.C.E. from the west coast of India.[10] Today, the sociocultural and economic situation of both the domestic working women and their home states raise some serious questions regarding their migration to metropolitan cities. Is migration the only way out? Can the plight of these women and the outsourcing of their talents, creativity, and tremendous energy be justified in the name of survival and subsistence? Can their labor not be used instead to transform their own homeland? These questions have been tormenting the tribal communities for a long time. The efforts to stop the outflow of women by the local people and the civic bodies have not yielded satisfactory results. The government of Jharkhand, for example, has offered compulsory free education to young women, midday meals to the students, and job opportunities in rural areas through the constructions of roads, bridges, wells, and ponds; but rampant corruption, malfeasance, and nepotism eat up more than half of the resources meant for the projects, and thus perpetuate the poverty and misery of the local population. For many, migration seems to be only answer for the moment.

Integration of Values in a Foreign Land

Simplicity, honesty, hard work, the spirit of sharing and communion, interdependence, and community life are some of the fundamental tribal values of India. Along with language, sociocultural traditions, customs, and practices, the tribal identity is encapsulated in five J's of their worldview—*Jan–Janwar–Jal–Jameen–Jungle* (humans, animals, water, land, and forest).[11] Being born and brought up in a closely knit community, the tribal domestic workers encounter the first culture shock when they are employed in a nontribal family—alone and isolated from the others. Often they succeed in adapting themselves to the new situation and integrate their traditional values with the values of the nontribal society. Sunday meetings and other social activities help them to maintain their tribal roots and avoid sociocultural annihilation.

Questions of Respect, Human Dignity, and Justice

The general ill treatment meted out to the tribal domestic workers is rooted basically in the *slave or servant-owning* Indian psyche. Their own tribal people, who are well educated, trained, and skilled, and are working in private or public sectors, show little or no respect for them and for their work. Even in their native villages, people are prejudiced against them. They are suspected of carrying sexually transmitted diseases, and so marriage remains a distant dream for them. Nevertheless, it is significant to note that "a majority of workers with a history of domestic work did not perceive it as disgraceful or undignified. Women who had no other support systems also did not view it as a humiliating or shameful."[12] After going through an ordeal of latent hatred and disrespect by their own people and by those in the cities, they do not seem to care anymore about other people's perception of them and of their profession.

The role of the church has been distinctive and commendable in seeking justice for the tribal domestic workers by offering them legal assistance and instilling in them self-esteem, self-respect, and dignity by organizing sociocultural and religious activities. For example, a common marriage ceremony of fourteen tribal couples was organized on May 17, 2014, in Mumbai by a church-run social forum, Chotanagpur Migrant Tribal Development Network. The ceremony was held at Jesuit-run St. Stanislaus School and was officiated by the Auxiliary Bishop Agnelo Gracias of Mumbai. Such initiatives help the tribal migrants "to see beyond their humdrum and wretched life."[13] The fact of being recognized and assisted by the authorities, and the prospect of establishing a family, fill them with confidence, even if they continue in the same work after their marriage. The reaction of those benefitted by such initiatives was extremely positive and encouraging. They minced no words to express their joy and gratitude to the church-run agencies because they felt that there are some who care for them and help them to realize their dignity and self-esteem.

Hope for a Better Future Grounded on Faith

The tribal domestic workers flock in huge numbers to participate in Sunday Holy Masses primarily for three reasons: (1) they get the opportunity to meet their friends and relatives; (2) they participate in some community activities organized by the church-run social forum; and (3) they are able to live their faith in Jesus Christ, which gives them hope, courage, and strength to combat the feeling of being abandoned, loneliness, separation from family, forced restriction, and exploitations.[14] "Sunday Mass is a must for me"—these words echo their innermost desire to be part of a faith community and to have deeper union with Jesus Christ who promises them liberation from their untold miseries, "Come to me, all who are weary and heavy-laden, and I will give you rest" (Matt. 11:28). They firmly believe that Jesus is the source of inspiration for the church-run agencies in their efforts to work for the poor and the marginalized.

In the Old and New Testaments, the structure of hope is "characterized by God's promise, fulfillment, and then promise of a sure and radical change of [human] existence into something which can only be understood as the formation of a new heaven and a new earth."[15] This hope requires commitment, perseverance, and faith in Jesus, because it is a promise about things yet unseen.[16] It is the hope of a time when God will "wipe every tear from their eyes" (Rev. 21:4) and "the incompleteness of their present experience of God will be resolved, their present thirst for God fulfilled, their present need for release and salvation realized."[17] For them, such hope is the source of their strength to fight the present-day despair, suffering, and the harsh realities of life with courage and faith in Jesus Christ.

Future Prospects Built on Hopes

The preamble of the International Labor Organization (ILO) on Domestic Workers Convention held in Geneva on June 1, 2011, recognized "the significant contribution of domestic workers to the global economy, which includes increasing paid job opportunities for women and men workers with family responsibilities." The convention outlined clear guidelines on terms and conditions of employment; wages; working hours; effective protection against all forms of abuse, harassment, and violence; social security; and the avoidance of child labor. Unfortunately, "domestic work is not recognized as 'work' by the Indian government. The state does not value or recognize this work as a contribution to society and the economy."[18] Still worse, women are stereotyped as domestic workers, which also raises the prevalent issue of gender justice. If the ILO recommendations were implemented by the government of India, the domestic workers would have enjoyed the rights and provisions like any other worker of the organized sector. This could help them acquire confidence, self-esteem, and dignity for what they are and for what they do.

Paradoxically, without the domestic workers, the thriving middle class of Indian metropolitan cities would crumble. Therefore, the "globalization of indifference" (*Evangelii gaudium*, no. 54) toward them must end. We must guarantee improved working conditions, adequate wages, access to much-needed health care, and other rights and privileges. The church, various charitable institutes, and nongovernment organizations are working to improve their situation and to persuade governments to ratify the recommendations of the ILO Convention on Domestic Workers. For example, the National Platform for Domestic Workers, which includes twenty organizations from fifteen states, recently submitted a petition demanding comprehensive legislation. They proposed an autonomous statutory body or tripartite board, with compulsory registration of employer, employee, and agency.[19] Indeed, there is hope for the future, but that hope can take a concrete form if, and only if, their work is recognized, their rights are guaranteed by some specific laws, and they are given due respect for what they do and what they are as human beings.

Notes

1. Prem Xalxo, *Current Ecological Crisis and Its Moral Dimensions: A Tribal Perspective* (Ranchi, India: Xavier Publications, 2008), 14.

2. J. Marianus Kujur and Vikas Jha, *Tribal Women Domestic Workers in Delhi* (New Delhi: ISI Publications, 2008), 25.

3. John Lakra, "Rewriting Tribal Anthropology," *Sevartham* 22 (1997): 14.

4. K. John, "Domestic Women Workers in Urban Informal Sector," *ABHINAV* 2, no. 2 (2014): 6.

5. Surabhi T. Mahrotra, *Domestic Workers: Conditions, Rights and Responsibilities* (New Delhi: JAGORI, 2010), 6–7.

6. Megha Shree, "Female Tribal Migrants as Domestic Workers: A Study of Their Compulsion and Working Conditions," *Man and Development* 34, no. 1 (March 2012): 58.

7. Mahrotra, *Domestic Workers*, 39.

8. Cf. Deepshikha Ghosh, "Horror in a South Delhi Home: Teen Help Tortured for a Year," *NDTV*, October 1, 2013, http://www.ndtv.com/india-news/horror-in-a-south-delhi-home-teen-help-tortured-for-a-year-536314.

9. Cf. Gethin Chamberlain, "The Delhi Child Servant Scandal That Has Outraged India," *The Guardian*, April 7, 2012, http://www.theguardian.com/world/2012/apr/07/india-child-labour-delhi-outrage.

10. Cf. Philip Ekka, *Tribal Movements: A Study in Social Change* (Pathalgaon, India: Tribal Research and Documentation Centre, 2003), 24–25.

11. Xalxo, *Current Ecological Crisis and Its Moral Dimensions*, 12.

12. Mahrotra, *Domestic Workers*, 36.

13. "Tribals' Community Marriage Blessed in Mumbai," *UCAN India Online News*, May 18, 2014, http://www.ucanindia.in.

14. Cf. Shree, "Female Tribal Migrants as Domestic Workers," 47.

15. Robert C. Doyle, *Eschatology and the Shape of Christian Belief* (Carlisle, Cumbria, UK: Paternoster Publishing, 1999), 298.

16. Cf. Ibid., 306.

17. Brian E. Daley, *The Hope of the Early Church: A Handbook of the Patristic Eschatology* (Grand Rapids, MI: Baker Academic, 2002), 1.

18. Mahrotra, *Domestic Workers*, 50.

19. Divya Trivedi, "The Invisible Workers," *The Hindi.com*, October 13, 2013, http://www.thehindu.com/features/the-yin-thing/the-invisible-workers/article5229435.ece.

BAKLÂ AND PAGLADLAD

Unfurling Boundaries of Self, Home, and Theological Imagination

Michael Sepidoza Campos

> An ability to articulate the world . . . may well be oriented around the tensely attributive specular axis between two closets: in the first place the closet viewed, the spectacle of the closet; and in the second its hidden framer and consumer, the closet inhabited, the viewpoint of the closet.
>
> —Eve Kosofsky Sedgwick[1]

"The Closet Inhabited"/Coming Out

When José Antonio Vargas came out as "undocumented" through a 2011 *New York Times* exposé, he unraveled American imaginaries of citizenship and nation.[2] This was magnified by his achievements: a Pulitzer Prize-winning journalist whose Asian face heralded seamless integration of foreign bodies into the national corpus. Hiding behind forged documents, Vargas lived a life of subterfuge while gaining success and accolades along the way.

In a later documentary, Vargas—who is gay—nuanced the burden of his sexual versus political coming out.[3] While both portended the potential for expulsion, the former came with less risk. Having been raised in the gay-friendly San Francisco Bay area, he would always find belonging among queer folks. As an undocumented American, however, Vargas risked deportation. By equating these two experiences, Vargas illuminated queer tropes latent in migration narratives.

Negotiating moments of concealment and unveiling, migrants like Vargas queer spaces of belonging, where coming out reconstitutes a spectral self. Both strokes evoke strategies of closeted lives that thrive in ephemera, condemned to the threat of unending displacement. Choosing to resignify himself an undocumented American, Vargas negotiates proposition and enunciation, the "third space" of a body neither here nor there.[4]

"The Closet Viewed"/Looking In

Well before Vargas broke onto the forefront of the immigration debate, a film parodying contemporary Filipino life was released to mild acclaim. *La Visa Loca* followed the adventures of Jess Huson who, like millions of Filipinos, desperately sought to leave an impoverished homeland.[5] Obsessed with the American dream, Jess spent his days peddling services to tourists as a limousine driver, cultural resource, and native informant—all in the hope of culling confidence and sympathy from potential overseas employers. Everything was for sale.

At a pivotal moment in the film, a twist of events forces Jess to take the place of another *Jesús* who was hired to be crucified on international TV for a Holy Week special. Desperate to please the foreign producer (who promised him an employment referral in exchange), Jess becomes Jesús, nailing his body to the cross. By reincarnating the crucified one, Jess literally dismembers self, a veritable martyr for migration. He exposes the gruesome exchange undergirding colonial transactions, between Filipinos peddling selves for the American dream and Americans paying to gawk at indigenous bodies to satiate a fetish for the strange. At this juncture, "Jess becomes part of this spectacle . . . his suffering . . . the currency through which his American visa is bought."[6] Jess hallucinates, glimpsing the truth of his condition as a body reduced to commodification by peddler and patron alike. Who fetishizes whom?

"The Viewpoint of the Closet"/ Filipino as Migrant and *Baklâ*

To speak of contemporary Filipino migration is to speak of displaced bodies, of homes both real and imagined. Migrant bodies stand in perennial moments of coming out. They simultaneously yearn for and resist belonging, queered by the impossibility of full integration to nation.

In the Filipino cultural universe, queerness is embodied in the transgressive figure of the *baklâ*—an essentialized femininity forged on a male body.[7] Inherent to the *baklâ* imaginary is *pagladlad,* a gesture of coming out that does not so much expose as unfurl a masculine body to consolidate a feminized self. In so doing, the *baklâ* undermines the masculine–feminine binary that undergirds the patriarchal scaffolding of Filipino culture and worldview.[8] To be *baklâ* is to be constituted through a dynamic process of disintegration and reintegration—a shift from (normative) masculinity to (*ab*normal) femininity.

To the extent that migrant bodies mirror this slippage from the normativity of home to the displacement of diaspora, migrants are *baklâ*. They unsettle citizenship, "produced as . . . stateless [abnormal bodies] at the same time that they are jettisoned from juridical modes of [normative] belonging."[9] Dismantling the impenetrability of identity and place, migrants intuit mechanisms of queerness embedded within the displacement of home. Diaspora, in a sense, interrogates the presumed normativity of nation and subjectivity. If this should be the case, theologies of migration cannot but disclaim and unfurl notions of embodiment and incarnation, reorienting the theological task toward apophasis.

As an exploratory piece, this chapter traces the expansive impulses of *pagladlad* to recontour the boundaries of a Filipino self and its specific strategies of meaning making. Rather than nuance migration from diaspora, immigrant from emigrant, body from self, I suggest that discrete categories of place and subjectivity elide into the other, illuminating theological strategies that break open imaginaries of body, blurring boundaries of self and God, home and dislocation, stability and possibility.

Bodies and States Condemned to *Pagladlad*

While they stand on opposite ends of the migration divide, Vargas and Jess unravel scaffoldings of nation, citizenship, and subjectivity in their aspiration for belonging. By exposing his undocumented status, Vargas identifies recurring moments of displacement within the state. By peddling his body, Jess affirms the arbitrary boundaries of nation and economy. As problematic bodies, Vargas and Jess are "contained within the polis as its interiorized outside."[10] They are "others" who thrive within, spectral reminders of the impossibility of belonging. Both articulate bodies that hide and expose parts of selves, illuminating the closet's specular potency as the place where one is both "viewed" and "inhabited."

Together, Vargas and Jess expose the state *as* a closet that functions not so much as a discrete place of belonging, but as a phantasmic boundary that simultaneously contains and repels foreign, unwanted, and abnormal bodies. As an apparatus of statehood and identity, therefore, citizenship forces bodies to straddle exposure and unveiling, grappling with "[moments] of absence, [where the self becomes its own] *re*-presentation."[11] Within the framework of migration, of bodies moving in between states, citizenship condemns one to unending *pagladlad*.

Eve Kesofsky Sedgewick once described coming out—and the closet for that matter—as a double-gesture "initiated . . . by the speech act of silence."[12] When Vargas comes out as undocumented, therefore, he embraces both his displacement and recontours the boundaries of the state itself. More than an act of disclosure, *pagladlad* deploys agency between exposure and strategic silence. One only partly comes out.

Akin to the *baklâ*, the migrant imposes a determinedly "other"—feminized?— body onto the presumably normative—masculine?—body of the state. Like the *baklâ*, the migrant reengages the normative body, splitting subjectivity, forcing one to blur the divide between the familiar and strange. What unfolds is a self that becomes a spectacle of itself.[13] To echo Homi Bhabha: "The [migrant/feminized self's] eyes breaks up the [normative/masculine self's] body and in that act of epistemic violence its own frame of reference is transgressed, its field of vision disturbed."[14]

Indeed, there is something poignant about Jess choosing to crucify himself for the elusive visa. Gasping for air, he finally sees the absurdity of his unrealistic departures. Apprehending the limits of his dismembered body, Jess enters psychic trauma, forced to reorient his gaze inward. Nailed to the very instrument of state expulsion, he is unfurled, *naladlad*. Vargas echoes this dance between belonging and expulsion. At the end of the documentary, Vargas challenges the Senate commission to apprehend his own split subjectivity: *What will you do with me, an undocumented American?* Undocumented. Other. American. Citizen. Vargas abdicates from citizenship while demanding belonging.

In this double gesture of expulsion/belonging, Vargas and Jess interrogate the presumed stability of selfhood and belonging. Coming out as undocumented to secure an ephemeral home, Vargas is split. Peddling his traumatized body to the state, Jess is unraveled. Both are unfurled, *naladlad*. Both are *baklâ*.

Interrogating Bodies

What is being interrogated is not simply the image of the person but the discursive and disciplinary place from which questions of identity are strategically and institutionally posed.

—Homi Bhabha[15]

Reconceiving Filipino migration *as baklâ* hedges identity against itself; one both claims and disclaims a stable self. Martin Manalansán traces this trajectory among his coterie of NYC-based *baklâ* informants who disavow place and home to affirm selves.[16] By locating home "in-between," these migrants deploy a kind of strategic meaning making that destabilizes "decontextualization . . . an opening to the future."[17] Refusing the stability of home, these *baklâ* deploy a different kind of "coming out"—unfurling ontological boundaries mandated by culture, location, and context. *Pagladlad* thus thrives at the ephemeral boundaries of reality, fantasy, and possibility. Unlike the trope of a singular "life-shattering-coming-out-event" of North American gay idiom, *pagladlad* situates one forever at the cusp of concealment and revelation.[18] One stands *in limine*—at the threshold of becoming. *Pagladlad* situates selves at the crux of embodiment, where "language—our own daily referentialism, or our poetic indirection, or our *theos logos*—makes contact with its world, [becoming] body, [becoming] flesh."[19] *Pagladlad* hints at a self repelled by ontology, drawn to dynamic incarnation.

As bodies consolidated over and again through *pagladlad*, migrants unfurl imaginaries of God and enfleshment. They illuminate incarnational events that resist fetish for stability, reorienting divinity toward irruption.[20] More than a mechanism for subjectivity, therefore, *pagladlad* unfurls theological language itself, exposing a kind of theology that John Caputo describes as "weak," standing at the cusp of "expectation and the possibility of shattering."[21] Opening the limits of theological language toward the displacement of diaspora, migrants cannot but disclaim incarnational events that allude to singular selves and moments. What unfolds is a body rendered "more real"—hyperreal—for its refusal to be rooted in a specific time and place.[22]

Interrogating Home and Belonging

Clamoring to name migrant selves, Vargas and Jess inevitably contend with America. It is this specter of empire that configures their imagined ontologies; it is this search for belonging that undergirds their ambivalent articulations of home and personal fulfillment. They are liminal subjects, standing in between place and time, exposing Filipino and American as arbitrary categories of home.

Theologians Rachel Bundang and Eleazar Fernandez unravel this complex engagement of self and home by reimagining Filipino as an ambivalent location within America. They expose multiple conceptions of diaspora: where they speak, for whom, and with whom they write reveals divergent/consonant engagements with empire. Fernandez locates his work clearly within the historical and geographical contours of the Philippines. He upholds accountability to an autonomous nation engaged with empire. Bundang, on the other hand, reflects on the religious culture of Filipinos in the United States, recognizing the centrality of diaspora in the articulation of Filipino subjectivity. Bundang thus stands unbeholden to an originary homeland, as Fernandez is grounded in one. While her notion of Filipino draws from the same historical and contextual framework as Fernandez's, Bundang challenges its epistemological scaffolding: Filipino cannot simply refer to shared history, shared ethnic roots, shared language, and memory. It is both none of these and all of these.[23]

Negotiating home and empire, Bundang and Fernandez evoke the fetish for/repulsion of belonging that haunt migrant subjectivity. To the extent that both disclaim Filipino–American bodies to theologize, Bundang and Fernandez unfurl theological imagination toward "the desires, the contexts of . . . constructed materialities; to the humiliations that distribute crucifixion more freely than any eucharist."[24] They intuit theological *pagladlad*. They call to mind the kind of unfurling that forces Jess to crucify self to secure an elusive belonging. His ambivalent sacrifice—to the extent that it is also borne of self-interest—holds both the United States and the Philippines accountable to the inevitable displacement of the colonial condition.

Migrants speak of homes that unfurl into the other. Rather than salvific fulfillment, Jess's crucifixion evades belonging. Instead, he hangs in-between, a sacramental reminder of an impossible yet necessary futurity. As a theological gesture, *pagladlad deconstructs* the incarnational moment, reorienting eschatological promise toward temporal displacement, where the act of naming/claiming self evokes the unnameability of God. To embrace *pagladlad* is to grasp that which is "uncontainable . . . restless with promise and the future, with memory and the past, with the result that names contain what they cannot contain."[25] Thus, one edges closer to apophasis. One disclaims fetish for the "name"—unfurling bodies beyond the entrapment of selves. Through *pagladlad*, God is enfleshed anew. God comes out.

"Many Closets to Come Out of"

When you're a gay person of color, there are many struggles to deal with. There are many closets to come out of.

—José Antonio Vargas[26]

By interrogating the stability of migrant bodies, I assert that diaspora inevitably hints at incarnational events. Migrants stand always at the threshold of *pagladlad*. One never fully crosses the threshold, thriving in the ambiguity of belonging/ disavowal. More than transnational anomalies, therefore, Filipino migrants cannot but be *baklâ*.

Rather than a place of rest, home for the migrant speaks of an "'inability' to stop mourning . . . a positive, perhaps even creative, ploy to 'resurrect' a 'buried' past into one's present social engagements and political struggles."[27] Indeed, the *baklâ* hints at the very potency of melancholy to consolidate self. More than grasp for belonging, the *baklâ* gravitates toward negative space, a deconstructive yearning for the im/possibility of grounding self.[28] One is thus unfurled, crucified onto multiplicity, standing "always on the track of 'hyperessentiality.'"[29] In its illumination of this hyperessential self, the *baklâ*—the migrant—exposes the artifice of identity politics and its obsession with categories of race, ethnicity, nation, and sexuality. Like the *baklâ* who must cull from femininity to articulate his silenced masculinity, migrants draw from the displacement of home to subvert the stability of state.

The *baklâ* is a migrant body. They muddle dichotomies of past/present, in/ stability, home/exile, reincarnating selves beyond limits of time and place. At these moments, "[one's] proximate self-presence, [one's] public image, comes to be revealed for its discontinuities, its inequalities, its minorities."[30] Both migrant and state are unfurled as multilocated, omni-cultural, polyamorous. The state is exposed as a closet of multiple openings, unable to fully contain. At this threshold of belonging and expulsion, the migrant re-creates/remembers/reincarnates self.

From Interrogation to *Pagladlad*

Jess and Vargas prod us to embrace migratory displacement as constitutive of self. Witnessing their desperate grasp for the American dream, we cannot but ask, whose body is really being peddled? By setting up for sale his crucified subjectivity, Jess exposes the commodification of the American Dream itself. He can sell only because the dream has always been for sale. For Vargas, citizenship can only be undocumented because citizenship was arbitrary to begin with. These migrants— queered and other-ed in their nonnormativity—expose the tenuous grasp of belonging. They illuminate the sacramental potency of *pagladlad* as repetitive practices that point to a reality more expansive than that immediately apprehended.

This unending grasping for self and home evokes liturgical repetition, gestures that Elizabeth Stuart describes as "[pointing] to [death's] defeat."[31]

Neither here nor there, Filipino migrants point to an impossible futurity. Reincarnating selves, they reanimate bodies that blur the line between normativity and the abnormal, space and time, self and other. Articulating a self caught in perennial unfurling, they speak "volumes about that which it deems worthy of unsaying," hinting at the plenitude of possibility.[32]

Notes

1. Eve Kosofsky Sedgwick, *Epistemology of the Closet* (Berkeley: University of California Press, 1990), 222–23.

2. José Antonio Vargas, "My Life as an Undocumented Immigrant," *New York Times*, June 22, 2011, sec. Magazine, http://www.nytimes.com.

3. José Antonio Vargas and Ann Raffaela Lupo, *Documented: A Film by an Undocumented American*, Documentary (Apo Productions, 2013).

4. Homi K Bhabha, *The Location of Culture* (London: Routledge, 2004), 53.

5. Mark Meily, *La Visa Loca* (Unitel Pictures, 2005).

6. Lisa B. Felipe, "Affective Cartographies: Transnational Labor and the Spectacularization of Suffering in Globalized Spaces" (PhD diss., University of California, Los Angeles, 2013), 47, http://escholarship.org/uc/item/4c27x2sx.

7. Michael Sepidoza Campos, "The 'Baklâ: Gendered Religious Performance in Filipino Cultural Spaces," in *Queer Religion: Homosexuality in Modern Religious History*, ed. Donald L Boisvert and Jay Emerson Johnson (Santa Barbara, CA: Praeger, 2012), 168.

8. J. Neil C. García, *Philippine Gay Culture: The Last Thirty Years: Binabae to Baklâ, Silahis to MSM* (Diliman, Quezon City: University of the Philippines Press, 1996), 117.

9. Judith Butler and Gayatri Chakravorty Spivak, *Who Sings the Nation-State?* (London: Seagull Books, 2007), 16.

10. Ibid. Emphasis added.

11. Bhabha, *The Location of Culture*, 67.

12. Sedgwick, *Epistemology of the Closet*, 3–4.

13. Martin Manalansán describes a similar dynamic in his study of a *santacruzan* (Catholic religious procession) among New York–based *baklâ* informants. Imposing campy elements onto a determinedly traditional religious practice enabled them to "return the gaze . . . to reinvent themselves according to their own terms." See Martin F Manalansán, *Global Divas: Filipino Gay Men in the Diaspora*, Perverse Modernities Series (Durham: Duke University Press, 2003), 151.

14. Bhabha, *The Location of Culture*, 60.

15. Ibid., 68.

16. Manalansán, *Global Divas*, 54.

17. John D. Caputo, *The Weakness of God: A Theology of the Event*, Indiana Series in the Philosophy of Religion (Bloomington: Indiana University Press, 2006), 5.

18. García, *Philippine Gay Culture*, 117.

19. Chris Boesel and Catherine Keller, eds., *Apophatic Bodies: Negative Theology, Incarnation, and Relationality* (New York: Fordham University Press, 2010), 10.

20. For a more robust discussion, see John D. Caputo, *The Prayers and Tears of Jacques Derrida: Religion without Religion*, The Indiana Series in the Philosophy of Religion (Bloomington: Indiana University Press, 1997).

21. Caputo, *The Weakness of God*, 110.

22. Ibid., 11.

23. Tat-Siong Benny Liew, *What Is Asian American Biblical Hermeneutics?: Reading the New Testament* (Honolulu, Hawaii: UCLA Asian American Studies Center, 2008), 7.

24. Catherine Keller, "The Cloud of the Impossible: Embodiment and Apophasis," in *Apophatic Bodies: Negative Theology, Incarnation, and Relationality*, ed. Chris Boesel and Catherine Keller (New York: Fordham University Press, 2010), 26.

25. Caputo, *The Weakness of God*, 3.

26. Sunnivie Brydum, "Undocumented, Gay, and Excluded: Jose Antonio Vargas," *Advocate.com*, June 27, 2014, http://www.advocate.com.

27. Liew, *What Is Asian American Biblical Hermeneutics?*, 105.

28. Caputo, *The Prayers and Tears of Jacques Derrida*, 3.

29. Ibid., 2.

30. Bhabha, *The Location of Culture*, 6.

31. Elizabeth Stuart, "Queering Death," in *The Sexual Theologian: Essays on Sex, God and Politics*, ed. Marcella Althaus-Reid and Lisa Isherwood (London: T & T Clark International, 2004), 67.

32. Keller, "The Cloud of the Impossible: Embodiment and Apophasis," 25.

THE ITINERANT FRATERNITY OF JESUS

Christological Discernment of the Migration Drama

Rafael Luciani

The "contemporary movements of migration" as Pope Francis affirms, "represent the largest movement of individuals, if not of peoples, in history."[1] He links this phenomenon of massive migration to the "scandal of poverty in its various forms":

> Violence, exploitation, discrimination, marginalization, restrictive approaches to fundamental freedoms, whether of individuals or of groups: these are some of the chief elements of poverty which need to be overcome. Often these are precisely the elements which mark migratory movements, thus linking migration to poverty. Fleeing from situations of extreme poverty or persecution in the hope of a better future, or simply to save their own lives, millions of persons choose to migrate. Despite their hopes and expectations, they often encounter mistrust, rejection and exclusion, to say nothing of tragedies and disasters which offend their human dignity.[2]

The poor and migrants are the faces of the new crucified victims, exposing the scandal of a globalized world that needs to be humanized. We are witnessing a death in life, condemned to a future without well-being. This is the case of the drama lived by millions of people enduring the effects of migration or itinerancy—willful or forced—representing a complex sociocultural, economic, and political issue, and presenting us new religious challenges.[3] It is an opportunity for us to build a universal fraternity among cultures,[4] which implies—as stated by the Latin American Church—"the transition from less than human conditions to true and more human ones."[5]

Theologically speaking, these dramas appear to us as new *signs of the times*[6] that cry out loud to God and humankind for a response (Ps. 85).[7] They—migrants, poor, sick, and victims—are sacraments of Christ, those for whom Christ himself gave his life, as they are the ones who suffer most and carry the burden of the world (Luke 17:7–8, 18:18–23).[8] In them, theology must put its gaze again and assume them as privileged recipients of the reign of God and sacraments of Jesus's praxis (Matt. 25:42ff.).

The Latin American church has denounced how "economic globalization has provoked a worsening of the conditions of the migrants."[9] *Ecclesia in America*

206

encourages "the international agencies of the continent to establish an economic order dominated not only by the profit motive but also by the pursuit of the common good of nations. . . . (no. 196)"[10] Following Pius XI, Pope John Paul II called the current order "the economic tyranny" or the "international imperialism of money," valuing reality based solely on economic profitability.[11]

Venezuela: From In-migration to Out-migration

Venezuela represents one of the most recent cases where migration has grown exponentially. Between 2000 and 2014 over 1.2 million people migrated.[12] This new phenomenon is producing a cultural transition, from being a country that was traditionally known as receiving immigrants to a country where young and well-educated women and men are becoming migrants.

During the twentieth century, Venezuela was known as a country of in-migrants. In 1938, the government created the Technical Institute of Immigration to regulate the entry of immigrants, distribute plantations, repopulate fields, and enhance the quality of life. This is in response to the need for a major plan to receive European refugees and displaced people who could not or would not return home after World War II. The former UN Committee of Refugees valued this initiative as the best existing program for migrants during the post war period, receiving more than one million Europeans between 1948 and 1958, especially from Italy, Spain, Portugal, and Germany. After the 1970s, the country received another migratory wave, this time from Latin America, particularly from Colombia. During this period, Venezuela was also recognized for receiving groups migrating from dictatorships such as Chile, Argentina, and Cuba.[13]

But in the beginning of the twenty-first century, when Hugo Chavez took power and oriented the country toward his so-called twenty-first-century socialism,[14] a new cultural transition began, transforming Venezuela into a nation where people are migrating due to political persecution and ideological discrimination. Liberation theologian Pedro Trigo, SJ, has expressed on various occasions that during his regime Chavez exercised the dictatorship of the proletariat as its military commander (*comandante*).[15] It was a form of political neototalitarianism, embraced by economic populism. It may be described as a sort of democratic Caesarism,[16] sustained by "the rule of the Majority through the government of the Tyrant," as argued by Jesuit sociologist Arturo Sosa, SJ.[17] This system continues under the current president, Nicolás Maduro, named by Chavez to be his successor.

The migration of Venezuelans is a phenomenon that has its own characteristics, differing significantly from other populations in Latin America and the Caribbean. According to the Pew Hispanic Center,[18] most Venezuelan citizens migrate to the state of Florida (United States) and have the highest educational level compared with other Hispanics and North Americans in general. In fact, 47 percent of them have undergraduate and postgraduate studies. In addition, 91 percent are bilingual, mainly speaking English and Spanish.

Among their reasons for migration is to seek asylum[19] as a result of political persecution and ideological discrimination. After 2014, the Venezuelan government assumed as a state policy the criminalization of public protests and, contrary to international standards of human rights, approved the use of firearms by security forces during public protests and rallies, a practice condemned by PROVEA, a nonprofit human rights organization.[20] The country is experimenting with a transition to military control of the state apparatus and society.[21] This led to the highest number of political prisoners in its history.[22] Even Pope Francis, referring to this situation, has declared, "I am aware of the pain experienced by so many Venezuelans, and while I express concern for what's happening, I renew my affection . . . particularly for the victims of violence and their families."[23]

Jesus's Itinerancy and Humanity

The migration phenomenon, beyond its rawness, can be a fountain of humanity, bringing out the best in ourselves. Jesus's praxis reveals to us the capacity to live humanly, even in situations of negativity, as well as the possibility to be subjects of our own history toward a better quality of life.[24]

Jesus is the paradigm of humanity; his itinerant lifestyle not only speaks to the situation of migrants and to host societies but challenges, as well, our conception of what it means to be human.

As an eschatological itinerant prophet,[25] Jesus was a rootless wanderer, living without house (Mark 8:20), always on the move (Luke 8:1ff.). He made short travels staying in people's houses. Sometimes, with time, they became friends, as happened with Martha and Mary (Luke 10:38). At times, he slept where the night fell, in a boat exhausted by the day (Matt. 8:25), or in the fields, homeless, in the open, taking the risk of encountering bandits and looters.

From living with his biological family, rooted within the Jewish traditions and learning the imaginaries of a concrete culture, Jesus adopted the lifestyle of an itinerant (Luke 9:58). Symbolically, this can be viewed as a prophetic protest against and detachment from all cultural and religious codes of honor, status, and social stability, and his rejection of these codes' definition of what it means to be human. He showed that our belonging to a culture, religious tradition, or biological family should not be absolutized. They are temporary roads toward the realization of our humanity but not the definite *path* that defines us.

Itinerancy allowed Jesus to encounter faces and stories never before imagined by him. In his encounters with the forgotten and excluded, Jesus was changing; an inner process was happening, and he found humanity where others saw negativity and sin. He could find faith where others did not believe there was any, like in the Syrophoenician woman (Mark 7:24–30), the centurion (Matt. 8:5–13), or the eunuchs (Matt. 19:11; Isa. 56:3–5). This transformed his understanding of his mission, which was not only for the chosen people but for all, especially the poor and excluded.

He himself suffered the brunt of poverty (Luke 2:7), the anguish and pain of exile (Matt. 2:13–15), the exhaustion from being always on the move, living life as a continuous trust in God's goodness and compassion.[26] Living in itinerancy marked the way Jesus prayed. He prayed in the midst of a possible death traveling in a boat, or before the fear of an attack on his life while walking, or even while sleeping in the open fields between villages. Psalms 31(30), 52(51), or 56(55) echoed in him, and he could release his fears by saying, "the day when I am afraid, I trust in you."

Itinerancy molded and shaped Jesus's character. It confronted him with the visage of the "other,"[27] and challenged him to include them in his circle of friends, while learning to look beyond the space of his own group of followers. This heart-felt experience of absolute trust in God and openness to others gradually led him to the so-called Galilean crisis, a result of his countless encounters with strangers and outcasts (Mark 7: 26). A self-questioning process and experience of metanoia is unmistakable during his encounter with the Syrophoenician woman that made him change and see faith with the eyes of the "other" (Matt. 15:24–28), with a mysticism of open eyes.[28]

The Welcome of Siblings and Reinsertion in a New Family

One day, Jesus's mother and brothers went looking for him. Jesus answered them with some harsh words: "my mother and my brothers are those who hear the word of God and do it" (Luke 8:21). He was not rejecting the relevance of the biological family, but rather decentering it. He understands that one's identity does not lie in our belonging to a biological family but in a personal faith-based relationship of hearing, wagering and trusting, like Abraham's faith.

Jesus called women and men, sinners and victims, despised and publicans, centurions and gentiles, to become brothers and sisters (Matt. 23:8). Eternal life begins in this historic bond of fraternity. Our relationship as brothers and sisters is the measure and height of our own humanity, of our identity and Christian calling. From it a new family is born, one in which all people are recognized as children and as brothers and sisters (Matt. 11:28).[29]

The itinerant character of Jesus shows that only those who broaden their ties and become brother/sister to all—including migrants and political exiles—can discover their own identity and vocation, as part of a nonbiological family, that of sons and daughters of God living in fraternity. This type of relationship involves a charismatic experience, moved by the spirit of God, but also prophetic deeds—social actions that foster fraternal and supportive relationships.[30]

Sharing Meals Together

God created this world as good (Gen. 1:31). The earth did not lack anything (Deut. 8:7–10). God placed us in the middle of a sublime abundance of fruits and gifts (Exod. 3:8; Deut. 6:3) that must be used (Lev. 25:1–17) with the original fraternal solidarity that existed (Lev. 25:14). The drama of the migrants, bread-less and homeless, represents a process of historic uncreation, denying the original promise to have a common land where all can "eat" and "work" (Deut. 27:7), especially the poor and needy (Deut. 14:28–29).

Jesus offers a way, a gesture: We have to eat together again! God wants us all to sit on the table, share the food and eat in God's banquet! (Luke 14:15–24). But *sharing meals* in Jesus's way has several implications. Religiously speaking, it means to overcome exclusionary practices (Luke 11:37–5). Socioculturally, it means to relate to each other not according to status and honor, healing the shame that might exist in the one who has nothing (Luke 19:1–10). Anthropologically, it implies the need to recognize the others in all their diversity, to give them a place at the table and reintegrate them in society (Luke 7:36–50).

Meals actualize the time of grace,[31] offering a way to heal our broken realities (Isa. 61:1). As in the banquets with Jesus, we too are called to create the social spaces needed to welcome and reinsert migrants into our societies. We have the challenge of restoring the gifts of creation, providing food and shelter to those who do not have it (Matt. 5:5) in order to be able to sit at the final banquet (Luke 24:30–31).

Jesus's Humanity, Migration, and the Venezuelan Drama

Jesus's itinerancy, which relativizes ideologies, poses a challenge to the Venezuelan crisis. Sociopolitical ideologies, even if intended to eradicate poverty, can only be justified to the extent that they are politically and economically inclusive, promote social processes of humanization, and are implemented with compassion. In the face of the Venezuelan sociopolitical drama that has created the surge in out-migration, the uniquely Christian option presented by Jesus's praxis of itinerancy challenges us to fight for freedom of expression and democracy, social and political reconciliation, and economic justice. The Venezuelan church has, in fact, advocated for the "strengthening of the democratic system, sustainable national development, and an education centered on the entire human person."[32]

As members of the one family of God, Christians in host societies in turn are called to create spaces of common good where the migrants/political exiles can feel welcomed and heard, just as the Venezuelans welcomed migrants to their home country in previous decades. As with Jesus, when we confront ourselves with the suffering of migrants, we open ourselves to an inner process of change and conversion in our way of thinking. We become receptive to the gifts they offer, learn to live according to the logic of gratuity and reciprocity, and even be converted by them.

The reign of God announced by Jesus evokes the liberating force of a creational will that rejects oppression, violence, and tyranny as ways of acting and treating people (Exod. 34:6–8). Jesus, foreigner and itinerant, is the model and paradigm to create a culture of justice, hospitality, and fraternal solidarity today.

Notes

1. Pope Francis, "Migrants and Refugees: Towards a Better World," *Message of Pope Francis for the World Day of Migrants and Refugees* (2014), http://w2.vatican.va/.

2. Ibid.

3. Pontifical Council for the Pastoral Care of Migrants and Itinerant People, *Instruction erga migrantes caritas Christi* (May 1, 2004), Introduction, no. 1, http://www.vatican.va/.

4. The Christian proposal for the good of the other is very clear, albeit harsh: "to deliver us from misery, more safely find our own subsistence, health, a stable occupation; to participate even more in the responsibilities, beyond oppression and protected from situations that offend the dignity of mankind." Paul VI, *Populorum progressio* (March 26, 1967), http://w2.vatican.va/.

5. CELAM, *Medellín: Conclusions of the II General Conference of Latinoamerican Bishops*, Introduction, 6, http://www.celam.org/doc_conferencias/Documento_Conclusivo_Medellin.pdf; See also *Populorum progressio*, no. 20.

6. Pope Benedict XVI, *Message of Pope Benedict XVI for the World Day of Migrants and Refugees:* "Migrations: A Sign of the Times" (October 18, 2005), http://w2.vatican.va/.

7. Second Vatican Council, *Gaudium et spes*, no. 4 (December 7, 1965), http://www.vatican.va/.

8. Second Vatican Council, *Lumen gentium*, no. 8 (November 21, 1964), http://www.vatican.va.

9. Jacyr F. Braido, "Migrantes y Refugiados en América Latina," in *People on the Move: V World Congress for the Pastoral Care of Migrants and Refugees* 93 (2003): 63–66, http://www.vatican.va.

10. Saint Pope John Paul II, *Ecclesia in America*, Post-synodal Apostolic Exhortation, no. 52 (January 22, 1999), 52, http://w2.vatican.va.

11. Pope Paul IV, *Populorum progression*, no. 26; Pius XI, *Quadragesimo anno*, nos. 105–9 (May 15, 1931), https://w2.vatican.va.

12. Iván De la Vega, *Mundos en movimientos: movilidad y migración de científicos y tecnólogos venezolanos* (Caracas, Venezuela: Fundación Polar, 2005), chap. 2; Iván De La Vega, "Emigración intelectual en Venezuela", in *Interciencia* 28, no. 5 (2003).

13. Froilán José Ramos Rodríguez, "La inmigración en la administración de Pérez Jiménez (1952–1958)," in *Revista Conhisremi*, 3 (2010): 29–43; Troconis de Veracochea, El proceso de la inmigración en Venezuela (Caracas, Venezuela: Academia Nacional de la Historia, 1986).

14. Rafael Luciani, "Politics and Church in Venezuela: Perspectives and Horizons," *Theological Studies* 70 (2009): 192–95.

15. See Pedro Trigo SJ, "Cómo vivimos la situación de Venezuela," in *Revista SIC* 1 (2015), http://revistasic.gumilla.org/2015/como-vivimos-la-situacion-en-venezuela-hoy/.

16. José Virtuoso SJ, "Balance y perspectivas," *Revista SIC* 691 (January–February, 2007): 5.

17. As declared by Arturo Sosa, SJ, former Superior of the Jesuits in Venezuela and former Rector of the Universidad Católica del Táchira (entrusted to the Company of Jesus), in a recent encounter held in Bogotá to the Jesuits in 2014.

18. Anna Brown and Eileen Patten, eds., *Hispanics of Venezuelan Origin in the United States,* Pew Hispanic Center, June 19, 2013, http://www.pewhispanic.org/2013/06/19/hispanics-of-venezuelan-origin-in-the-united-states-2011/.

19. Adalberto Urbina, *Derecho internacional de los refugiados* (Caracas, Venezuela: UCAB-SJR, 2012), 153–57.

20. See PROVEA's annual report from 2006, http://www.derechos.org.ve.

21. "Editorial," *Revista SIC* 768 (September–October 2014).

22. *Venezuela Awareness Foundation*, located in Miami, FL: http://www.venezuelaawareness.com.

23. Pope Francis, *Personal address to the President and the Government of Venezuela* (April 10, 2014), https://w2.vatican.va.

24. Pedro Trigo SJ, "Horizonte cristiano de la pastoral de la movilidad," *Revista Latinoamericana de Teología* 91 (2014): 8.

25. Differing from other scholars, I describe how I understand this expression in my work: "*El Jesús histórico como norma hermenéutica para la teología y criterio para ser testigos en el seguimiento,*" in *ITER Teología* 37 (2005): 17–116.

26. And "in the same way Mary, the Mother of Jesus, can be equally well contemplated as a living symbol of the woman emigrant. She gave birth to her Son away from home (cf. *Lk* 2:1–7) and was compelled to flee to Egypt (cf. *Mt* 2:13–14). Popular devotion is right to consider Mary as the Madonna of the Way." *Instruction erga migrantes caritas Christi*, no. 15.

27. He may have experienced what Lévinas expresses as "the other faces me and puts me in question and obliges me." Emmanuel Levinas, *Totality and Infinity* (Pitsburgh, PA: Duquesne University Press, 1969), 207.

28. Jesus observes suffering in history and yet never ceases to pray to God as a sign of trust and hope for a better and more humane future. For further development of this concept, I recommend reading Johann B. Metz, *Faith in History and Society* (New York: Crossroad Publishing, 2007).

29. "The Beatitudes do not refer to the *apparently* miserable ones, but to the *really* miserable (. . .). These miseries are confronted with the Kingdom of God. We now say that a precise light breaks into that situation which, was neither caused nor desired or loved by them—the miserable—. This situation has an unpleasant, negative and resembling character similar to *death*. In their misery they find themselves in the highest boundary of the cosmos, called to renew itself through the man Jesus and to be confronted with the Kingdom of God." Karl Barth, *Die kirchliche dogmatik* IV, 2 (Zürich: ZTV, 1964), 211–12. (Translated by me.)

30. To deepen this perspective, I recommend reading José Ignacio González Faus, *La humanidad nueva: Ensayo de Cristología* (Bilbao, Spain: Editorial Sal Terrae, 1984), chap. 5.

31. John Meier, *A Marginal Jew: Rethinking the Historical Jesus* (New York: Doubleday, 1994), 350–51.

32. See *Exhortation of the Venezuelan Bishops*: *Tiempo de diálogo para construir juntos* (Caracas, Venezuela: CEV, 2007).

Toward an *Ubuntu* Trinitarian Prophetic Theology

A Social Critique of Blindness to the Other

Nontando Hadebe

For many motorists in Johannesburg, South Africa, the sight of blind women, men, and children begging at traffic lights is a daily occurrence. These are migrants from Zimbabwe who, together with their compatriots, and other African nationals have left their countries of origin in search of a better life in South Africa. Their presence for many South Africans is unwanted, as they are perceived to be competitors for limited resources that rightfully belong to South African citizens. Negative stereotypes abound depicting migrants as criminals and illegal aliens taking *jobs and opportunities* from South Africans while enjoying the benefits of democracy that they did not *fight for.*

The struggle for economic resources has led to nationwide xenophobic violence against African migrants. The worst incidents were in 2008, when over sixty migrants were killed. Xenophobia is racialized, as it targets migrants from African countries leaving other migrant populations like Europeans and Chinese untouched.[1] These migrant groups are seen favorably as *investors* and *tourists* who bring money that leads to jobs for locals, whereas African migrant are seen as takers whose needs drain economic resources and do nothing to contribute to economic growth. In reality, research has shown that many African migrants are entrepreneurs who boost the local economy by employing locals and promoting cross-border trade. These contributions are not widely publicized or as widely known as the negative stereotypes. This creates a mutual blindness that separates migrants and South Africans. In this context, the *intrusion* of blind migrants into the public space of xenophobia is not only an audacious act of dangerous vulnerability but a rallying call to migrants to come out of their shadows and face their opponents with their stories of courage, resilience, and survival. It is also a call to South Africans to take off their blinders of prejudice toward an encounter with migrants at the level of shared humanity and dignity embodied in the concept of *ubuntu.*

There are fears from South Africans that *ubuntu* will increase their vulnerability to migrant invasion, and so, as will be discussed later, *ubuntu* becomes an in-group practice that sustains the cohesion and sense of identity of the group. The challenge is to rehabilitate *ubuntu* and reformulate it into a liberating practice that has no winners or losers and where the common good born out of a realization of interdependence is fostered.

Ubuntu, as an anthropology of relatedness, community, difference, and oneness, aligns naturally with Trinitarian anthropology. In the Trinity, God is expressed as a communion of people, each distinct and yet radically related and united to the other. Thus, to be made in the image of the Trinity means that related-ness, difference, equality, interdependence, and community define what it means to be human. The mission of Christians in the context of xenophobia is to unite the concepts of *ubuntu* and Trinitarian theology as the model for inclusive and just communities of difference that promote the common good where none is excluded. The experiences of multiple exclusions and vulnerabilities by people living with disabilities provide a nonthreatening framework for migrants to name their experi-ences of exclusion as well as their othering of migrants with disabilities. Similarly, South Africans need to be invited to face their *othering* of African migrants.

The *ubuntu* Trinity paradigm allows Christians to exercise their prophetic role as they did during times of national crisis like apartheid and the Truth and Recon-ciliation Commission in South Africa. Xenophobia is a scandal for the church in South Africa and requires a prophetic witness that will steer the nation to a different and nonviolent encounter with migrant Africans. This essay will address the context of African migrants and the challenge of xenophobia in South Africa; it will also examine lessons from disability studies on exclusion and *Trinitarian–ubuntu* theology as prophetic witness to an inclusive postxenophobic South Africa.

African Migrants and Xenophobia in South Africa

As mentioned in the introduction, large numbers of migrants have moved to South Africa from different parts of Africa. Media reports have helped fuel rising antiforeign sentiments through negative stereotyping of foreigners. In their research on the role of media in fueling xenophobia in South Africa, Ransford Danso and David A. McDonald found that the local media perpetuated three common stereo-types: "migrants as job-stealers, migrants as criminals and migrants as illegals."[2] These three stereotypes reinforced the perception of migrant Africans as a threat to their democracy. They were criminals draining the resources of the justice system and their repatriation was costly to the government. These resources, argued many South Africans, could have been used to meet their basic needs. Some media outlets actively perpetuated negative stereotypes, while others presented alternative stories that showed migrants as actively contributing to the local economy. The media continues to be polarized on this issue, as described in the following quotation:

> Two polarized views currently characterize press coverage of foreign migration in South Africa. One section of the press (the majority) portrays immigration from an antiforeigner perspective and calls for stringent and immediate controls, even an outright banning of immigrants. This

media coverage also tends to be unanalytical, reproducing problematic research and anti-immigrant terminology uncritically. The other section of the press (the minority) is more accommodating and thoughtful in its coverage and attitude toward immigration.[3]

A strong undercurrent in these debates is the notion that citizens have the right to benefit exclusively from the resources of the country. In this rhetoric of nationalism and nation-building, migrant Africans are seen as threats to the prosperity of the nation: "the new oppositional 'other,' is essentially defined as 'non-South African.'"[4]

The contribution of migrants to the local economy, however, has been documented by numerous scholars. Maharaj and others have set out to prove that African migrants contribute to the growth of the local economy through businesses that employ foreigners and cross-border trade: "Migrants contributed to the economy by buying goods and services, and importing skills. A significant body of research has suggested that migrants actually created job opportunities, especially in the small, medium and micro-enterprise sectors."[5]

These contributions by migrants are often underreported, and the negative stereotyping continues to fuel incidents of xenophobia across South Africa. This essay will draw on disability studies as a resource for understanding the experience of exclusion and discrimination based on a biological trait. The racialization of xenophobia in South Africa that targets African migrants falls into this category of exclusion. The next section will summarize some of the key principles in disability studies that offer resources for understanding and overcoming exclusion.

The Experience of Disability and Disability Studies

People living with disabilities account for 10 percent of the world's population, and, according to Stein, 80 percent live in developing countries.[6] He further adds that

historically, persons with disabilities have been among the most politically marginalized, economically impoverished, and least visible members of society. Many societies have viewed and continue to view this social exclusion as natural, or even a warranted consequence of the inherent inabilities of disabled persons.[7]

The above quotation points toward the multiple levels of exclusion and discrimination that people with disabilities experience. There are two contrasting theories of disability, namely, the biomedical model that locates disability in the body as an impairment that needs to be fixed and a social model that locates the experience of disability not in biology but in the social context: "it is society, not the impairment, that disables, through social, cultural, economic, and environmental barriers."[8] Feminist scholars also argue that the exclusion of people with disabilities reflects the dominant paradigm of exclusion based on difference.[9] Their experiences of multiple forms of oppression provide a nexus for migrants to explore their experiences as the persecuted other.

In the context of xenophobia, the exclusion of African migrants based on their race as a biological feature that is outside their control aligns with experiences of exclusion that are commonplace to people with disabilities. This resource of experience from people with disabilities allows for their integration in this discourse as authorities and agents of change in society. Myroslaw Tataryn argues in favor of understanding disability as a "fresh stance for seeing the world" and that "in essence, understanding disability as human diversity facilitates meaningful community as we reach out to each other and discover ourselves more deeply."[10]

Xenophobia violates the giftedness of difference and the uniqueness of the other and undermines the ideals of South Africa, particularly the virtue of *ubuntu*. The next section will begin with a discussion of *ubuntu* in government discourse and then move on and merge *ubuntu* with Trinitarian theology as a prophetic response to xenophobia and the call for communities of inclusion and difference.

Ubuntu, Government, and Trinitarian Theology

According to Outwater et al., *ubuntu* is a central ethos of government policy as reflected in the following quotation taken from *Government Gazette, The South African Governmental White Paper on Welfare*. According to this document, the South African Government

> officially recognizes *ubuntu* as the principle of caring for each other's well-being [. . .] and a spirit of mutual support. Each individual's humanity is ideally expressed through his or her relationship with others and theirs in turn through a recognition of the individual's humanity. *Ubuntu* means that people are people through other people. *Umuntu ngumuntu ngabantu*. It also acknowledges both the rights and the responsibilities of every citizen in promoting individual and societal well-being (p.18, par. 18).[11]

The emphasis on citizenship seems to continue the discourse of exclusion by limiting *ubuntu* to citizens only. The domestication of *ubuntu* to serve national interests betrays the essence of the radical call to relatedness with all human beings irrespective of their nationalities, because *ubuntu* is possessed by all. In this regard, the partnering of *ubuntu* with Trinitarian theology offers a much wider universal message grounded on the inherent dignity of all people based on their being made in the image of God. Of particular interest is that contemporary social models of the Trinity have continuities with *ubuntu* and therefore can become a resource in the African context, where a person is understood as a relational being formed in community with others.

Ubuntu and Social Models of the Trinity

Social models of the Trinity can reflect understandings of *ubuntu* that are already present in Western anthropologies. Stanley Grenz speaks of social personalism as follows:

> Social personalism might be described as the realization that the self is not ultimately merely a "what," an essence, but a "who." Moreover, this "who" emerges communally rather than in isolation; that is, it emerges together with other "whos" and from within a conversation of persons-in-communion, but ultimately from a conversation with Another, who thereby constitutes the identity of the "who" as a person-in-relationship.[12]

This is a Western way of saying *umuntu ngumuntu ngabantu*!—that is, a *person-in-communion* and *person-in-relationship*.

Another theologian who develops this idea using the Trinity is John Zizoulas. He goes back to the theology of the Greek fathers who formulated the creed. He applies their Trinitarian theology to the understanding of a person.

> The [Greek] Fathers developed and bequeathed to us a concept of God who exists as a communion of free love and out of which unique, irreplaceable and unrepeatable identities emerge i.e. true persons in the absolute ontological sense. It is of such a God that man is meant to be an "image." There is no higher and fuller anthropology than this anthropology of true and full personhood.[13]

From this, Zizioulas identified three characteristics of a person, that is, sacredness, relatedness, and uniqueness.

- The sacredness of people: "nothing is more sacred than the person since it constitutes the 'way of being' of God Himself."[14]
- The relatedness or social nature of people, that is, people cannot exist in isolation because "God is not alone; He is *communion*."[15] Since God exists in communion human beings are social and communal.
- Lastly, the uniqueness of people that makes them unrepeatable and irreplaceable: "persons can neither be reproduced nor perpetuated like species; they cannot be composed or decomposed, combined or used for any objective whatsoever."[16]

These three characteristics of personhood reflect and deepen our understanding of *umuntu ngumuntu ngabantu*. The uniqueness of each person is not a threat to *ubuntu*, but rather contributes to the communion. The witness of the Trinity is that "uniqueness flourishes within a true community of mutual relations."[17] Robert

Vosloo describes otherness as an ethic of hospitality that "challenges 'enclosed' identity which isolates people from each other."[18] He explains further that "otherness is sustainable only through an ethic of hospitality based on *perichoresis*."[19] According to David Cunningham, the Triune God calls us to "difference and to oneness" and to "differentiation and convergence."[20] It is in communities and relationships with others that people discover themselves as sacred, social, and unique.

Leonard Boff integrates the justice element in communities modeled after the Trinity. He says,

> in the Trinity there is no domination by one side, but convergence of the Three in mutual acceptance and giving. They are different but none is greater or lesser, before or after. Therefore a society that takes its inspiration from Trinitarian communion cannot tolerate class differences, dominations based on power (economic, sexual or ideological) that subjects those who are different to those who exercise that power and marginalizes the former from the latter.[21]

The vision of human society based on the Trinity is one of justice, equality, and new economic and political systems that deal with concrete needs of the poor so that the whole community benefits. These are ideals of *ubuntu* that offer an alternative to xenophobia.

Steve Biko, who through the black consciousness movement fought for the dignity of black people, spoke similarly of blackness as a positive difference rather than a stigma:

> Merely by describing yourself as black you have started on a road towards emancipation, you have committed yourself to fight against all forces that seek to use your blackness as a stamp that marks you out as a subservient being.[22]

This quotation in the context of xenophobia is prophetic, as it affirms blackness without qualification.

Conclusion

This essay sought to draw in the experiences of blind women, men, and children who beg daily as a rallying call for new ways of seeing the other and removal of blindness from those who see. The inclusion of people with disabilities aligns with the ethos of *ubuntu* as well as that of Trinitarian theology. It calls for a return to black pride that is inclusive of all who are black rather than relying on a xenophobia that divides the black community and marginalizes the other. In the above quotation, Biko called on Africans to return to their cultural roots and reclaim their dignity and identity in community. In such a return, *ubuntu* becomes a tool of resistance and restoration of black pride and identity.

Notes

1. During the apartheid era, political refugees, mostly black South Africans, fled to countries in southern Africa where they were hosted and protected. The situation changed after apartheid as South Africa became the country of choice for many political and economic refugees from this region and other parts of Africa. Most migrants worked in entry-level jobs competing with locals while others started their own business. The competition for scarce resources is a contributing factor of xenophobia, which affects African migrants. For further information, read Cindy Warner, Gillian Finchilescu, and Gillian Finchelescu, "Living with Prejudice: Xenophobia and Race," *Agenda: Empowering Women for Gender Equity* no. 55 (2003): 36.

2. Ransford Danso and David A. McDonald, "Writing Xenophobia: Immigration and the Print Media in Post-Apartheid South Africa Source," *Africa Today Evaluating South African Immigration Policy after Apartheid* 48, no. 3 (2002): 124.

3. Ibid., 117.

4. Belinda Dodson, "Locating Xenophobia: Debate, Discourse, and Everyday Experience in Cape Town, South Africa," *Africa Today Special Issue: Africa's Spaces of Exclusion*: 56, no. 3 (2010): 9.

5. Brit Maharaj, "Economic Refugees in Post-apartheid South Africa—Assets or Liabilities? Implications for Progressive Migration Policies," *Geojournal: Geography and Refugees* 56, no. 1 (2002): 52.

6. Michael Ashley Stein, "Disability Human Rights," *California Law Review* 95, no. 1 (2007): 121.

7. Ibid.

8. Sue, Coe, "Practical Lessons from Four Projects on Disability-inclusive Development Programming," *Development in Practice* 20, no. 7 (2010): 881.

9. Rosemarie, Garland-Thomson, "Feminist Disability Studies," *Signs* 30, no. 2 (2005): 1558.

10. Myroslaw Tataryn and Maria Truchan-Tataryn, *Discovering Trinity in Disability: A Theology for Embracing Difference* (Maryknoll, NY: Orbis Books, 2013), 27.

11. Anne Outwater, Naeema Abrahams, and Jacquelyn C. Campbell, "Women in South Africa: Intentional Violence and HIV/AIDS: Intersections and Prevention," *Journal of Black Studies* 35, no. 4 (2005): 136.

12. Stanley J. Grenz, *The Social God and the Relational Self: A Trinitarian Theology of the Imago Dei* (Louisville, KY: Westminster John Knox Press, 2000), 12.

13. John D. Zizoulas, "The Doctrine of the Holy Trinity: The Significance of the Cappadocian Contribution" in *Trinitarian Theology Today: Essays on Divine Being and Act*, ed. Christoph Schwöbel (Edinburgh: T & T Clark, 1995), 58.

14. Ibid., 56.

15. Ibid.

16. Ibid., 57.

17. Patricia A. Fox, RSM, *God as Communion: John Zizoulas, Elizabeth Johnson, and the Retrieval of the Symbol of the Triune God* (Collegeville, MN: Liturgical Press, 2001), 254.

18. Robert Vosloo, Robert. "Identity, Otherness and the Triune God: Theological Groundwork for a Christian Ethic of Hospitality" *Journal of Theology for Southern Africa* 119 (2004): 69.

19. Ibid., 88.

20. David S. Cunningham, *These Three Are One: The Practice of Trinitarian Theology* (Oxford: Blackwell Publishers, 1998), 271.

21. Leonardo Boff, *Trinity and Society,* trans. Paul Burns (Oregon: Wipf & Stock Publishers, 1998), 151.

22. Aelred C.R. Stubbs, ed., *Steve Biko. I Write What I Like. A Selection of His Writings* (Oxford: Heinemann, 1987), 48.

Part VII

A Future with(out) Borders

A Future beyond Borders

Reimagining the Nation-State and the Church

David Hollenbach, SJ

The movement of people across the borders of nation-states is one of the major signs of the times in our increasingly interconnected globe. This essay will sketch some of the facts about the massive migratory movements occurring today. It will consider whether the common humanity of all people requires countries to open their borders to all who wish to migrate across them. It will raise the question of how the sovereignty of nation-states defined by borders relates to the idea that all people are members of a single human family. Finally it will propose some priorities that can help determine who has a legitimate claim to migrate into or to be granted asylum within a country. The approach taken will be based on a description of some of the political and social issues raised by migration, and it will assess these issues from an ethical perspective shaped by Catholic social thought.

The Realities of Migration and Refugee Movement

It will be useful to begin with a few facts about the movement of people across borders that is occurring today. Migration has, of course, been occurring throughout the entire scope of human history. People have been on the move since leaving eastern Africa for Arabia and the rest of the world between 60,000 and 70,000 years ago.[1] They have been seeking to improve their lives or are fleeing war, oppression, famine, or other threats to their well-being. Major surges in migratory movement were the European expansion to other parts of the world that began in the sixteenth century and the large migrations from Europe to the Americas between the mid-nineteenth century and World War I. Since World War II, and especially since 1985, migration has been occurring in all parts of the world, not principally from Europe to elsewhere. In recent decades, migration has been increasing in magnitude, complexity, and impact.

In 2013, the number of international migrants worldwide (the global migrant stock) reached 232 million, up from 154 million in 1990 and from 76 million in 1960. Currently, the global number of international migrants is growing at about 1.6 percent per year.[2] This growth in the numbers of migrants and the scope of their movements has led a major social scientific study to call our epoch *The Age of Migration*. The number of migrants and the range of their movement are making migration "part of a transnational revolution that is reshaping societies and politics around the globe."[3] The mass movement of people is a key aspect of the reality of the globalization that is an important characteristic of our age. Like globalization, migration is bringing both benefit and harm to large numbers of people.

The single greatest source of increased migration is economic. Though the extent of extreme poverty in the developing world has declined slightly in very recent years, the gap has been growing between the incomes of people in the rich countries of the global north and those poorest people of the global south whom Paul Collier has called the "bottom billion." Collier has observed that "other things being equal, the wider the gap in income, the stronger the pressure to migrate."[4] The rate of migration is also significantly influenced by the level of income of the people who are considering movement. Making a major move costs money. The very poorest are not likely to be able to afford to migrate. But those who have benefited slightly from the decline of global poverty but whose incomes are still below the levels common in the global north have strong motivation to move and may have enough to afford doing so. The huge gaps in income between north and south combined with slight decreases in global poverty thus leads to rising migration.[5] It is not surprising, therefore, that between 1990 and 2013, the number of people who moved from less developed to more developed countries increased by over 100 percent, from 40 million in 1990 to 82 million in 2013. In addition, almost 60 percent of all international migrants were living in more developed regions, where they represented 10.8 percent of the population.[6] The migration, which these economic pressures lead to, calls for reflection from an ethical standpoint on the importance of national borders and state sovereignty.

The movement of refugees raises similar questions of an ethical nature. A refugee is a specific kind of migrant. The United Nation's 1951 Convention Relating to the Status of Refugees defines a refugee as a person who "owing to well-founded fear of being persecuted for reasons of race, religion, nationality, membership of a particular social group or political opinion, is outside the country of his nationality and is unable or, owing to such fear, is unwilling to avail himself of the protection of that country."[7] Refugees, therefore, have little or no choice about their movement. The persecution they face means that their lives or their most basic freedoms are on the line. The phrase *forced migrants* has recently been coined to take into account the fact that persecution is not the only coercive pressure that drives people from their homes. For example, environmental degradation or long-standing conflict may make it necessary for people to flee to other countries to secure their safety. In addition, people can be driven from their homes and yet still remain within their own country as *internally displaced people*. These internally displaced people are not refugees according to the convention definition, but they have often been forced to migrate by pressures as severe as those faced by refugees strictly defined. People facing extreme poverty may have a moral claim for admission to another country that is as serious as a refugee's claim for asylum.

The UN High Commissioner for Refugees (UNHCR), António Guterres, has argued that response to the extraordinary levels of movement occurring in the world today must take into account the many diverse reasons people have for moving. Guterres anticipates that the twenty-first century will be characterized by the mass movement of people pushed and pulled within and beyond borders by conflict, human rights violations, severe poverty, climate change, and environmental degradation.[8] He also argues that we urgently need a new legal and policy framework, based on humanitarian principles, for a more adequate response to the multiple kinds of forced migration that are occurring today, including the migration caused by "serious economic, social, and environmental crises."[9] Such a framework, needless to say, has not yet been developed.

In his role as commissioner, Guterres, is, of course, particularly concerned with the stark plight of refugees as traditionally defined. In June of 2013, the most recent date for which worldwide data are available, the number of people of concern to the UNHCR reached 39.7 million, the highest number ever recorded, and it was expected that this number would surpass 40 million by the beginning of 2014. These people included 11.1 million refugees, over 20 million IDPs, and a variety of other displaced people such as asylum seekers and the stateless.[10] The civil war in Syria is the leading source of this massive human suffering. As of March 2014, 9 million Syrians had been forced to flee from their homes, more than 2.5 million to neighboring countries, and 6.5 million within Syria itself. This means that more than 40 percent of Syria's total population is in flight, and at least half of these are children. This mass movement of people is placing a huge burden on Syria's neighbors. For example, approximately 25 percent of all the people within the borders of politically fragile Lebanon are Syrian refugees.[11] Other conflicts are also sources of grave suffering. The conflict under way within South Sudan since December 2013 has driven more than a quarter million refugees into Uganda, Ethiopia, and other neighbors, while 800,000 people have been displaced within South Sudan itself. These have to be added to the nearly quarter million people from Sudan to the north who are now refugees within South Sudan. South Sudan is the newest country in the world and one of the very poorest, so it hardly has the resources to deal with the massive needs of all these displaced people. The High Commissioner has therefore recently warned that "If there is no peace in the next few months, the humanitarian situation risks becoming catastrophic."[12] One could add similar statistics for other countries in crisis such as Central African Republic, Democratic Republic of Congo, Afghanistan, and Colombia. But the need to address the ethics of response to migration in all its forms should be clear from these illustrations.

Open Borders?

The suffering of people displaced by war and natural disasters and the deep economic disparities of our world give many a powerful motivation to seek to enter those countries that are peaceful and prosperous. This raises the question of whether preventing people from following their desire to migrate or flee across a national boundary is a legitimate act. Do national borders have moral status, and, if so, what sort of status do they have? As the pressure to migrate caused by the sharp economic inequalities of our world has grown, and as the number of people seeking asylum from grave threats to their well-being has risen, there have been increasingly pointed calls for open borders. For example, political philosophers, such as Joseph Carens, and refugee scholars, such as Philip Marfleet, have argued that the time has come to consider making borders fully open to migration and to asylum for all who are forced to flee from conflict, oppression, or disaster.[13] In a similar spirit, several years ago, philosopher Martha Nussbaum argued that the cosmopolitan community of all human beings has primacy over narrower communities defined in terms of nationality, ethnicity, or religion. Indeed she called nationality a "morally irrelevant" characteristic of personhood.[14] By relativizing the nation-state and its borders in this way, Nussbaum was implicitly endorsing the opening of borders to all seeking to enter.

This support for open borders was given Christian religious backing in an opinion piece by Christopher Hale interpreting the appeal a group of nine US Catholic bishops made on behalf of immigrants at the US–Mexico border. Hale commented that the bishops' activity was a proclamation that "in Jesus Christ, there are no borders."[15] This stance has biblical roots. In Luke's Gospel, for example, Jesus presents the parable of the Good Samaritan to illustrate that the commandment to love one's neighbor as oneself reaches across religious and ethnic boundaries. When a man on the road from Jerusalem to Jericho falls among thieves and is left half dead by the roadside, it is not the Jewish priest or Levite who comes to his aid, but rather a Samaritan—someone whom the Jews of Jesus's time regarded as an outsider. When the parable ends with the words "go and do likewise," it challenges Christians to see in-group/out-group boundaries of religion, ethnicity, or nationality as irrelevant to their response to human need.[16]

The Gospel of Matthew also highlights the importance of concern for those driven from their homes by crisis. In Matthew's narrative, just after his birth, Jesus, with Mary and Joseph, was driven from home by King Herod's effort to destroy the infant as a threat to his regime. This can be seen as a form of persecution, and since it involved flight across a border, anachronistically we could say that Jesus met the contemporary international convention's definition of a refugee. Also in Matthew's Gospel, Jesus teaches that on the Day of Judgment, one of the criteria that will determine an individual's salvation or damnation at the last judgment will be whether one has welcomed the hungry; the thirsty; and, most relevant here, the stranger (Matt. 25:40). Thus, Christians should understand their relation with Jesus and with God as closely linked with the way they respond to suffering people who are not members of their own communities, including migrants and refugees.

Jesus's inclusive understanding of neighbor-love reflects the book of Genesis's affirmation that all people have been created in the image of God and are brothers and sisters in a single human family no matter what their nationality or ethnicity.

This common creation gives every person a shared worth that reaches across national borders. As St. Paul put it, "From one single stock [God] ... created the whole human race so that they could occupy the entire earth" (Acts 17:26). This challenges any understanding of the moral significance of borders that restricts the respect and care required by the love commandment to members of one's own religious, national, or ethnic community. *Sub specie aeternitatis* there are no foreigners; all humans are equally brothers and sisters to one another. Thus, Christian care and concern must surely reach across borders. The universality of human dignity and the universal scope of Christian love led Pope John XXIII to insist that "the fact that one is a citizen of a particular State does not detract in any way from his membership in the human family as a whole, nor from his citizenship in the world community."[17]

The Role of States and Their Sovereignty

The question, of course, is whether a philosophically based cosmopolitanism and a Christian affirmation of the universal reach of the love commandment means that one should conclude with Nussbaum that state borders have no moral relevance. In fact, the issue is more complex. An adequate appreciation of the common humanity of all people must not only support the oneness of the human family but must also respect the differences among peoples, cultures, and nations.[18] A thoroughgoing stress on what we have in common will have difficulty explaining why being forced from home, either as a refugee or within one's own country, has such negative moral significance. Similarly, it is objectionable for one community to be compelled to live under colonial control by another not only because this limits the freedom of the colonized but also because it undermines their shared identity. Being able to live in one's own home and with one's identity and culture intact are moral values.

We need, therefore, a more differentiated approach to how responsibilities reach across borders than the stress on the unity of the human family, taken alone, can provide. In one of her more recent writings Nussbaum has changed her approach and now argues for respecting the sovereignty of countries that are organized in sufficiently accountable ways. Drawing on the thought of Hugo Grotius and Immanuel Kant, Nussbaum argues that people exercise their freedom and express their dignity as people when they join together to shape the political institutions and laws of their own nation-state. In her view, the nation-state is the largest presently existing institution through which people are likely to be able to govern themselves and to conduct politics in a responsible way. Thus, Nussbaum now argues that protecting the independence of accountable states is a way of protecting human dignity. In her view, large, distant international bodies like the United Nations cannot be held accountable in this way, at least not yet. State sovereignty and borders, therefore, should ordinarily be respected, unless there is good reason to override them. Certainly this means avoiding colonial and imperial threats to people's freedom and dignity. More generally, it implies that state borders are not morally irrelevant but can be important protections for the dignity of those living within them.[19]

In a similar way, though Christian love requires universal concern for all one's neighbors, it also requires respect for the distinctive identities of people or groups. Such respect includes abiding by the requirements of the particular moral relationships one has with others. St. Augustine and St. Thomas Aquinas both affirm a Christian duty to love all humans as our neighbors. At the same time, they also acknowledge that there is an order of priorities among diverse loves (an *ordoamoris*). Those with whom we have special relationships, such as our parents, spouses, or the fellow citizens of our political community, deserve distinctive forms of treatment as an expression of our love for them.[20] Thus, Christian love requires both *universal* respect for all and *distinctive* concern for those with whom we have special relationships. Christian ethics forbids discrimination among people that effectively treats those of other countries as nonpeople. But Christian ethics also affirms that one has special duties to one's cocitizens, just as one does to one's siblings and friends. We need to balance these two requirements of love with each other. Much wisdom is needed in the effort to find such a balance.

The principle of subsidiarity that has been developed in modern Catholic social thought and that has also been adopted by secular organizations, such as the European Union, can provide additional help in finding the right balance between duties to the entire human family and to one's cocitizens. Subsidiarity sees social vitality coming from many social agents and institutions in society, especially from those at more local levels who are closer to the grass roots. In his classic articulation of this principle, Pope Pius XI observed that we should not "assign to a greater and higher association what lesser and subordinate organizations can do." Nevertheless the pope recognized that the developing conditions of social life called for increasing engagement by larger or more extensive communities. If a problem cannot be handled effectively on a more local level, larger organizations should take action. When such larger agents become involved, however, they should "provide *help (subsidium)*" to the organizations that are closer to the grass roots and "never replace and absorb them."[21] The action taken on the broader or higher social level should avoid overwhelming local agents with bureaucratic control or treating them in ways that undermine their distinctive identities.

The principle of subsidiarity was applied to the international level by Pope John XXIII in his 1963 encyclical *Pacem in terris*. John XXIII argued that the growing interdependence of global society means that nation-states are no longer able to respond adequately to a number of the political and economic problems they are facing. Thus, larger institutions of transnational governance are needed to protect human dignity and rights in this interdependent world. Each country's own government carries the primary responsibility for the well-being and human rights of its citizens. But when a country's government lacks the capacity to protect its own citizens, or for some reason is unwilling to do so, action by regional and global institutions can be both legitimate and required. Such larger agents, however, must not stifle the life of communities that have less than global scope such as national and cultural groups.[22] Thus, Pope John insisted that the international authority he advocated must support the important role the nation-state continues to play in the protection of the distinctive identities of local communities. Indeed the tragic suffering that accompanies the phenomenon of failed states shows how important it is to support the continuing role of the state even as transnational responsibilities are being exercised.[23] The pope thus insisted that national communities have serious duties to their members but that the larger international community also has such duties. These reflections in Catholic thought have been echoed in some recent secular discussions of transnational and global governance. For example, the principle of subsidiarity is explicitly referred to in the treaty governing the structure of the European Union, where it specifies the respective roles of both the union and of its member states.[24]

In the face of the grave need of those being driven to migrate, therefore, neighboring countries and even countries at considerable distances may have genuine moral obligations to respond to those in distress. From both a theological and ethical standpoint, there are important duties both to one's fellow citizens, on the one hand, and to potential migrants and those who have already crossed the border into one's country, on the other hand. Neither of these duties, however, is absolute. Duties to fellow citizens do not always trump duties to migrants, nor do duties to migrants always override duties to cocitizens.

The Need for Priorities

The question, therefore, becomes whether the responsibilities to cocitizens or to migrants from other countries are more binding in particular circumstances. In most circumstances, we have apparent or prima facie duties to respond to the needs both of cocitizens and of migrants and refugees. We need, therefore, to determine which of these duties is more stringent. Reflection on the historical and social contexts of different migratory movements can help establish some priorities among the competing obligations that can arise in efforts to shape just policies.

The competing claims of duties to one's cocitizens and to migrants from other countries have been made poignantly evident by Paul Collier in his recent book on migration policy, *Exodus: How Migration Is Changing Our World*. The discussion that follows will draw on Collier's work, agreeing with some aspects of it and disagreeing with others.

Collier notes that open borders, with rich countries readily welcoming immigrants from poor countries, are of real benefit to those who migrate. As noted above, however, it is rarely the very poorest who migrate. Also, since the better off in developing countries are frequently better educated, easy migration can facilitate a "brain drain," that reduces the capacities of very poor countries to move toward greater development. On the other hand, Collier notes that since good education facilitates migration, the opportunity to migrate creates incentives to seek such education. The results of these incentives can be an overall "brain gain," despite the emigration of some who are better educated. Collier believes that such gain has been occurring in most developing countries except the very poorest, which lack the capital to make education possible except for very few. Thus in Collier's view, easy migration to the developed world may raise the educational level in moderately poor countries, thus supporting their development, but may make the very poorest countries even worse off.[25]

An additional consideration is that migrants from poor countries to the developed world often provide sizable incomes to the families they have left behind through the cash they send home. The World Bank has recently recorded that such remittances to developing countries in 2013 reached $414 billion and are expected to reach $540 billion by 2016. The power of these remittances is clear from the fact that for India, the top receiver in the world, remittances in 2013 were three times greater than the total foreign direct investment in the country, and in Tajikistan remittances amounted to half of total gross domestic product.[26] The movement of more educated people to developed countries thus has the further positive effect of supporting incomes in their home countries. The countries to which these educated people have migrated also benefit from taxes on the incomes of the immigrants. Host country governments receive these taxes because of the productivity enabled by the education the migrants bring with them when they move. Since this education was financed by the poor country left behind, such education is in effect a form of aid from the poor home country to the rich destination country. Collier has calculated that if rich countries were to compensate poor countries for the gains they receive from the taxes paid by these immigrants due to their education, these rich countries should transfer 0.4 percent of their national income to the poor countries per annum.[27] Very few rich countries provide aid at this level. The education poor countries provide to those who migrate is therefore an inadvertent aid program by developing to developed countries. This hardly seems just.

We also need to consider the effects of migration on receiving countries, particularly how it affects the functioning of host countries economically. It may have negative effects on the poorest members of receiving countries by displacing some of them from jobs for which migrants are willing to accept lower wages. Overall, however, Collier calculates that this effect is quite small and that migration actually increases the wages of all but the poorest in the global north due to the way it stimulates growth in the economy as a whole. In addition, because of their slightly increased incomes, those who are better off can more easily come to the assistance of the indigenous poor. Overall, however, Collier concludes that the effects of migration on wages "are trivial compared to the fuss that has been made about them."[28] The possible social consequences of migration are much more important than the economic ones. Collier fears, however, that the presence of unassimilated groups of people from other societies and cultures can weaken the trust needed to sustain national unity. Diminished national unity can, in turn, weaken the commitment of the better off to support social welfare programs that aid the poor, assist the unemployed, and provide health care. This is illustrated in the way culturally more unified European countries have stronger social welfare and health care programs than does the more diverse United States, with its rich history of immigration.[29]

Collier thus appeals to the need for national unity as an ethically defensible reason to prevent immigration from increasing faster than migrants are assimilated into the host society. He insists that in reaching this conclusion, he has no intention of supporting racism or xenophobia. Nonetheless, Collier's appeal to national unity as a reason for limiting migration only makes sense if fear or distrust of those who are different is an important force in society. When he argues that policies should restrict the number of people who enter from cultures that are significantly different from the receiving country, he fails to note that when past US immigration policies pursued this goal, the result was reserving over 85 percent of US immigration slots for white Europeans.[30] In my judgment, Collier's rejection of racism and xenophobia should lead him to policies that seek to overcome distrust toward those who are different, not to policies of exclusion based on fear of social division.

Where, then, does this leave us in the effort to establish priorities for immigration policy that take duties to cocitizens and potential migrants into account? How can these contextual considerations help shape an intermediate approach between totally open and totally closed borders?

We can begin by agreeing with Collier that asylum should be provided to people who are facing persecution, civil war, or other serious threats to their lives and basic freedoms. In particular, once an asylum seeker has crossed a host country's border, the 1951 international refugee convention unambiguously opposes forced return (*refoulement*) when the dangers that led to flight still exist. An adequate response to refugees also requires efforts to find *durable solutions* that will enable refugees to return home or find a permanent new residence quickly. The importance of *nonrefoulement,* safe repatriation, and resettlement of refugees is grounded in Christian concern for the most vulnerable members of society. It is also supported by practical wisdom formed by political experience, for when displaced people live in uprooted situations for protracted periods they often become sources of growing conflict, including terrorism, thus leading to further displacement.[31]

When a country's military activity has been one of the causes or occasions of refugee movement, the country will have particular duties to those who have been displaced. The United States recognized such a special duty to receive large numbers of migrants and refugees from Vietnam following the US–Vietnam war, which ended in 1975. Though US military engagement in Iraq was not the sole reason for the displacement of Iraqi people, US intervention was the occasion for a huge forced migration of Iraqis. Thus, the United States and its allies have serious duties to admit refugees seeking asylum from Iraq and other migrants driven from their homes by poverty caused by the Iraq war. They also have continuing responsibilities to help rebuild the political and economic life whose destruction has been the source of this huge movement of Iraqi people.

Second, Collier is surely right that migration policies should not be based on xenophobia and racism. However, he is far too confident that his recommendation that policies should give overriding importance to preserving national unity and culture can avoid excluding strangers because of their race, ethnicity, or religion. In wealthy nations such as the United States, European countries, and Australia, negative attitudes toward migrants are often based on such stereotypes. To exclude people solely on the basis of their race, ethnicity, or religious identity is clearly contrary the Christian and humanistic commitment to the dignity of every person. Since migration does not pose substantial threats to the jobs and income of those in host countries, advocates of just policies should work to overcome these stereotypes. Advocates should also seek policies that recognize the ways that migrants make positive contributions to receiving countries by enriching the receiving cultures, by doing essential jobs that citizens are often unwilling to do, and by paying taxes.

Rich countries of the global north are often inclined to give preference to the well educated when deciding whom to admit. Collier thinks policy should favor those who are better educated and more employable, for they are more likely to help sustain national unity and to contribute economically to the self-interest of the receiving country. They also submit significant remittances to those they have left behind. Nevertheless, this recommendation conflicts with his concerns that brain drain will have harmful effects on the poorest countries. It is also in tension with his concern that migration of the educated is a contribution by poor countries to rich countries because the education of emigrants in their home countries increases tax income in their new homes. As an alternative, I would suggest that policy should not discriminate among immigrants on the basis of education or skills. Indeed the people most needed in the economies of rich countries are often the unskilled, for indigenous citizens of these countries are frequently reluctant to accept low-skill jobs. In addition, when people are admitted as guest workers for jobs that indigenous citizens prefer not to do, they should be granted citizenship within a reasonably short time. When people contribute through their work to the life and well-being of the society they have entered, they should be able to become full, participating members of the community they are supporting—they should be welcomed as citizens.[32]

The historical relation between sending and receiving countries can also have relevance in determining admissions policies. For example, European countries, such as France and England, have surely reaped rich benefits from the poor regions of Africa or Asia they colonized in the nineteenth and twentieth centuries. This benefit gives them a special duty to be open to migrants from their former colonies. The benefits gained by the United States through its dominant role in Central American nations like Guatemala, in Caribbean nations like Haiti, and in Asian nations like the Philippines also lead to special duties to those countries. These duties include making significant contributions to the development of these countries and admitting migrants in ways that will benefit both the migrants and those remaining in their home countries. Seeking these objectives will call for careful consideration of the economic and political context today.

There is no doubt additional grounds for granting priority to the admission of migrants from a particular background if not all can be received. The priorities suggested here are illustrations of the kind of contextual considerations that are needed in the development of wise and ethically responsible policy. It would, of course, be much easier to say that the moral unity of the human race means that all who want to enter should be admitted or that state sovereignty means that no one should be admitted. Neither of these options, however, would be either Christian or reasonable. From a Christian perspective, belief that all people have been created "in the image of God" (Gen. 1:27) and that God "created the whole human race so that they could occupy the entire earth" (Acts 17:26) suggests concern cannot be limited by the borders of nation-states. But the conditions of finitude require judgments about how to love one's neighbors when not all can be loved in an equally effective way. Acknowledging that not all needs can be met or all struggles overcome simultaneously calls for the development of priorities of the sort suggested here. These priorities certainly do not address all the ethical issues that arise in developing migration policy in a world of states. Each of them can surely be debated in the interest of developing more adequate proposals. They do suggest some of the concrete implications of an ethical stance that affirms the contributions states and their borders make to human well-being and that also insist that sovereignty is limited and borders never absolute. One hopes that the sketch of these priorities will lead to further reflection on the challenges of our *age of migration*.

Notes

1. See "The Human Journey: Migration Routes," https://genographic.nationalgeographic.com.

2. United Nations Department of Economic and Social Affairs, *World Population Policies 2013* (New York: United Nations, 2103), 8, http://www.un.org/.

3. Stephen Castles and Mark J. Miller, *The Age of Migration: International Population Movements in the Modern World*, 4th ed. (New York: Guilford Press, 2009), 7.

4. Paul Collier, *Exodus: How Migration Is Changing Our World* (New York: Oxford University Press, 2013), 38.

5. Ibid., 39.

6. UN Department of Economic and Social Affairs, *World Population Policies 2013*, 108.

7. United Nations, Convention Relating to the Status of Refugees, 1951, art. 1(A)(2), http://www.unhcr.org/.

8. António Guterres, "Millions Uprooted: Saving Refugees and the Displaced," *Foreign Affairs* 87, no. 5 (September/October 2008): 90.

9. Ibid., 92.

10. UN High Commissioner for Refugees, *Mid-Year Trends 2013* (Geneva: UNHCR, 2013), 3, 6, and 22 (tbl. 2, world totals), http://www.unhcr.org/.

11. UN High Commissioner for Refugees, "Syria Tops World List for Forcibly Displaced after Three Years of Conflict," March 14, 2014, http://www.unhcr.org/.

12. UN High Commissioner for Refugees, "UNHCR and World Food Programme Alarmed at Scale of Needs in South Sudan," April 1, 2014, http://www.unhcr.org/.

13. Joseph Carens, "Aliens and Citizens: The Case for Open Borders," *Review of Politics* 49, no. 2 (Spring 1987): 251–73; Philip Marfleet, *Refugees in a Global Era* (New York: Palgrave Macmillan, 2006), 288–90.

14. Martha C. Nussbaum, "Patriotism and Cosmopolitanism," in *For Love of Country*, ed Martha C. Nussbaum and Joshua Cohen (Boston: Beacon Press, 2002), 5. Nussbaum subsequently changed her view on the importance of nation-states, as will be noted below.

15. Christopher J. Hale, "Cardinals Prove Borders Cannot Block the Love of Jesus Christ," April 2, 2014, http://time.com/.

16. See Drew Christiansen, "Movement, Asylum, Borders: Christian Perspectives," *International Migration Review* 30, no. 1 (1996): 7–11; and Avery Dulles, "Christianity and Humanitarian Action," in *Traditions, Values and Humanitarian Action*, ed. Kevin Cahill (New York: Fordham University Press and Center for International Health and Cooperation, 2003), 5–20.

17. Pope John XXIII, *Pacem in terris*, no. 25, http://www.vatican.va.

18. See Kwame Anthony Appiah, *Cosmopolitanism: Ethics in a World of Strangers* (New York: W. W. Norton, 2006), xiv–xviii.

19. Nussbaum develops this argument in her *Frontiers of Justice: Disability, Nationality, Species Membership* (Cambridge, MA: Belknap Press of Harvard University Press, 2006), 255–62. Seyla Benhabib develops an analogous treatment of the importance of states in *The Rights of Others: Aliens, Residents and Citizens* (Cambridge: Cambridge University Press, 2004). Both Nussbaum and Benhabib also insist that sovereignty be understood in a way that fully supports the fundamental human rights of all, including migrants and refugees. They seek to protect these rights, however, by calling for what might be called porous borders rather than open borders.

20. On the need for an order of priorities among different loves (an *ordo amoris*), see Augustine, *De doctrina Christiana*, bk. 1, xxviii; and Thomas Aquinas, *Summa theologiae*, II^{a}II^{ae}, q. 26, arts. 6, 7, 8.

21. Pius XI, *Quadragesimo anno*, no. 79, http://www.vatican.va.

22. John XXIII, *Pacem in terris*, nos. 135–45.

23. For an insightful discussion of the need to combine appreciation of the continuing role of the nation-state with a cosmopolitan commitment to responsibilities across borders, see Nussbaum, *Frontiers of Justice*, esp. 255–62.

24. The Treaty on the European Union states the principle this way: "Under the principle of subsidiarity, in areas which do not fall within its exclusive competence, the Union shall act only if and in so far as the objectives of the proposed action cannot be sufficiently achieved by the Member States, either at central level or at regional and local level, but can rather, by reason of the scale or effects of the proposed action, be better achieved at Union level." Consolidated Version of the Treaty on the European Union, 2010, art. 5, no. 3, http://eur-lex.europa.eu.

25. Collier, *Exodus*, 252–53.

26. World Bank, "Migrants from Developing Countries to Send Home $414 Billion in Earnings in 2013," October 2, 2013, http://www.worldbank.org.

27. Collier, *Exodus*, 226–27.

28. Ibid., 113.

29. See ibid., 61.

30. For this and other objections to Collier's conclusions, see the highly critical review by Michael Clemens and Justin Sandefur, "Let the People Go: The Problem with Strict Migration Limits," *Foreign Affairs*, 93, no. 1 (January/December 2014): 152–59.

31. See Gil Loescher and James Milner, *Protracted Refugee Situations: Domestic and International Security Implications* (Abingdon, NY: Routledge, 2005).

32. See Michael Walzer, *Spheres of Justice: A Defense of Pluralism and Equality* (New York: Basic Books, 1983), 56–61.

The Ambivalence of Borders and the Challenge of an Ethics of Liminality

Marianne Heimbach-Steins

Borders structure the lives of human beings, societies, and states. Borders define, divide, and connect spaces and differentiate identities. By allowing inclusion, borders necessarily also produce exclusion. They stabilize collective identities, both bridging spaces of mutual recognition and dividing groups of people from each other, and they function as means and symbols of power.

This essay deals with the obvious ambivalence of borders from a social–ethical point of view. My reflection starts from a strong expression of racial division shaping our world presented by a contemporary artist. Then I briefly sketch political and anthropological dimensions of borders. In the last part of my essay, the moral question provoked by the ambivalent experience of political and social borders is examined. To present but one aspect of an answer in the context of Christian faith, I go back to biblical impulses that might nourish an *ethics of liminality*. The term *liminality*, as introduced by French ethnologist Arnold van Gennep,[1] is more easily associated with the transitus between differing experiences of time (within ritual practices) than with the transgression of spaces. But I would argue it may also express a certain ethical attitude toward borders as defining social, cultural, and political spaces in favor of human cooperation, interchange, and inclusion instead of dividing groups of people and representing antagonisms between them and their respective way of living together. The basic idea of what I want to express with the term *ethics of liminality* is that although human societies will not function without borders, they need a moral guidance of how to transcend borders—or how to make them porous—on the basis of recognition of the other. Eurocentric Christianity, having strongly promoted colonial structures during the last five hundred years, in our days is called to take responsibility and action in order to overcome this kind of border regime.[2] To take responsibility at the same time means not to follow an illusionist attitude that tends to forget about the anthropological reason of borders.

Borders: Cracks, Walls, or Bridges?

In 2007, Colombian artist Doris Salcedo presented her work "Shibboleth" in Tate Modern Gallery in London. She had fractured the concrete floor of the great Turbine Hall with a long crack, running through the whole length (146 meters) of the hall. Starting near the entrance as a fine, almost invisible line, it gets broader and deeper; at the end, it is about twenty-five centimeters broad and is dug into the ground by the height of half a meter. It looks like a 'canyon' embedded with chain-link wire fence. The material the artist used—the concrete and the wire fence—is the material that is used to fortify borders in order not to let unwanted immigrants through. After the end of the presentation the *canyon* was filled again and sealed so that a permanent scar remains in the concrete floor keeping the memory of the *wound* alive.

The artist created "a negative space: it addresses the w(hole) in history that marks the bottomless difference that separates whites from non-whites. The w(hole) in history that I am referring to is the history of racism, which runs parallel to the history of modernity, and is its untold dark side."[3] She deals with the logic of borders within the global context of colonial and postcolonial history. She reminds the Europeans and all first-world citizens of the hidden but still relevant colonialist and hierarchical structure.[4] The ongoing dynamics of inclusion and exclusion, of belonging and rejection shape the experiences of migrants at the borders of the European Union as well as at the Mexican–American border.

The artist explains,

> Shibboleth is a piece that refers to dangers at crossing borders or to being rejected in the moment of crossing borders. So I am making a piece about people who have been exposed to extreme experience of racial hatred and subjected to inhuman conditions in the first world. This piece is trying to introduce into the Turbine Hall another perspective, and the idea is that we all look down and maybe try to encounter the experience of these people that I have been referring to somewhere herein within this deep division that has been generated in the Turbine Hall. The presence of the immigrant is always unwelcome. The presence of the immigrant is seen as jeopardising the culture of Europe. Europe has been seen as a homogenous society, a democratic society that has learned, through centuries of development, has learned to resolve the issues through dialogue. And if that is the case then where do we place these outbreaks of racial hatred? So I think that society is not so homogenous and is not so democratic and there is [sic!] some people that are experiencing that. So wherever the world the earth opened . . . in the first world there is mesh keeping people out or inside as you want to see it, anyway keeping people away so it's a piece that is both in the epicentre of catastrophe and at the same time it is outside catastrophe. As you look in you can get the feeling of catastrophe in there but nonetheless outside is quite subtle and I wanted a piece that intrudes in the space, that it is unwelcome like an immigrant that just intrudes without permission, just gets in slowly and all of a sudden it's there and it's a fairly big presence.[5]

Salcedo's piece of art leads right into the center of what constitutes the challenge and ambivalence of borders. Borders form a means of division and—from the outside perspective—of exclusion. For those who are inside, borders create or define a space of belonging and of power that is exercised by a state or by a supranational political entity in order to let those within live securely and peacefully and to keep disturbing elements out. Within these borders, those who are included cultivate a certain identity such as Salcedo exemplifies with regard to the European former colonial powers: borders assure living in a democratic way, solving conflicts in dialogue, and following high standards of modernity. Borders within these contexts may bridge the differences between modern, civilized societies, like those European societies Salcedo addresses as seemingly democratic, dialogue-oriented, and homogenous, and at the same time, they defend the defined space against unwanted influences that might threaten the presumed harmony. Salcedo challenges this image by reminding the insiders of their colonialist attitude as a source of influence still alive and by contrasting it with the outside perspective of migrants seeking to get in. For them, borders serve as a means of continued separation, hierarchy, or racism. The insiders' benefits of borders are earned on the cost of those unwanted immigrants remaining excluded, be it by physically invincible or life-threatening fortifications or by the social discrimination of those who managed to get in but without gaining a status of citizenship and experiencing being accepted as members of the *host* society.

A World Structured by Borders

As basic structures of the human existence and of human societies, borders are found in all dimensions of human experience and self-construction. Nation-states are shaped by borders. This is a legally and politically relevant fact since borders define the space wherein a specific rule of law and politics is exercised. At the same time, these borders divide one state from the other and symbolize distinct national identities (finding expression in national symbols such as anthems, flags, and national holidays). They may allow easy permeability like, for example, the borders within the legal space of the Schengen Treaty[6] by which an area of free movement of citizens of the European Union was established. In contrast, they may draw a sharp line of division like the outer borders of the European Union fortified in order to keep immigrants from the global south out.

National borders thus define the space of influence wherein the sovereign of a state exercises political power and the rule of law. This is the rationale of the modern state as developed in the Westphalian system since the mid-seventeenth century. Despite recent developments of supranational law and the law of peoples, the Westphalian system still dominates the relation between state power and the human rights of individuals seeking a status of belonging apart from their nation of origin. The human rights system defines a right to emigrate and a right to seek asylum. But it does not guarantee those who do so (because of severe experiences of pressure—be it warfare, political persecution, ecological catastrophes, or poverty) the right to immigrate into a specific state of their choice. The right to let people in or to keep them out remains reserved to the sovereign of the nation-state with the only exception of the legal obligation defined by the Geneva Convention (1951) to protect victims of political persecution. Based on the doctrine of sovereignty, borders function as an instrument of division between in and out, between those who are considered to be members and enjoy a status of citizenship and those who are considered not to have or to gain any status of membership.[7]

The existence of borders also represents an anthropological necessity. Borders define the space wherein societies develop social and cultural conventions and cultivate a collective sense of historical, social, cultural, and maybe also religious belonging. This refers to the anthropological capacity to form and stabilize individual and collective identities, based on the experience of difference.[8] Citizenship or the belonging to a social and political entity cannot be claimed unless a distinct and limited group can be identified.

It seems quite obvious that borders, in terms of identity markers, are not necessarily *national* borders; one may also think of borders defined by criteria of ethnic, religious, or gender-specific belonging. Various contexts and fields of conflict of our contemporary world show clearly that, for example, tribal structures and religious borders are much more relevant as sources of identity-building than national borders.

Generally speaking, borders form a necessary means of organizing societies and enabling individuals and groups to enjoy the advantages of a specific cultural, social, and political context, and to participate within its legal, social, political, and economic structures. From my European perspective and experience, the rationale of national borders goes along, to a great extent, with the rationale of social and cultural borders as a means of identity-building. On the one hand, this has a rather strong impact on the cohesion of European societies and, on the other hand, exerts great influence on the political treatment of borders. Whereas borders form necessary conditions for inclusion and participation for those who are recognized as citizens, they, at the same time, function as a means of exclusion for those who are considered to be strangers. Refugees, asylum seekers, labor migrants, noncitizens of any kind can be prevented from crossing the border of a foreign state or, if they manage to do so, can be denied the status of a citizen with full rights to participate.

Whereas borders can be used to keep people out, they cannot hinder global influences from intruding. Phenomena of the ecological crisis and the consequences of climate change or the dynamics of the worldwide economic crisis and growing social disparities are not limited to any kind of politically defined borders. But people in different parts of the world, living under diverse social and economic conditions, are affected by these phenomena in highly different degrees of intensity. The more people live under precarious economic and political conditions, within weak civil societies and more or less failed states, the more they suffer from ecological risks or catastrophes and from the social and economic pressure those events provoke. Those who live in economically and socially well-developed countries, with functioning social security systems and a prosperous national economy, face much better conditions for meeting difficulties and building programs to secure the ecology and livelihood of people against the risks of climate change and various phenomena of crisis. The unequal chances of meeting the global ecological risks and profitting from economic and cultural globalization have a specific impact on how borders work as means of inclusion or exclusion. Borders do not and cannot keep out unwanted and possibly disturbing influences from a certain territory or society. War and violence, poverty, and the devastation of nature create pressure on people, politics, and the economy not only in the areas where they happen but—with different intensity—in the global world as such. Thus, in a particular nonideal-istic way a *future without borders* seems to have already come into existence by the growing density of global, though asymmetric, dependencies and by the increasing pressure created by the worldwide ecological and social problems.

The Ethical Challenge to Transcend Borders

The above-mentioned factors, influencing the life of people in all parts of the world, seriously question the expectation that borders might defend a certain status of security and standard of living in specific, enclosed geographical spaces of nation-states. At the same time, these factors shed light on the urgent task of global cooperation in order to save and improve the living conditions of those suffering most from the destroying influences of warfare, violence, and power asymmetries, as well as climate change, lack of resources, and extreme poverty. Ethical reflec-tion therefore meets the challenge of transcending political borders and elaborates arguments for struggling for a future shaped by a border regime beyond colonialist hierarchy and racism: the suffering from unequal opportunities to meet the risks of life in our globalized world and the experience of injustice resulting from these inequalities cannot be limited by whatever kind of borders. These universal expe-riences transcend political, as well as social and cultural, borders, although *what* makes people suffer and *what* will be identified as unjust depends, at least to a certain degree, on contextually bound experiences. In a similar way the search for justice and the longing for a good life are global dynamics, whereas the concepts of justice and the ideas of what is necessary for a good life differ with regard to the political, cultural, and religious horizons moral experience and ethical reflection are embedded in. The longing for integrity of the ecological basis of all life tran-scends the borders of states, societies, and cultures. The claim for a universal legal and moral order, which nourishes the hope that peace and well-being is reachable for all human beings, is deeply rooted in the notion of a global society—despite many conflicts about human rights and their implementation.

Those strong ideas may inspire longing for a world without borders, insofar as they divide the world into haves and have-nots, and exclude parts of humankind from the resources of living. But these longings cannot be met by the idea of merely opening or closing national borders. To make borders permeable is a task primarily to be accepted *within* societies. It is a question of realizing and transcending or erasing *hidden* borders that impede mutual recognition of people. Thus, it is at the same time a question of virtues the members/citizens of a society perform and a question of the structures by which a society provides education, guarantees participation, and organizes a peaceful exchange between its diverse members. Borders of hierarchy, exclusion, and racism have to be detected and deconstructed in everyday life; within social relationships, schools, and universities; in the space of the civil society; within religious communities and political circles. It is not very likely that the state-dominated legal regime of borders will change toward inclusiveness, participation, and hospitality toward immigrants and strangers living within the society, whereas the society as such remains shaped by a hidden *racist* agenda.

In Search of an Ethics of Liminality in the Context of Faith

The ambivalence of borders challenges Christian ethical reflection. It will start from the above-mentioned insights that, on the one hand, borders are anthropologically necessary with regard to the building of collective identities, whereas, on the other hand, legal, political, and sociocultural borders must not function as absolute and exclusive divisions between in and out, continuing racist attitudes, and colonial structures—often denying humane standards of living and belonging for those who are kept out. Different philosophical and theological approaches to the subject can be imagined and would have to be elaborated in order to broadly discuss the issues at stake. As such an enterprise would go far beyond what can be presented in this essay, I confine myself to the reflection of major biblical topics that may provide further inspiration for Christian political and social engagement in the line of an ethics of liminality. My reflection aims at identifying resources that nourish an understanding of borders as opening a space of life, not of death; of inclusive, not exclusive identities; and of hospitality between individuals and groups who acknowledge each other as basically related though different.

Within biblical narratives and theological traditions, manifold inspirations can be found that may help formulate elements of an ethics of liminality. It may contribute to the framing of a societal future not without borders, but with borders made permeable and bridging. The socioanthropological understanding and the ethical challenge mirrored in the biblical motifs to be reflected here may serve as background for political and legal arguments that, of course, need to be further elaborated. Four inspiring aspects are introduced into the discussion; although none of them is new, they might not all be present in an ethical reflection on how to overcome the exclusiveness of (political and social) borders.

Creation—The Dynamics of Transcendence

The biblical notions of the human being created *in the image of God*, of all human beings as children of the same father and thus as brothers and sisters, provide elements of foundation for an ethical universalism prior to all relevant differences. The metaphor of one entire human family, currently used in Catholic social teaching, evokes the image of global kinship and solidarity. From a Christian social ethics point of view, it may appear too plain an image to provide orientation for modern global political ethics. Nonetheless it expresses an ideal and a moral claim not to stick to seemingly *natural* divisions and hierarchies that, in fact, stem from political decision making and historically framed constructions of asymmetric power relations. The biblical motifs of human relatedness to God as creator and to any other human being as creature equally made in the image of God nourish a universalistic ethical understanding. They prioritize the experiences of equality, connectedness, and mutual recognition of all humans albeit with manifold differences in terms of ethnic belonging, gender, sexual orientation, religious belief, and other sources of diversity. Humankind is to be found at either side of any border, and no border of whatever society and regime must be interpreted as a border of humanity as such.

Thus, to refer to the biblical narrative of creation serves as a faith-based argument for the universal recognition of human dignity. No borders whatsoever can legitimize the ignorance of human dignity. As human dignity needs to be protected by basic human rights, none of the aforementioned factors of diversity must be claimed to justify the denial of human rights for specific people or groups of people. Once these fundamental convictions are accepted, they form a vital source of critique against excluding border regimes in the specific sense of exclusion from the protection of basic human rights. This specification is important as to the insight that borders cannot generally be abandoned but need to be made porous in order to safeguard basic standards of humanity.

Incarnation—A Fundamental Change of Perspectives

The gospel of *God incarnate* in Jesus Christ forms another strong impulse for an ethics of liminality. The experience of God having fully adopted humanity in the life and violent death of Jesus of Nazareth expresses the radical change of the divine perspective in order to restore human integrity without giving up divinity as such. The theological pattern of kenosis is perhaps the most radical experience of liminality. It may be ethically interpreted as defense of humanity at its very limits where the dignity of the person, as created in the image of God, is in the utmost danger of being destroyed. According to the Christian creed, it is the very *nature* of God not to deliver humanity to the fate of (self-)destruction. It is then the option for the poor that ethically answers to the incarnation of Christ as the gospel of salvation. It is the humane answer to the divine unconditioned readiness to recognize the deprived *other* as the one for whom Jesus Christ has delivered himself into death and in whose face the *image of God* needs to be saved. Thus, it is the center of the Christian creed that provokes Christians to switch from the inside to the outside perspective wherever exclusion takes place. This change of perspective may be discovered as necessary in order to overcome the logic of exclusion within a regime of borders dividing spaces of possession and participation from spaces of misery and exclusion from what is necessary for a truly humane life. Christian political and social responsibility implies criticizing dehumanizing exclusive structures and helping build an inclusive society.

Exodus—A Dynamic of Liberation and of Society-building

The experience of Exodus marks the centerpiece of the Old Testament gospel. It is this foundational narrative that constitutes the collective identity of the Israelites as God's people and as a society with its own rules and norms corresponding to their foundation owed to the experience of being liberated from slavery by God. This basic experience is at the core of the ethical formation of ancient Israel as to be seen, for example, in the preamble of the Decalogue. This means that the constitutive act that has brought the biblical people of God into existence is an act of transcending borders and implies the creation of new spaces of belonging. The formation of God's people enrolls itself in a process of wandering through the desert—a space that forces the people to be on the move in order to stay alive. The narratives of the Israelite history and the books of the prophets memorize the experience of liberation and the constitutive transcendence of borders as a constant challenge. It is repeatedly referred to as normative source or argument for the framing of a society that not only mirrors the experience of having been liberated but reiterates the dynamics of liberation for those miserable people who need to be liberated by practices of justice and mercy. This same dynamic is set forth in the New Testament by Jesus himself who constantly goes beyond the borders of religious and social exclusion in favor of the poor and the needy, the disabled and the strangers—in short, all those who are not (fully) recognized as members of the contemporary, Jewish community of that time.

Relation to God—Identity of Strangers

The Old and New Testaments give expression to the basic experience that the relation of faith implies an essential moment of foreignness within the world. The faithful gives priority to the relation with God, and this preference creates a specific distance toward the world. Whereas this does not mean a disregard or nonrecognition of the world's dignity, it basically underpins its relatedness to God and its relativity within the horizon of faith. The faithful constantly experiences that the border of worldly—material, human, social—reality has to be transcended by the longing for the greater God, the source of all that in an earthly sense, *is*. This makes the faithful feel as *strangers* in the world. It is a kind of existential strangeness, which, if accepted as a dimension of faith itself, may reveal a new sense of the relativity of borders, on the one hand, and create certain solidarity with those who experience borders as hostile and antihuman barriers, on the other hand.

Conclusion

Biblical inspiration cannot replace political decision making, of course, and it does not by itself provide precise moral orientation for action in the contemporary globalized world. But carefully reflected, it can promote an awareness of and deliver arguments for a border-transcending relatedness and a responsibility to adjust conditions of living and participation to a global situation that urges people to transcend existing—and indeed often hostile—borders, in order to look for a better life far from their home places. The entire biblical narrative of God as creator, liberator, and savior of humankind thus provides strong motifs to overcome enslaving and oppressing borders. This allows us to more precisely describe the practical impact of a liminal ethics within the biblical horizon of understanding.

The biblical option for the poor as a challenge of Christian practice originally evolves from God's option for the oppressed and marginalized Israelites and from the option of Christ for the excluded or marginalized of his time. It drives Christians to identify within their different social contexts the poor, to recognize the areas of marginalization of our days, and to make the church become present and engage herself at the margins where people suffer from deprivation and nonrecognition. Commemoration of the biblical narratives can help cultivate our individual and collective memories, which preserve the knowledge—and for many people the experience—of having been migrants or refugees or displaced people themselves, or being descendants of those who had experienced such fates.

Awareness of the religious images, roots, and traditions of the option for the poor may drive people to personal engagement—be it on the level of working for the welfare of migrants, asylum seekers or other refugees, or be it in politics to struggle for more humane border regimes and a human rights–oriented cooperation on the national as well as on a supranational level. Not least, they may inspire Christians to publicly criticize ideological tendencies of separation or isolation, which, in recent times, are obviously growing in the heads of many European contemporaries fortifying their mentalities against the challenges of open societies, increasing numbers of migrants, and the needs of active integration strategies.

The very first step to overcome the spaces of exclusion and reorganize social structures in favor of inclusion and recognition for Christians and for the church should be to illuminate the areas of marginalization and to bring those suffering from experiences of exclusion from dark to light. This is exactly what Pope Francis did when he decided to take the first trip of his papacy to the isle of Lampedusa to meet groups of shipwrecked refugees. The entire world then had to take notice of the masses of refugees from the African continent left alone in overcrowded boats in the Mediterranean Sea and of the asylum and migration politics of the European Union, which, to date, still has not succeeded in elaborating a reasonable and humane solution for the challenges of migration from the south. To make a substantial change, of course, further steps have to be taken. It is not enough to make the unseen visible. But actions like the pope's visit to Lampedusa strengthen the social and political engagement of Christians for the sake of migrants and refugees, and draw public attention to the political level. What is necessary is to give the needy access to humane living conditions. For those on the move who cannot return to their home countries under humane conditions, possibilities for gaining legal status in a society and being allowed to work and to get access to at least basic social services need to be created.

Notes

1. Arnold van Gennep, *Übergangsriten* (Frankfurt, Germany: Campus, 2005).

2. Cf. Marianne Heimbach-Steins, "Migration in a Post-colonial World," in *Religious and Ethical Perspectives on Global Migration*, ed. Elizabeth Collier & Charles Strain (Lanham, MD: Lexington Books, 2014), 87–107.

3. Doris Salcedo, "Proposal for a Project for the Turbine Hall, Tate Modern, London 2007," in *Doris Salcedo: Shibboleth*, contributors Mieke Bal et al. (London: Tate Publishing, 2007), 65.

4. Cf. Heimbach-Steins, "Migration in a Post-colonial World," 93–97.

5. Doris Salcedo, Interview on Her Work *Shibboleth*, transcription, http://www.tate.org.uk/.

6. The Schengen Treaty (1985) established a European space with open borders "with compensating internal security measures including immigration and asylum." Anthony Geddes, *Immigration and European Integration: Towards Fortress Europe?* (Manchester, UK: Manchester University Press, 2000), 131. It was intended to allow the member states "to pursue market integration accompanied by restrictive immigration and asylum policies." Although this was the main focus on the level of state interests, Schengen also "put[s] in place structures that indicated deeper integrative intent among a core group of member states." Ibid., 132.

7. Cf. Claus Leggewie, "Zugehörigkeit und mitgliedschaft. Die politische kultur der weltgesellschaft," in *Handbuch der kulturwissenschaften, vol. 1: Grundlagen und schlüsselbegriffe*, ed. Friedrich Jaeger & Burkhard Liebsch (Stuttgart, Germany: Metzler, 2004), 316–33.

8. Konrad P. Liessmann, *Lob der grenze: Kritik der politischen unterscheidungskraft* (Wien, German: Zsolnay, 2012).

CONTRIBUTORS

DIEGO ALONSO-LASHERAS, SJ, was born in Madrid, Spain. He holds a BA/MA in law and business, from ICADE, Madrid and a doctor in theology degree from Boston College. He teaches at the Pontifical Gregorian University, Rome. His fields of research are history of moral theology, religious freedom, and ethics and economics.

AGNES M. BRAZAL is associate professor at De la Salle University, Manila and planning committee member of the Catholic Theological Ethics in the World Church since 2007. She is coauthor of *Intercultural Church: Bridge of Solidarity in the Migration Context* (Borderless Press, 2015), coeditor of *Moving Body: The Church in Migration around the World* (Palgrave Macmillan, 2015), *Faith on the Move: Toward a Theology of Migration in Asia* (AdMU, 2008), and three other Asian anthologies.

MAURICIO ALARCÓN BURBANO is an Ecuadorian Jesuit. He studied philosophy in Colombia, theology in Brazil, and migration studies and moral theology in Spain. He holds a PhD in Social Sciences (University of Deusto—Bilbao Campus) where he wrote a thesis on migrant associations in Ecuador. In the last fifteen years, he has worked in various contexts of human mobility: those forcibly displaced in Colombia, Colombian refugees in Ecuador, Peruvian immigrants in Brazil, refugees in England, and Latin American immigrants in Spain.

MICHAEL SEPIDOZA CAMPOS studies Filipino–American diaspora, queer and postcolonial theories, and critical pedagogy. His writings include "Embracing the Stranger: Reflections on the Ambivalent Hospitality of LGBTIQ Catholics" in *More Than a Monologue: Sexual Diversity and the Catholic Church* (Fordham University Press, 2014); and "In God's House: Of Silences and Belonging," *Theology and Sexuality* 17, no. 3 (Equinox, 2011). Campos coedited *Queering Migrations towards, from, and beyond Asia* (Palgrave Macmillan, 2014) with Hugo Córdova Quero and Joseph N. Goh.

GEMMA TULUD CRUZ is senior lecturer in theology at Australian Catholic University. She is author of *An Intercultural Theology of Migration: Pilgrims in the Wilderness* (Brill, 2010), *Toward a Theology of Migration: Social Justice and Religious Experience* (Palgrave Macmillan, 2014), and a number of essays on other topics such as mission and women and gender issues.

MARÍA TERESA DÁVILA is associate professor of Christian ethics at Andover Newton Theological School. Her current research focuses on the intersection of Christian discipleship, activism, and social transformation. She has published in the areas of

Latino/a theology and ethics, the role of the social sciences in Christian ethics, the use of force, racism in theological ethics, immigration, and the option for the poor in the US context.

CHRISTINE E. GUDORF is Emeritus Professor of Religious Studies (June 2015) at Florida International University in Miami. She has published nine books and two hundred articles on issues in ethics and comparative ethics.

NONTANDO HADEBE has a doctorate in theology from St Augustine College of South Africa. She is a native of Zimbabwe and is currently residing in South Africa. She recently spent ten months in the United States (August 2014–May 2015): five months as an international fellow at the Jesuit School of Theology, Santa Clara University, and five months as a Fulbright scholar-in-residence at Emmanuel College, Boston, where she taught two undergraduate courses. She teaches part time at St Augustine College of South Africa in pastoral and systematic theology, and she is also the coordinator of the Circle of Concerned African Women Theologians in Southern Africa. Her areas of research are Trinitarian theology; contextual–liberation–feminist–African theologies in response to contemporary issues facing the African context particularly HIV and AIDS; and poverty, including migration.

MARIANNE HEIMBACH-STEINS was born in Cologne (Germany), and is a doctor in theology. She studied Catholic theology and German literature at different universities in Germany and Switzerland. From 1996 to 2006, she was professor of Christian social teaching and religious sociology at the University of Bamberg (Bavaria). Since 2009, she is professor of Christian social sciences and director of the Institute of Christian Social Sciences at the Catholic Theological Faculty of the University of Muenster/Westfalia in Germany. She is editor in chief of the *Jahrbuch für Christliche Sozialwissenschaften*. For her list of publications, see http://www.uni-muenster.de/FB2/personen/ics/heimbach-steins.html.

KRISTIN E. HEYER is professor of theology at Boston College. Her books include *Kinship across Borders: A Christian Ethic of Immigration* (2012); *Prophetic and Public: The Social Witness of U.S. Catholicism* (2006); and the edited volume *Catholics and Politics: Dynamic Tensions between Faith and Power* (2008); *Conscience and Catholicism* (2015). She co-chairs planning committee for the Catholic Theological Ethics in the World Church, and she is an editor for Georgetown University Press's Moral Traditions series.

DAVID HOLLENBACH, SJ, holds the University Chair in Human Rights and International Justice at Boston College, where he teaches Christian social ethics. His research interests are in human rights, justice, and responses to humanitarian crises. His books include *Driven from Home: Protecting the Rights of Forced Migrants*, and *The Common Good and Christian Ethics*. He often serves as a visiting professor of social ethics at Hekima College in Nairobi, Kenya.

Maryanne Loughry is a psychologist who has been associated with Jesuit Refugee Service (JRS) since 1988 when she commenced work in the Indochinese refugee camps in the Philippines and Vietnamese Detention Centers in Hong Kong. She has conducted research, program evaluations, and humanitarian training in the Middle East, Africa, the Balkans, South East Asia, and the United Kingdom. Presently, Dr. Loughry is associate director of JRS Australia and a visiting professor at the Center for Human Rights and International Justice and the School of Social Work at Boston College, and a research associate at the Refugee Studies Centre, University of Oxford. Prior to this, she was the Pedro Arrupe tutor at the University of Oxford Refugee Studies Centre. She is a member of the Australian government's minister of immigration's advisory council on asylum seekers and detention (MCASD) and serves on the governing committee of the International Catholic Migration Committee (ICMC). Maryanne was made a Member of the Order of Australia (AM) in 2010 for service to refugees and the displaced.

Rafael Luciani holds a doctorate in theology and a licenciate in dogmatics from the Pontificia Università Gregoriana; a baccalaureatum in philosophy and in theology from the Università Pontificia Salesiana; a licenciate in education from the Universidad Católica Andrés Bello; and postdoctoral activities at the Julius-Maximilians Universität in Würzburg. He has been director of the School of Theology at the Jesuits' Andrés Bello University, where he is a full professor, focusing on Christology and political theology. He is also *Professore Stabile* at the Salesian University in Rome and visiting professor at Boston College.

Alexandre Andrade Martins is a religious of the Order of St. Camillus from Brazil. He holds bachelor degrees in philosophy and theology and a license in nursing. He holds a master of science in religious sciences from the Pontifical University of São Paulo, and a master of arts in bioethics from Saint Camillus University, São Paulo, and is currently a PhD candidate in health care ethics at Marquette University in Wisconsin.

Patrick T. McCormick received an STD in moral theology from the Gregorian University, is professor of Christian ethics at Gonzaga University in Spokane, Washington, and is the author of *A Banqueter's Guide to the All-Night Soup Kitchen of the Kingdom of God* and *God's Beauty: A Call to Justice* (both from Liturgical Press).

Nader Michel, SJ, was born in Cairo in 1956. He is professor of moral theology and medical ethics at the High Institute of Religious Studies and the Coptic Catholic Seminary in Cairo, and visiting professor at St. Joseph University in Beirut. He is a medical doctor (cardiology), with a PhD in Islamic studies (Bordeaux University-France) and a PhD in moral theology (St Joseph University—Lebanon). He has written twelve books in Arabic in moral theology, medical ethics, and spirituality, and many articles in different languages.

NANCY PINEDA-MADRID   is associate professor of theology and Latina/o ministry at Boston College. Her published work includes *Suffering and Salvation in Ciudad Juarez* (Fortress Press, 2011); a co-edited book, *Hope: Promise, Possibility and Fulfillment* (Paulist Press, 2013); and numerous articles. She is President of the Academy of Catholic Hispanic Theologians of the United States (ACHTUS), and Vice President of the International Network of Socities of Catholic Theology (INSeCT).

WILLIAM O'NEILL, SJ, is an associate professor of social ethics at the Jesuit School of Theology of Santa Clara University and a visiting professor at the Jesuit School of Theology, "Hekima" in Nairobi. He received his doctorate from Yale in 1988. His writings address questions of social hermeneutics, human rights, social reconciliation, restorative justice, and refugee and immigration policy. He has worked with refugees in Tanzania and Malawi, and done research on human rights in South Africa and Rwanda.

PETER C. PHAN came to Georgetown University in 2003 and currently he holds the Ignacio Ellacuría Chair of Catholic Social Thought. He is the founding director of graduate studies of PhD programs in theology and religious studies. He has earned three doctorates: STD from the Universitas Pontificia Salesiana, Rome; and PhD and DD from the University of London. He has also received two honorary degrees: doctor of theology from the Catholic Theological Union and doctor of humane letters from Elms College. Professor Phan began his teaching career in philosophy at the age of eighteen at Don Bosco College in Hong Kong. He is the first non-Anglo to be elected president of the Catholic Theological Society of America.

DEOGRATIAS M. RWEZAURA, SJ, is currently serving as socius to the provincial of the Eastern Africa Province of the Society of Jesus. He finished his three-year term as regional director for Jesuit Refugee Service (JRS) Eastern Africa in April 2015. He obtained his doctorate in social ethics with specialization in forced migration issues from the Jesuit School of Theology of Santa Clara University in California. His Jesuit life has been challenged and spiritually enriched by working with refugees and by researching on forced migration related topics.

SASKIA SASSEN is Robert S. Lynd Professor of Sociology, and cochair of the Committee on Global Thought at Columbia University, New York. Her expertise is in the areas of globalization, immigration, global cities, and new transnational networks. Her many publications include *The Global City: New York, London, Tokyo* (2001), *Territory, Authority, Rights: From Medieval to Global Assemblages* (2008), and her most recent *Expulsions: Brutality and Complexity in a Global Economy* (2014).

PETER ŠTICA studied Catholic theology in Prague and Erfurt. He obtained a ThD in theological ethics in 2009, and his doctoral dissertation on "Migration and State Sovereignty—Justification and Limits of Migration Policies from the Perspective of Christian Social Ethics" was published in Czech (Červený Kostelec: Pavel Mervart,

2010). He has been a research associate at the Institute for Christian Social Studies at the University of Muenster since 2013. His current fields of research are political ethics, migration ethics, global ethics, and fundamentals of Christian social ethics.

REGINA WENTZEL WOLFE, PhD, is associate professor of theological ethics at Catholic Theological Union, Chicago, Illinois, and Senior Wicklander Fellow, Institute for Business and Professional Ethics, DePaul University. She was Christopher Chair in Business Ethics in the Brennan School of Business Dominican University. Prior to that, she was associate professor at Saint John's University Collegeville, Minnesota. Wolfe has worked in the fields of market research and economic research and forecasting and was on the editorial staff of *The Tablet*, in London, England.

PREM XALXO, SJ, an Indian Jesuit, is an associate professor of moral theology at the Pontifical Gregorian University, Rome. He studied philosophy and theology in Pune, Delhi, and Rome, and was previously trained in sciences and statistics in Chennai, India. He obtained a licentiate in moral theology from Accademia Alfonsianum, Rome, and a doctorate from the Pontifical Gregorian University, Rome. He specializes in environmental ethics and in the dialogue between moral theology and communications.

Index